UN Emergency Peace Service and the Responsibility to Protect

This book examines the attitudes of political, military and non-state actors towards the idea of a United Nations Emergency Peace Service (UNEPS), and the issues that might affect the establishment of this service in both theory and practice.

UNEPS is a civil society-led idea to establish a permanent United Nations service to improve UN peace operations as well as to operationalise the emerging norm of the 'responsibility to protect' civilians from atrocity crimes. The UNEPS proposal has received limited support. This book argues that interest in, and support for, the UNEPS proposal is influenced by perceptions that it would erode state sovereignty, the extent to which the principles of the proposal are consistent with actors' views on the world and perceptions on whether UNEPS will realistically contribute to the workings of the UN and regional peacekeeping systems in areas where these are seen to be deficient.

This book makes the case for localising the UNEPS proposal so that it is more consistent with the attitudes of those consulted for this research. It concludes that developing less controversial proposals could be the first steps to creating a rapidly deployable service with the mandate to prevent atrocity crimes.

This book will be of great interest to students and scholars of peace operations, the Responsibility to Protect, international organisations, international relations and security studies.

Annie Herro is a lecturer at the Centre for Peace and Conflict Studies, University of Sydney, Australia, and has a PhD in Peace and Conflict Studies.

Global politics and the responsibility to protect

Series Editors:
Alex J. Bellamy
Griffith University
Sara E. Davies
Griffith University
Monica Serrano
The City University of New York

The aim of this book series is to gather the best new thinking about the 'responsibility to protect' into a core set of volumes that provides a definitive account of the principle, its implementation and its role in crises, and that reflects a plurality of views and regional perspectives.

Global Politics and the Responsibility to Protect
From words to deeds
Alex J. Bellamy

The Responsibility to Protect
Norms, laws and international politics
Ramesh Thakur

Humanitarian Intervention and the Responsibility to Protect
Security and human rights
Cristina G. Badescu

Sri Lanka and the Responsibility to Protect
Politics, ethnicity, genocide
Damien Kingsbury

International Responsibility and Grave Humanitarian Crises
Collective provision for human security
Hannes Peltonen

Global Justice, Kant and the Responsibility to Protect
A provisional duty
Heather M. Roff

UN Emergency Peace Service and the Responsibility to Protect
Annie Herro

UN Emergency Peace Service and the Responsibility to Protect

Annie Herro

LONDON AND NEW YORK

First published 2015
by Routledge

2 Park Square, Milton Park, Abingdon, Oxon OX14 4RN
711 Third Avenue, New York, NY 10017, USA

Routledge is an imprint of the Taylor & Francis Group, an informa business

First issued in paperback 2016

Copyright © 2015 Annie Herro

The right of Annie Herro to be identified as author of this work has been asserted by her in accordance with sections 77 and 78 of the Copyright, Designs and Patents Act 1988.

All rights reserved. No part of this book may be reprinted or reproduced or utilised in any form or by any electronic, mechanical, or other means, now known or hereafter invented, including photocopying and recording, or in any information storage or retrieval system, without permission in writing from the publishers.

Notice:
Product or corporate names may be trademarks or registered trademarks, and are used only for identification and explanation without intent to infringe.

British Library Cataloguing-in-Publication Data
A catalogue record for this book is available from the British Library

Library of Congress Cataloging-in-Publication Data
Herro, Annie.
The UN Emergency Peace Service and the responsibility to protect / Annie Herro.
 pages cm. – (Global politics and the responsibility to protect)
 Includes bibliographical references and index.
 1. United Nations. Emergency Peace Service. 2. United Nations–
Peacekeeping forces. 3. Responsibility to protect (International law)
4. Atrocities–Prevention. I. Title.
 JZ6374.H47 2014
 355.3′57–dc23   2014016392

ISBN: 978-0-415-71919-3 (hbk)
ISBN: 978-1-138-20081-4 (pbk)

Typeset in Times New Roman
by Wearset Ltd, Boldon, Tyne and Wear

For my mother, and in loving memory of my father

Contents

Acknowledgements viii
List of abbreviations x

1 Introduction: an idea whose time has come? 1

2 The history of UNEPS 14

3 Normative and problem-solving ideas 38

4 An un-armed UNEPS 58

5 The use of force 74

6 The UN and regional organisations 92

7 Towards a pragmatic policy proposal 115

8 Conclusion: moving beyond the UNEPS proposal? 137

Selected bibliography 157
Index 162

Acknowledgements

This book is based on a PhD thesis I wrote at the Centre for Peace and Conflict Studies (CPACS) at the University of Sydney. I would like to thank the following people who have all contributed to my research journey.

My sincere thanks go to my former PhD supervisors, Wendy Lambourne and Stuart Rees. Wendy has shown an unwavering commitment to and genuine enthusiasm for my work. Her willingness to read multiple versions of the thesis and book has exceeded all expectations. Both the thesis and book have benefitted enormously from her sharp and insightful feedback. Stuart introduced me to the UNEPS proposal and encouraged me to undertake a PhD on this topic. He has been an inspiring, generous and steadfast mentor.

I thank Jake Lynch for creating a relaxed and motivating space at CPACS that is conducive to generating politically bold and academically rigorous research. All my friends and colleagues in the CPACS research community, including Cammi Webb-Gannon, James Tonny Dhizaala, Eyal Mayroz, David Penklis, Vivianna Rodriguez Carreon, Peter King, Rachael Hart, Neven Bondokji, Punam Yadav, Lydia Gitau, Bona Mkandawire, Annabel McGoldrick, Paul Duffill, Leticia Anderson, Lucy Fiske, Lynda Blanchard, Ken Macnab and Gary Trompf, have provided a stimulating source of ideas and discussion. Thushara Dibley, especially, was always available to help me with all sorts of research-related stumbling blocks and to celebrate my successes. I also thank Louise Chappell, Franklin Obeng-Odoom, Raymond Apthorpe and Vesselin Popovski for the little gems they shared with me during the transition from PhD to book.

I am grateful to colleagues at the Centre for Peace and Conflict Studies at Cornell University, where I spent time as a visiting scholar in 2013, for offering a welcoming and thought-provoking environment in which to write this book. I am particularly grateful to Matthew Evangelista for his feedback on Chapter 3.

I thank Bob Zuber from Global Action to Prevent War with whom I have spent many hours discussing the subject of a UNEPS. Bob has offered important encouragement for this research and organised a series of UNEPS-related events which generated rich data that I draw on in the pages that follow. Kavitha Suthanthiraraj has also been a delightful colleague who has contributed valuable ideas to how I think about a UNEPS. Certain insights in this book are taken from the chapter "Framing a Protection Service" which I co-authored with Kavitha. It was published in the 2012 book *Norms of Protection: Protection of Civilians and the Responsibility to Protect*, edited by Angus Francis, Vesselin Popovski and Charles Sampford. Parts of this chapter have been reproduced with permission from the United Nations University Press.

I also thank Peter Langille, Saul Mendlovitz and William Pace for sharing their experiences on the early days of the UNEPS advocacy initiative and their perspectives on the UNEPS proposal.

I owe thanks to Lyn Dickens, Leah Chan and Gabrielle Herro for their valuable editorial comments. I am especially grateful to Adam Courtenay for offering a journalist's perspective on my writing, and to Gina Courtenay for providing important advice on this book. Thanks to my other family and friends, too many to mention by name, who have travelled with me on this research journey.

Finally, to my parents, who have given me everything. It is with gratitude and love that I dedicate this book to them.

Abbreviations

ADF	Australian Defence Force
ALP	Australian Labor Party
ASEAN	Association of South East Asian Nations
ASF	African Standby Force
AU	African Union
C34	Special Committee on Peacekeeping Operations
CAR	Central African Republic
CSCAP	Council for Security Cooperation in the Asia Pacific
DFAT	Australian Department of Foreign Affairs and Trade
DRC	Democratic Republic of the Congo
ECOSOC	Economic and Social Council
ERDC	Enhanced Rapid Deployment Capacity
FORD	Friends of Rapid Deployment
G77	Group of 77
GAM	Gerakan Aceh Merde or the Free Aceh Movement
GAPW	Global Action to Prevent War
GPPAC	Global Partnership for the Prevention of Armed Conflict
ICISS	International Commission on Intervention and State Sovereignty
INTERFET	International Force for East Timor
NATO	North Atlantic Treaty Organization
NGO	Non-Governmental Organisation
OHCHR	Office of the High Commissioner for Human Rights
P-5	Permanent Five
POC	Protection of Civilians
QUNO	Quaker UN Office in Geneva
R2P	Responsibility to Protect
TAN	Transnational Advocacy Network
TNI	Tentara Nasional Indonesia or Indonesian armed forces
UN	United Nations
UNAMIR	United Nations Assistance Mission in Rwanda
UNDFS	UN Department of Field Support
UNDPKO	UN Department of Peacekeeping Operations
UNEF	UN Emergency Force

UNEPS	UN Emergency Peace Service
UN ES	UN Emergency Service
UNGA	UN General Assembly
UNMIL	UN Mission in Liberia
UNPBC	UN Peacebuilding Commission
UNSAS	UN Standby Arrangement System
UNSC	UN Security Council
UNSG	UN Secretary-General
WFM	World Federalist Movement
WSOD	World Summit Outcome Document

1 Introduction
An idea whose time has come?

Violence against civilians and mass atrocities have been the hallmarks of too many conflicts in recent years. You only have to switch on the news to see reports of the slaughter of innocents by government and rebel forces in Syria, acts which the United Nations (UN) has called war crimes and crimes against humanity.[1] Rewind to 2009 and we see a similar picture in Sri Lanka. Here, the UN estimates that up to 40,000 innocent people were killed during the war between the government and the insurgency group, the Tamil Tigers.[2] Let's not forget Darfur: the mass killing and displacement of the ethnically African, Muslim, civilian population, most likely instigated and coordinated by the Sudanese government.[3] Tragically, this is just a snap-shot of extreme violence perpetrated in the twenty-first century.

The world has increasingly looked to the UN, and in particular to UN peace operations, to prevent or to halt such crimes. In the early 1990s, it seemed that the UN could accomplish anything in the realm of international peace and security. The optimism was palpable, but it did not last long. The UN either deployed peacekeeping forces 'too little, too late' in response to conflict, or not at all. When they were deployed, peace operations suffered from delays and a lack of willingness from governments to provide adequate numbers of well-trained and equipped peacekeepers and supplies needed to fulfil the mandates of missions. Missions failed to provide security in notoriously complex crises such as Somalia. They were also unsuccessful in protecting civilians from genocide such as in Rwanda in 1994, where 800,000 people died in under three months, and in Bosnia in 1995, when over 8,000 Muslim men and boys who sought refuge in a UN safe zone were 'ethnically cleansed' by Serb forces as UN peacekeepers looked on.[4]

Such tragedies tested the central principles and capabilities of UN peace operations and demonstrated that reform was urgently needed. As a result, in 1999 the UN recognised that the plight of civilians was fundamental to its mission.[5] The UN Security Council (UNSC) started to reference the protection of civilians "under imminent threat of physical violence" in mandates for peace operations and such language is now a mainstay in this arena. The responsibility to protect (R2P) doctrine was unanimously endorsed by member states in 2005 at the World Summit hosted by the UN. World leaders agreed that all states had the responsibility to protect their populations from genocide, war crimes, ethnic cleansing and crimes against humanity, and committed to take "timely and decisive action" in cases where governments "manifestly failed to protect their populations" from such atrocities.[6]

This chapter explains the problems the UN faces in responding rapidly and effectively to (imminent) conflict and mass atrocities. It also introduces a possible solution: a UN Emergency Peace Service (UNEPS) proposal. It presents the sources of information on which this book is based and briefly reviews the literature on the topic of a permanent UN service. I assert that this is an under-researched subject and show how this book stands out from the others. It ends with an outline of the chapters to follow.

Challenges facing UN peace operations

Despite the political head-nodding at 2005 at the World Summit, UN peace operations are still minimally resourced due to the lack of capacity or political will for the task of protecting large numbers of civilians in conflicts. Peace operations that possess the mandate to use force to protect civilians are a relatively new phenomenon. Traditional peacekeepers are deployed in the so-called calm between a ceasefire and a political settlement, with the goal of building confidence between belligerents in order to establish a process of political dialogue.[7] They adhere strictly to the principles of neutrality, impartiality and the non-use of force except in self-defence.[8]

After the cold war, peacekeepers increasingly found themselves in volatile situations where there was no peace to keep and were often unprepared to respond.[9] At the same time, peacekeeping operations began to grow in size, composition and function. The UN in general – and peacekeepers in particular – began to play a larger, more active role in managing conflict. There has not only been a dramatic increase in the number of coercive peace operations[10] but peacekeepers now comprise police, military and civilian personnel performing a range of tasks in multidimensional missions with the goal of building the foundations of sustainable peace.

The first operational challenge that the UN faces in its efforts to protect civilians from violence in conflict zones is the sluggish pace at which peacekeepers are deployed.[11] This partly explains why preventative deployments are rare and why it takes an average of 46 days for missions to deploy after they have received the green light from the UNSC.[12] There is no set sequence of events and each operation must be formed 'from scratch'.[13] In 1993, the UN Standby Arrangements System (UNSAS) was created to improve access to readily available deployment capabilities. A few years later, the Multinational Standby High Readiness Brigade was established with comparable goals in mind. It succumbed to pressure, however, from Sweden and certain other Nordic states to close its doors, allegedly because of a renewed interest in the Nordic Coordinated Arrangement for Military Peace Support which has a similar scope and mandate to the Brigade.[14] These mechanisms, however, resulted in similar deployment delays and shortages of personnel and equipment to those faced by the UN's Department of Peacekeeping Operations (UNDPKO).[15] There are also similar regional peacekeeping arrangements including the European Union Battlegroups and the North Atlantic Treaty Organisation (NATO). These groups still depend on political will and the provision of national standby personnel. When lacking these essential ingredients, rapid deployment does not occur.[16]

The second challenge is that governments might be unable or unwilling to contribute personnel, advanced weaponry, 'enabling units' and 'strategic airlift' to peacekeeping operations.[17] Specifically, operations might lack the necessary number of troops, police, civilians and engineering and communications systems. They may be short on logistics or intelligence or lack the ability to employ long-distance transport facilities.[18] Often the reasons for an ineffectual response are political – the country to which the operation is deployed is of little perceived strategic, geopolitical or economic interest. In other instances, the member states either do not have the resources or cannot afford to hand them over to a peacekeeping operation.[19] Consequently, a mission such as the African Union/United Nations Hybrid Operation in Darfur, Sudan, was both under-staffed and under-resourced.[20] It is the civilians, in the end, who must bear the brunt of this lack of capacity.

Third, peacekeepers lack uniform training, especially in the protection of civilians.[21] The recommendations affecting troop quality are among the most important in the *Report of the Panel on United Nations Peace Operations* which argues that without well-trained (and well-equipped) troops the UN cannot meet the Report's standards for robust operations and is liable to waste member states' money in supporting low-performing military personnel.[22] Not only are the troops often under-trained, but the UN is still struggling to deploy well-trained police[23] and civilian peacekeepers, especially those from the global South.[24]

Fourth, while many of the world's peacekeepers come from the global South, virtually all missions that are deployed rapidly are led by a pivotal state(s) or regional organisation, with the resources – troops, armoured equipment and supplies – mainly coming from the West. This has sometimes led to claims of neo-colonial interference and a subsequent backlash against peacekeepers of Western origin.[25]

An example of this was in Somalia where the US Rangers broke from the principle of impartiality and became directly engaged in the conflict, which compromised their efforts to protect civilians.[26] It was also recently illustrated in NATO's 2011 military intervention in Libya which raised questions about the motivations of the interveners – did they seek to advance their political interests through the intervention?

Such challenges have had an impact on both peacekeepers' capacity to protect as well as the legitimacy of UN peace operations and, indeed, the organisation itself.[27] This raises an urgent question for the international community: how can the UN's ability and preparedness to prevent and halt atrocities and protect civilians be improved? This book explores attitudes towards a possible answer to this question: the UNEPS proposal.

4 *An idea whose time has come?*

The United Nations Emergency Peace Service proposal

UNEPS is a proposal for a permanent service that would be directly recruited, trained, equipped and controlled by the UN. Peter Langille can be credited as the catalyst for the global initiative for a UNEPS in 2003. He developed the concept, case, model and initial plans in 2002 and has devoted much of the last decade to their promotion and to further research.[28] Since then, numerous civil society organisations and others have provided intellectual contribution to the concept and committed to its advocacy. This book is based on both Langille's idea and output from the wider UNEPS network.

In addition to receiving support from civil society organisations in various parts of the world, the proposed UNEPS receives the backing of UN officials, including Juan Mendez, the UN's former Special Rapporteur on Torture and Other Cruel, Inhuman and Degrading Treatment or Punishment.[29] Other prominent advocates include parliamentary representatives such as a former Japanese Senator, Tadashi Inuzuka, who incorporated UNEPS into his policy platform as well as two former members of the US Congress – Al Wynn and James Walsh – who drafted a bill in support of UNEPS to the US House of Representatives.[30]

The UNEPS proposal is not the first attempt to create a permanent UN service – what some have called a UN 'Legion'.[31] The idea can be traced back to the inter-war years when the impressive fighting record of the French Foreign Legion in World War I inspired a model for an international police force.[32] Some of the UN's architects also proposed an international army at the Dumbarton Oaks Conference in Washington DC in 1944. Way back then, international leaders formulated and negotiated the establishment of the UN, which makes the concept of a standing military force older than the organisation itself.[33] The idea, however, received a cool reception from the Soviet and French representatives, among others.[34]

From 1948 to 1995, proposals for a standing peacekeeping capacity periodically resurfaced and were championed by strange bedfellows in academic, diplomatic and political circles. They ranged from former UN Secretary-General Trygve Lie's appeal for a UN "Guard Force", to Ronald Reagan's call at the end of his presidency for a "standing UN force – an army of conscience".[35] The motivation behind some of these proposals was to improve the UN's ability to respond rapidly and effectively to mass human rights violations, while others sought to augment the UN's readiness and capacity to prevent and respond to conflict.[36]

In 2005, 35 experts drawn from far-flung regions of the world agreed on the general principles of a UNEPS at the University of Castilla–La Mancha in Cuenca, Spain. All participants were united in the belief that "the international community urgently needs an effective United Nations rapid reaction capability if it is to honor its responsibility to protect innocent people from genocide, war crimes, and crimes against humanity".[37] Below is a summary of the proposal from this significant and early meeting on a UNEPS.[38]

UNEPS would:

1 prevent genocide, war crimes and crimes against humanity that are not being addressed by other responsible parties. It could also respond to environmental and natural disasters if other governments, intergovernmental organisations or humanitarian agencies were unable or unwilling to avert major loss of human life;
2 be a permanent service that is highly mobile;
3 comprise individuals who volunteer, reflecting the diversity of all major cultural regions of the world and an equal representation of men and women;
4 deploy within 48 hours of UNSC authorisation;
5 be self-contained with readily available personnel (up to 15,000[39] at the start), equipment and supplies at the disposal of the UN;
6 comprise carefully screened personnel with a range of professional and language skills covering these areas: human rights, gender, police, military service, humanitarian assistance, judicial proceedings and penal matters, conflict transformation and environmental protection;
7 uphold women's human rights and have a fully integrated gender perspective, as specified in UNSC Resolution 1325, in all aspects of UNEPS;
8 operate within and enforce international humanitarian and human rights law;
9 be financed through the regular UN budget;
10 have the UNSC as the preferred mode of authorisation but it could also be authorised through the UN General Assembly;
11 be based at UN-designated sites, including field headquarters, and function under a unified command under UN authority;
12 complement – not replace – existing regional or UN security arrangements.[40]

Despite the apparent contribution of a UNEPS in providing the UN with another tool to protect civilians in conflict, and prevent atrocities, persuading governments of the merits of the proposal "remains an uphill battle".[41] This book is an attempt to explore the obstacles the proposal faces with a view to considering how this ambitious idea might be implemented.

Sources of information

Much of the information used in this book is based on over 80 interviews conducted between 2007 and 2013 with political, military and non-state actors concerned with international peace and security issues. Respondents represented themselves as individuals and as members of groups or institutions to which they belonged. Three, often intersecting, types of people were consulted. The first comprises decision-makers, such as members of the Australian Parliament, senior members of government bureaucracies or senior UN officials in relevant departments. They were in positions of power and consequently were able to advise what it would take for the proposed UNEPS to receive support in their respective domains – a key step towards the establishment of a UNEPS.

6 *An idea whose time has come?*

The second group of people both reflect and influence the views of these kinds of decision-makers. This group can be divided into two sub-groups. First, there were those who were previously in powerful positions within government, the UN, the military or regional organisations (specifically the Association of Southeast Asian Nations) but had recently retired. These respondents were generally still associated with colleagues in their respective professional spheres and, consequently, could illuminate the views of those in power on the proposal. They also expressed their own views on topics related to the proposed UNEPS in different forums, such as conferences, reports and in the media, and were therefore informative and influential figures in their own right. Second, there were unofficial observers such as those working for, or closely affiliated with, non-governmental organisations (NGOs), media organisations, universities or prominent think tanks who (try to) influence governments through their advocacy and analysis on UNEPS-related issues. Through their knowledge of, and experience in, fields related to the proposed UNEPS, they were able to shed further light on the types of responses that the proposal might confront and strategies that might shift a decision-maker who is unsupportive to a more supportive posture.

I conducted the majority of these semi-structured, exploratory interviews (at times with a colleague, Stuart Rees) but also draw upon interviews by Kavitha Suthanthiraraj of Global Action to Prevent War (GAPW) in New York. My interviews took place in Singapore (2009); Kuala Lumpur, Malaysia (2008, 2009); Jakarta and Aceh, Indonesia (2008, 2009); Canberra, Melbourne and Sydney, Australia (2007, 2008, 2009); and New York, USA (2013). In 2010, Suthanthiraraj conducted eight interviews with representatives from UN Country missions (Australia, Bangladesh, Croatia, Uganda and Uruguay) and three with senior officials in the UNDPKO, the Office of the High Commissioner for Human Rights (OHCHR) and the UN Office of the Special Advisor on Genocide Prevention. Her respondents comprised decision-makers as well as those who influence them.

It is important to understand that most respondents had multifaceted identities. For example, one academic respondent was formerly in the Australian Defence Force and previously worked as a senior bureaucrat at the Australian Department of Foreign Affairs and Trade. Similarly, several respondents based in Singapore for work were nationals of other countries in Asia, such as the Philippines and India. Many of the interviews were conducted in the Asia-Pacific region with respondents who had different professional, political, and cultural backgrounds and a variety of interests, which resulted in a range of responses to the UNEPS proposal.

I triangulate the interviews with other primary as well as secondary sources of information to sharpen and elaborate responses from the key informants mentioned above. These additional sources include transcripts and reports from conferences and workshops on the proposed UNEPS interviews on UNEPS conducted by colleagues at GAPW, documents released by UNEPS advocates and literature on previous proposals for a UN Legion. I also consulted institutional data that were publically available in government statements and UN reports, and media reports and scholarly analyses of issues related to the central claims of the UNEPS proposal.

Standing out from the crowd

The subject of a UN standing force or service has been perennially under-researched. Scholars writing about these proposals, including about UNEPS, tend to expound on and promote the technical and normative merits of a given idea without providing an in-depth critical analysis of the obstacles confronting it.[42] Others have presented the creation of a permanent UN force as a solution to various institutional shortcomings facing the international community's response to conflict and humanitarian crises. However, after doing so, they promptly distance themselves from such suggestions, noting the lack of political consensus and the practical challenges plaguing proposals of this kind.[43]

This book is not an advocacy piece for a UNEPS nor does it shirk the practical and normative obstacles such a proposal might face. It engages with hard questions, some of which have confronted previous ideas for a standing UN capacity, but also considers opportunities for the UNEPS proposal to be 'localised' or recalibrated to increase the support it could receive or pave the way for its implementation.

Stephen Kinloch-Pichat has produced an in-depth study on a standing peacekeeping capacity or UN Legion.[44] While his valuable book is thorough and comprehensive, there are at least three key differences between Kinloch-Pichat's approach and mine.

The first relates to the object of Kinloch-Pichat's study which spans dozens of proposals, each with a different composition and mandate. By contrast, the primary focus of this book is the UNEPS proposal, which would have the mandate to prevent genocide, war crimes and crimes against humanity. Consequently, the relationship between attitudes towards R2P and the interest in and support for the UNEPS proposal are central to this discussion.

The second point concerns the temporal scope of Kinloch-Pichat's study, which traverses some 50 years, and the sources of information used to compile his book. These are restricted to document analyses, such as official UN reports and speeches. This book examines attitudes towards the UNEPS proposal, based largely on interviews at a given point in history – between 2007 and 2013. The interviews were with the three groups of people mentioned above. The book brings in historical perspectives on previous efforts to establish a standing peacekeeping capacity (as well as other theoretical, primary and secondary sources) to help contextualise attitudes towards UNEPS today, and to provide further insight into the extent to which the UNEPS proposal might be implemented.

This leads us to the third and final point – Kinloch-Pichat does not make any concrete suggestions on how to make the idea of a UN Legion more palatable. Other, shorter studies on proposals for UN standing forces, such as those by Adam Roberts[45] and Andrew Miler,[46] are similarly restricted to a critical historical account and fail to consider ways in which such ideas might enjoy greater support. Conversely, this book identifies different variations on the UNEPS proposal that were suggested by respondents and other actors, and evaluates the feasibility and desirability of these alternatives.

8 *An idea whose time has come?*

Two recent studies on the proposed UNEPS go some way towards considering how to overcome some of the obstacles facing this ambitious idea. Because of the small size of the proposed UNEPS and the lack of legitimacy of the UN, James Pattison suggests strengthening national militaries and the capabilities of regional organisations to respond to crises. According to him, these would be pragmatic "first steps" towards the eventual creation of a much larger, autonomous force authorised by a reformed United Nations.[47]

Jonathan Gilmore also identifies some practical and political obstacles confronting the UNEPS proposal – such as its short-term deployment philosophy and the proposed role of UNEPS forces as well as larger issues of political will within the UN – and recommends incremental steps at national levels to make the UNEPS concept part of a coherent policy process.[48] The breadth of issues discussed by both scholars, however, are far narrower than those addressed in this book.

Structure of the book – bringing ethics and problem solving together

This book examines the attitudes of military, political and non-state actors towards the UNEPS proposal. It also explores issues that might affect the establishment of UNEPS in theory and in practice. Finally, it considers how the UNEPS proposal could best be designed and promoted in order to facilitate its eventual implementation.

Chapter 2 places the UNEPS proposal within a historical, political and legal context, while Chapter 3 identifies the central ideas on which the UNEPS proposal is based – normative and practical – and discusses the theoretical framework used in this book.

The remainder of the book is structured around these central ideas and is concerned with understanding different perspectives on them. Chapters 4 to 8 also consider how to move stakeholders from a lukewarm response to the proposal to one which the advocates of UNEPS (or those interested in preventing atrocities and other humanitarian crises) might be able to work with.

Chapter 4 explores two responsibilities: states have a responsibility to prevent their populations from being subjected to atrocities and the international community has a responsibility to assist states – potentially through the proposed UNEPS – in preventing atrocities from happening. Chapter 5 deals with the often taboo subject of force – would it be acceptable for the proposed UNEPS to use force without the consent of the state in question, as a means of preventing atrocities? Chapter 6 is based on the idea that the UN ought to be the institution to control such use of force and therefore to manage a mechanism like UNEPS. I also explore the idea that the UN ought to be upheld and strengthened as the principal institution for conflict prevention and resolution.

Chapter 7 looks at the practical arguments justifying the creation of a UNEPS such as the lack of prompt, well-trained and equipped peacekeepers to respond to a crisis and the projected cost of the service. A proposed UNEPS would cost US$2.5

An idea whose time has come? 9

billion to create and around US$1 billion per year to maintain – is it a feasible and cost-effective investment for the international community to sustain in order to prevent mass atrocities and protect civilians from violence in armed conflict?

The final chapter canvasses suggestions on how UNEPS might be recalibrated to accommodate the views of respondents and other sources. It evaluates these suggestions from both practical and principled perspectives – in other words, the necessity, feasibility and desirability of such ideas. The motivation driving this chapter – indeed this book – is to integrate the attitudes of those consulted by proposing new ideas that might increase support from, and adoption by, the international community for a UNEPS or a capacity like it.

Notes

1. Cowell and Myers, "UN Panel Accuses Syrian Government"; Cumming-Bruce, "UN Rights Officials".
2. United Nations, *Report on Accountability in Sri Lanka*.
3. Flint and de Waal, *Darfur*, 101–6.
4. Dallaire, *Shake Hands with the Devil*, xvii; Teson, "The Liberal Case", 122.
5. UN Security Council, *Protection of Civilians in Armed Conflict*.
6. UN General Assembly, *2005 World Summit Outcome*, paras 138–9.
7. Bellamy, Williams and Griffin, *Understanding Peacekeeping*, 174; Durch, "Paying the Tab", 3–4.
8. UN General Assembly, *Report of the Panel on United Nations Peace Operations*, paras 48–64.
9. Ibid., paras 15–28.
10. Bellamy, Williams and Griffin, *Understanding Peacekeeping*, 214; United Nations Department of Peacekeeping Operations and Department of Field Support, *Principles and Guidelines*, 22–4.
11. Roessler and Prendergast, "Democratic Republic of the Congo".
12. Suthanthiraraj, *Enhancing Capacity for Rapid and Effective Troop Deployment*.
13. United Nations Department of Peacekeeping Operations and Department of Field Support, *Principles and Guidelines*, 63; Suthanthiraraj and Quinn, *Standing for Change*, 47.
14. Koops and Varwick, *Ten Years of Shirbrig*, 26.
15. Langille, "Preventing Genocide", 40; *Bridging the Commitment–Capacity Gap*, 40.
16. Langille, "Preventing Genocide", 299–300.
17. Holt and Berkman, *The Impossible Mandate?*, 6.
18. Durch, *Twenty-First-Century Peace Operations*, 72–73; "Cross-Cutting Issues", 15; Solli *et al.*, "Training in Vain?"
19. Durch, "Paying the Tab", 50.
20. Herro, Lambourne and Penklis, "Peacekeeping and Peace Enforcement in Africa".
21. UN General Assembly, *Report of the Panel on United Nations Peace Operations*, para. 108.
22. Ibid.
23. Smith, Holt and Durch, *Enhancing United Nations Capacity*, xvi; Durch and England, *International Police*, 2.
24. Coning, "Civilian Peacekeeping Capacity", 590; *Civilian Capacity in United Nations Peacekeeping*, 2.
25. Anderson, "Timor-Leste", 74; Ahmed, Keating, and Solinas, "Shaping the Future", 6.
26. Wheeler, *Saving Strangers*, 198.
27. Holt, Taylor and Kelly, *Protecting Civilians*, 3–4.

28 Langille, *Bridging the Commitment–Capacity Gap*.
29 GAPW, "To Prevent Genocide"; Mendez, "The Prevention of Genocide".
30 US House of Representatives, *Resolution 213*; Inuzuka, "Terror Elimination Bill".
31 Kinloch, *A UN 'Legion'*.
32 Ibid., 14.
33 Lorenz, *Peace, Power, and the United Nations*, 36.
34 Anthony Eden, 1960 cited in Kinloch, *A UN 'Legion'*, 24.
35 Urquhart, "Preface".
36 Roberts, "Proposals for UN Standing Forces", 99; Kinloch, *A UN 'Legion'*.
37 Johansen, "Cuenca Report", 43.
38 Krieger, Mendlovitz and Pace, "Introduction", 17.
39 This number has since been increased to 18,000. See Langille, "Preventing Genocide".
40 Johansen, "Cuenca Report".
41 Bellamy, Williams and Griffin, *Understanding Peacekeeping*, 27.
42 Unterseher, "Domesticating Military Interventions"; Johansen and Mendlovitz, "The Role of Enforcement of Law"; Johansen, "UN Peacekeeping"; Langille, *Bridging the Commitment–Capacity Gap*; Conetta and Knight, *Vital Force*; Hehir, *The Responsibility to Protect*; Kaysen and Rathjens, "The Case for a Volunteer UN Military Force"; Langille, "Conflict Prevention".
43 Lang, *Just Intervention*; Government of Canada.
44 Kinloch, *A UN 'Legion'*.
45 Roberts, "Proposals for UN Standing Forces".
46 Miller, "Universal Soldiers".
47 Pattison, "Humanitarian Intervention and a Cosmopolitan UN Force"; *Humanitarian Intervention and the Responsibility to Protect*, 229–39.
48 Zuber and Curran, "Peacekeeping and Rapid Reaction".

References

Ahmed, Salman, Paul Keating and Ugo Solinas. "Shaping the Future of UN Peace Operations: Is There a Doctrine in the House?" *Cambridge Review of International Affairs* 20, no. 1 (2007).
Anderson, Tim. "Timor-Leste: The Second Australian Intervention". *Journal of Australian Political Economy* 58 (2006): 62–93.
Bellamy, Alex J., Paul Williams and Stuart Griffin. *Understanding Peacekeeping*. Second ed. Cambridge: Polity, 2010.
Conetta, Carl and Charles Knight. *Vital Force: A Proposal for the Overhaul of the UN Peace Operations System and for the Creation of a UN Legion*. Cambridge, Mass: Commonwealth Institute, 1995.
Coning, Cedric de. *Civilian Capacity in United Nations Peacekeeping and Peacebuilding Missions*. Policy Brief 4. Oslo: Norwegian Institute of International Affairs (NUPI), 2011.
Coning, Cedric de. "Civilian Peacekeeping Capacity: Mobilizing Partners to Match Supply and Demand". *International Peacekeeping* 18, no. 5 (2011): 577–92.
Cowell, Alan and Steven Lee Myers. "UN Panel Accuses Syrian Government of Crimes against Humanity". *New York Times*, 23 February 2012. www.nytimes.com/2012/02/24/world/middleeast/un-panel-accuses-syria-of-crimes-against-humanity.html?pagewanted=all.
Cumming-Bruce, Nick. "UN Rights Officials Urge Syria War Crimes Charges". *New York Times*, 18 February 2013. www.nytimes.com/2013/02/19/world/middleeast/un-rights-panel-says-violence-in-syria-is-mounting.html?_r=0.

Dallaire, Romeo. *Shake Hands with the Devil: The Failure of Humanity in Rwanda.* Toronto, Canada: Random House, 2005.

Durch, William J. "Paying the Tab: Financial Crises". In *The Evolution of UN Peacekeeping*, edited by William J. Durch, 39–58. New York: St. Martin's Press, 1993.

Durch, William J. *Twenty-First-Century Peace Operations.* Washington DC: United States Institute of Peace Press, 2006.

Durch, William J. "Cross-Cutting Issues in Protection of Civilians for UN Peace Operations". In *Challenges of Protecting Civilians in Multidimensional Peace Operations.* Canberra: International Forum for the Challenges of Peace Operations. 27 April 2010. http://challengesforum.org/cms/images/pdf/Forum2010_WilliamDurch.pdf.

Durch, William J. and Madeline L. England. *International Police: Improving Professionalism and Responsiveness.* Issue Brief. Washington DC: The Henry L. Stimson Center, 2009 www.stimson.org/images/uploads/research-pdfs/Police_Issue_Brief.pdf.

Flint, Julie and Alex de Waal. *Darfur: A Short History of a Long War.* London: Zed Books, 2005.

Global Action to Prevent War. "To Prevent Genocide and Crimes against Humanity: Diverse Perspectives on a Standing, Rapid-Reaction UN Emergency Peace Service". Symposium Report on the United Nations Emergency Peace Service Initiative. Convened at Rutgers Law School, Rutgers University, New Jersey, 29 March 2007. www.globalactionpw.org/wp/wp-content/uploads/rutgers_uneps_conference_report_2007.pdf.

Government of Canada. *Towards a Rapid Reaction Capability.* Ottawa: Government of Canada, 1995.

Hehir, Aidan. *The Responsibility to Protect: Rhetoric, Reality and the Future of Humanitarian Intervention.* Basingstoke, UK: Palgrave Macmillan, 2012.

Herro, Annie, Wendy Lambourne and David Penklis. "Peacekeeping and Peace Enforcement in Africa: The Potential Contribution of a UN Emergency Peace Service". *African Security Review* 18, no. 1 (2009): 49–62.

Holt, Victoria K. and Tobias C. Berkman. *The Impossible Mandate? Military Preparedness, the Responsibility to Protect and Modern Peace Operations.* Washington DC: The Henry L. Stimson Center, 2006.

Holt, Victoria, Glyn Taylor and Max Kelly. *Protecting Civilians in the Context of UN Peacekeeping Operations: Successes, Setbacks and Remaining Challenges.* Independent study jointly commissioned by the UN Department of Peacekeeping Operations and the UN Office for the Coordination of Humanitarian Affairs, 2009. www.peacekeepingbestpractices.unlb.org/pbps/Library/Protecting%20Civilians%20in%20the%20Context%20of%20UN%20PKO.pdf

Inuzuka, Tadashi. "From Article 9 to Chapter 6½: Perspectives from the Discussion on the Terror Elimination Bill". Paper submitted at the Workshop on the Eradication of Armed Conflict, co-sponsored by the Australian Centre for Peace and Conflict Studies, the World Federation of United Nations Associations, and the project for a United Nations Emergency Peace Service, Brisbane, Australia, 8–10 February 2008.

Johansen, Robert C. "UN Peacekeeping: The Changing Utility of Military Force". *Third World Quarterly* 12, no. 2 (1990): 53–70.

Johansen, Robert C. "Expert Discussion of the United Nations Emergency Peace Service: Cuenca Report". In *A United Nations Emergency Peace Service: To Prevent Genocide and Crimes against Humanity*, edited by Robert C. Johansen, 43–74. New York: World Federalist Movement – Institute for Global Policy, 2006.

Johansen, Robert C. and Saul H. Mendlovitz. "The Role of Enforcement of Law in the Establishment of a New International Order: A Proposal for a Transnational Police Force". *Alternatives: Global, Local, Political* 6, no. 2 (1980): 307–37.

Kaysen, Carl and George Rathjens. "The Case for a Volunteer UN Military Force". *Daedalus* 132, no. 1 (2003): 91–104.

Kinloch, Stephen. *A UN 'Legion': Between Utopia and Reality*. Abingdon, UK: Routledge, 2012.

Koops, Joachim and Johannes Varwick. *Ten Years of Shirbrig: Lessons Learned, Development Prospects and Strategic Opportunities for Germany*. GPPi Research Paper Series No. 11. Berlin: Global Public Policy Institute, 2008.

Krieger, David, Saul Mendlovitz and William Pace. "Introduction". In *A United Nations Emergency Peace Service: To Prevent Genocide and Crimes against Humanity*, edited by Robert C. Johansen, 11–19. New York: World Federalist Movement – Institute for Global Policy, 2006.

Lang, Anthony F. *Just Intervention*. Georgetown, Washington D.C: Georgetown University Press, 2003.

Langille, H. Peter. "Conflict Prevention: Options for Rapid Deployment and UN Standing Forces". *International Peacekeeping* 7, no. 1 (2000): 219–53.

Langille, H. Peter. *Bridging the Commitment–Capacity Gap: A Review of Existing Arrangements and Options for Enhancing UN Rapid Deployment*. New York: Center for UN Reform Education, 2002.

Langille, H. Peter. "Preventing Genocide". In *The World and Darfur: International Response to Crimes against Humanity in Western Sudan*, edited by Amanda Grzyb, 281–327. Montreal, Canada: McGill Queens University Press, 2009.

Lorenz, Joseph P. *Peace, Power, and the United Nations: A Security System for the Twenty-First Century*. Boulder, Colo: Westview Press, 1999.

Mendez, Juan. "The Prevention of Genocide and Its Challenges". In *Standing for Change in Peacekeeping Operations: Project for a United Nations Emergency Peace Service (UNEPS)*, UNEPS Secretariat, 43–9. New York: Global Action to Prevent War, 2009.

Miller, Andrew S. "Universal Soldiers: UN Standing Armies and the Legal Alternatives". *Georgetown Law Journal* 81 (1992): 773–828.

Pattison, James. "Humanitarian Intervention and a Cosmopolitan UN Force". *Journal of International Political Theory* 4, no. 1 (2008): 126–45.

Pattison, James. *Humanitarian Intervention and the Responsibility to Protect: Who Should Intervene?* Oxford: Oxford University Press, 2010.

Roberts, Adam. "Proposals for UN Standing Forces: A Critical History". In *The United Nations Security Council and War: The Evolution of Thought and Practice since 1945*, edited by Vaughan Lowe, Adam Roberts, Jennifer Welsh and Dominik Zaum, 99–130. New York: Oxford University Press, 2008.

Roessler, Philip and John Prendergast. "Democratic Republic of the Congo". In *Twenty-First-Century Peace Operations*, edited by William J. Durch, 229–318. Washington, DC: United States Institute of Peace, 2006.

Smith, Joshua, Victoria Holt and William Durch. *Enhancing United Nations Capacity to Support Post Conflict Policing and Rule of Law*. Washington DC: The Henry L. Stimson Center, 2007. www.stimson.org/pub.cfm?ID=483.

Solli, Audun, Benjamin de Carvalho, Cedric de Coning and Mikkel F. Pedersen. "Training in Vain? Bottlenecks in Deploying Civilians for UN Peacekeeping". *International Peacekeeping* 18, no. 4 (2011): 425–38.

Suthanthiraraj, Kavitha. *United Nations Peacekeeping Missions: Enhancing Capacity for Rapid and Effective Troop Deployment*. New York: Global Action To Prevent War, 2008. www.globalactionpw.org/wp/wp-content/uploads/troop-deployment-paper.pdf.

Suthanthiraraj, Kavitha and Mariah Quinn. *Standing for Change in Peacekeeping Operations: Project for a United Nations Emergency Peace Service (UNEPS)*. New York: Global Action to Prevent War, 2009.

Teson, Fernando R. "The Liberal Case for Humanitarain Intervention". In *Humanitarian Intervention: Ethical, Legal and Political Dilemmas*, edited by J.L. Holzgrefe and R.O. Keohane, 93–129. Cambridge: Cambridge University Press, 2003.

US House of Representatives. *Resolution 213*. March 2007. www.govtrack.us/congress/billtext.xpd?bill=hr110-213.

United Nations. *Report of the Secretary-General's Panel of Experts on Accountability in Sri Lanka* of 31 March 2011. www.un.org/News/dh/infocus/Sri_Lanka/POE_Report_Full.pdf.

United Nations Department of Peacekeeping Operations and Department of Field Support. *United Nations Peacekeeping Operations Principles and Guidelines*. New York: United Nations, 2008.

UN General Assembly. *Report of the Panel on United Nations Peace Operations*. A/55/305 of 21 August 2000.

UN General Assembly. *Resolution Adopted by the General Assembly: 60/1. 2005 World Summit Outcome*. A/RES/60/1 of 24 October 2005.

UN Security Council. *Report of the Secretary-General to the Security Council on the Protection of Civilians in Armed Conflict*. S/1999/957 of 8 September 1999.

Unterseher, Lutz. "Domesticating Military Interventions and the Creation of a UN Standing Force". In *Righteous Violence: The Ethics and Politics of Military Intervention*, 137–59. Melbourne, Australia: Melbourne University Press, 2005.

Urquhart, Brian. "Preface". In *United Nations Emergency Peace Service: To Prevent Genocide and Crimes against Humanity*, edited by Robert Johansen, 7–10. New York: Global Action to Prevent War, Nuclear Age Peace Foundation and World Federalist Movement, 2006.

Wheeler, Nicholas J. *Saving Strangers*. New York: Oxford University Press, 2000.

Zuber, Robert and David Curran. "Peacekeeping and Rapid Reaction: Towards the Establishment of Cosmopolitan Capacities for Rapid Deployment". Workshop report, 8 July 2013. Division of Peace Studies at the University of Bradford, Global Action to Prevent War and Armed Conflict, the World Federalist Movement Canada. www.bradford.ac.uk/ssis/media/ssis/peacestudies/Bradford-Write-Up-Sept.pdf

2   The history of UNEPS

Introduction

Ideas for a permanent, individually recruited UN force have borne many titles: a "UN Guard",[1] a "UN Volunteer Military Force"[2] and a "UN Peace Force",[3] to name just a few. All these proposals have at least three common features: (1) they aim to empower the UN to take timely and effective action on matters related to international peace and security; (2) their personnel would be composed of individuals from diverse nations, at the permanent disposal of the UN; and (3) none of them has ever been implemented.

This chapter places the concept of a UN 'Legion' within a historical, political and legal context, and traces the emergence of the UNEPS proposal and its network of advocates. I begin by discussing the seeds of the idea of an international police force. While there is no provision for a directly recruited force in the UN Charter, the national forces contemplated in Chapter VII were more coordinated – especially in terms of training, organisation and readiness – than the peacekeeping system which eventually materialised. Despite the lack of legal provision for a UN Legion, a case can be made that the creation of such a force would be constitutional.

I explore several proposals that emerged during the cold war and post-cold war period, which succumbed to bipolar tensions and norms of nationalism as well as other perceived political, logistical and financial obstacles. Part of the compromise over calls to improve the UN's ability to respond rapidly and effectively to crises, and the lack of political will to do so in a meaningful way, was to strengthen UN standby arrangements in which states retain control of their armed forces.

This chapter also discusses the context from which the UNEPS proposal emerged, tracing its direct lineage to Peter Langille's 2002 idea of a UN Emergency Service.[4] The UNEPS initiative can best be described as a transnational advocacy network; however, it lacks the necessary groundswell to advance the proposal politically in a significant way. In recent years, advocates have framed the proposal as a tool to operationalise the responsibility to protect and have merged UNEPS-related activities with similar proposals for UN and regional standing capacities. Some of the implications of these strategies are discussed below.

The seeds of an international (police) force

Perhaps the first example of an international police force was in the city-states of ancient Greece under the umbrella of the first Delian League (478–404 BC). States in the League, an association led by Athens, contributed ships or money to a force designed to protect it from Persia and eradicate piracy in the Aegean Sea.[5] There are other examples too, later in history. Henry IV of France, William Penn and Jean-Jacques Rousseau all drafted plans for all-European governments with police power. None, of course, was ever implemented.[6] The one occasion in modern history when there was a truly international police force, with troops from Britain, Italy, the Netherlands and Sweden, was through the League of Nations – the UN's predecessor. It was deployed during the 1935 plebiscite when the Saar basin was returned to Germany.[7]

But this was a far cry from the kind of ideas proposed by politicians from small and great powers, UN Secretaries-General, civil society organisations and individual citizens since the inter-war years. The modern roots of a UN Legion stretch back to the 1930s in Britain and captured the interest of prominent politicians, academics and publicists. For example, Liberal MP Lord David Davies, a federalist, believed the creation of a permanent international police force would constrain aggressor states.[8]

The idea also has roots in World War II and the birth of the UN. Such forces would have either replaced or complemented the failing League of Nations (before the war) or served as model for its replacement (during and immediately after the war).[9] For example, in the final years of World War II, Harold Stassen, the governor of Minnesota, proposed an international force as part of his "blueprint for a world government". Stassen's truly international service would have been composed of air, sea and land forces and been more powerful than the US military. Its goal would have been to "enforce justice", help administer the air and sea, and disarm aggressor states.[10] By the end of the war, the world would be a few steps closer to realising such cosmopolitan ideas through the creation of the UN but still a long way from seeing their full implementation.

The UN Charter and a standing force – close but not close enough

Despite the aspirations of some representatives who were present when the rules of the UN were being negotiated, states did not agree on a standing army made up of personnel independent of national control. Instead, Chapter VII of the Charter calls on member states to make their armed forces available when the UN Security Council (UNSC) calls for them. This, in itself, was quite ambitious and went some way to implementing the UN's collective security agenda. Under the Charter, national armed forces would be available through "special agreements" made between the UNSC, with support from the Military Staff Committee,[11] and the member state.[12] Special agreements basically refer to the size, composition and basing arrangements of national contributions.[13] But when the

Military Staff Committee, which was supposed to be composed of representatives of the Permanent Five (P-5) members of the UNSC, was formed, there were major disagreements about establishing a framework for how forces at the disposal of the UNSC were to be maintained and deployed. And so the whole task was abandoned, along with the Military Staff Committee itself.[14] This meant that an ad-hoc system of military cooperation, in which national contingents needed to be assembled at the last minute, became the status quo. There is no guarantee that adequate numbers of forces will be available, nor that such forces would be sufficiently prepared and integrated for the tasks assigned to them by the Council. The arrangement envisaged by the architects of the Charter whereby national forces would report to a common Military Staff Committee in peacetime and prepare themselves for their mission according to common instructions turned out to be merely a pipe dream.[15]

Would the creation of a directly recruited standing force composed of individuals independent of state control require a revision of the UN Charter? Some claim that there is no insurmountable legal obstacle to the creation of a standing UN rapid deployment capability. They argue that just because it is not mentioned in the Charter does not mean that it is unconstitutional. They cite the emergence of UN peacekeeping, which itself was not mentioned in the Charter, as a case in point. Peacekeeping has been labelled "Chapter 6½" because it falls somewhere between the chapter governing the peaceful settlement of disputes (Chapter VI) and that governing the use of force (Chapter VII). Furthermore, both military and non-military provisions of the Charter give the UNSC great discretion over what action needs to be taken on matters relating to international peace and security.[16] Indeed, the Council is authorised to decide what *constitutes* a threat to international peace and security, the *action* that should be taken in response and by what *means*.[17] In other words, the Charter does not preclude the use of any other forces available to the UNSC.[18] On the other hand, some have used the "original intent" argument which says that because there was no intention to create a directly recruited force, any attempt to establish one would be "illegal".[19] It is likely that people will opt for one legal argument over the other depending on whether or not they believe a UN Legion is politically desirable and practically viable.

UN forces and the cold war period

Trygve Lie, the first UNSG, is probably the most well known early champion of a permanent UN force. He proposed the idea just after the UN Truce Supervision Organisation was established in response to the Arab invasion of Palestine in May 1948. Lie conceded that in light of cold war tensions there was little chance that the P-5 would agree on the number of forces with which they would provide the UNSC (thus fulfilling their obligations under Article 43 of the UN Charter). So he thought it was his duty to propose an alternative. While light on detail, his idea was for a supranational, self-contained, directly recruited permanent force that would be at the disposal of the UNSC. He called it a small Guard Force. His proposal underwent several modifications but, originally, its projected size was between 5,000 and 10,000 men. Lie clarified, however, that it would be distinct from any type of Article 43 arrangement. It would have authority, thanks to its UN imprimatur, and, at the same time, give the UN the means to "exert its authority".[20] The Guard Force would perform fairly innocuous tasks compared with today's standards of multidimensional peacekeeping, such as monitoring plebiscites and the conditions of a truce.[21] Even though Lie watered down the proposal in name, size and function in response to concerns from the UN General Assembly (UNGA), the idea quietly died because of lack of government support.[22] This was only the beginning of proposals of this kind.

The next stream of proposals emerged around the time when UN peacekeeping was in its infancy. The first 'peacekeeping' mission deployed was in 1956 – the United Nations Emergency Force (UNEF), which provided a buffer in the Sinai between British, French and Israeli forces and their Egyptian opponents. On the one hand, UNEF provided the impetus for the codification of the UN's approach to peacekeeping for the next 45 years and demonstrated the UN's role as a neutral third party attempting to prevent the escalation of conflict between the superpowers.[23] On the other hand, the ad-hoc nature of peacekeeping where forces needed to be cobbled together at the last minute was cumbersome. The UN operation in the Congo (1960 to 1964), the only UN-led operation in the cold war period to be authorised under Chapter VII and to have a humanitarian mandate, further demonstrated this problem, especially the need for faster deployment and improved training of peacekeepers.[24]

Unsurprisingly, these two early missions prompted calls for the creation of something more permanent.[25] Some proposals were on the modest side. For example, in 1957, a commission of military experts and politicians chaired by Lord Packenham recommended creating a permanent, directly recruited, internationally balanced, well-equipped and lightly armed force of around 20,000 soldiers. The force would have only deployed in permissive environments and have conducted fairly non-confrontational peacekeeping tasks such as supervising elections.[26] Other proposals were further reaching. The idea for a "UN Peace Force", perhaps as well known for its ambitious scope as for the length and detail of the proposal, was designed by two American lawyers, Grenville Clarke and Louis Sohn. It was part of their wider plan for global disarmament. The Peace Force would have comprised a standing force of up to 600,000 people in addition to a reserve force of up to 1.2 million.[27] It would have been charged with preventing or responding to international violence,[28] "specifically violent aggression or serious defiance of the authority of the UN".[29] Reflecting the mood of the cold war where the UNSC was perennially deadlocked, Clarke and Sohn's Peace Force would have been under the strategic direction of the Military Staff Committee but the General Assembly could have deployed it.[30]

Other proposals also emerged during the cold war, especially among academic and NGO communities;[31] however, the cold war rivalry in part stymied the realisation of such ambitious ideas and almost all discussions on UN peacekeeping reforms focused on improving standby arrangements.[32] The reform proposals that did emerge during this time (for example Frye's 1957 proposal)[33] seemed to meet a tortured fate which would go on to plague subsequent plans and studies on a UN Legion in the post-cold war era. On the one hand, the architects of these ideas recognised the political intransigencies that would hinder proposals for standing forces but, on the other hand, they noted that only a force that does not rely on national contingents would be truly effective and reliable.

One proposal, notable partly because its architects had been involved in the UNEPS campaign from the early days, was Saul Mendlovitz and Robert Johansen's 1980 prototype of a "standing international constabulary or police force".[34] Mendlovitz and Johansen were full-time academics at the time but they released their proposal under the banner of the New York-based Institute for World Order with which they were both affiliated. The authors were prophetic in some ways because they anticipated that the UN would play a much larger role in international peace and security in the coming years – a prediction that was realised a decade later. Their idea of an individually recruited international police force has much in common with the proposed UNEPS. Besides the fact that both proposals envisaged individually recruited forces under one command structure to address the problem of slow-deploying peacekeepers, they would each conduct "humanitarian interventions"[35] through, for example, creating humanitarian corridors (or 'safe areas' as they are known today) in conflict zones "from which all belligerents were excluded". They would both also address structural violence through diplomacy.[36] The mandate of the Mendlovitz and Johansen police force, however, was broader than that of the proposed UNEPS and encompassed a range of tasks which would contribute to upholding "peace, economic well-being, social justice and environmental balance".[37] The projected size of the international police force – an initial 5,000-person force, supplemented by earmarked national contingents, if necessary[38] – was also smaller than that of UNEPS. Plus, unlike UNEPS, it would be composed solely of police and not personnel from other professions. Needless to say, their proposal, like others of the era, was never realised.

Post-cold war proposals

Between 1992 and 1995, there were more proposals relating to standing forces under UN control than at any other time before or after.[39] Civil conflicts that were festering during the cold war erupted and many people felt that, now that the deadlock in the UNSC had relaxed, the UN could finally fulfil its mandate to maintain international peace and security. In the early 1990s, Kofi Annan, who was Under-Secretary General for Peacekeeping at the time, reflected that "we were all expectant. It was thrilling and we saw possibilities of doing ... what the organization was expected to do [in 1945]".[40] As the number of UN peacekeeping operations significantly increased so too did the world's expectations of them. They were not just supposed to 'keep the peace' already established between belligerents, they were also expected to prevent conflict from erupting, enforce peace where there was none to keep, halt mass human rights violations and build peace to maximise the likelihood that an unstable state would not slide back into turmoil. This was also a time of tragic failures for the organisation, especially in the inability and unwillingness of UN peacekeeping forces to protect civilians.

An Agenda for Peace – edging towards a standing capacity

UNSG Boutros Boutros-Ghali's seminal 1992 report, *An Agenda for Peace*, captured the UN's position during the post-cold war years on the cumbersome peacekeeping system. Radically, he asked member states to make their armed forces available to the UNSC for enforcement purposes under Article 43 of the UN Charter "not only on an ad hoc basis but on a permanent basis".[41] The UNSG was not recommending directly recruiting personnel and was still relying on the goodwill of states to hand their forces over to the UNSC Council; yet he was asking them to do so *permanently*, a call suggestive of a standing force. He recognised that such armed forces would be no match for sophisticated military machines but could still counter a threat "posed by a military force of a lesser order".[42]

In addition, Boutros-Ghali specifically called for the creation of "peace enforcement units" that would be used "in clearly defined circumstances and with their terms of reference specified in advance".[43] These would be available on-call from member states. They would "consist of troops that have volunteered for such service", and would be "more heavily armed than peacekeeping forces".[44] Their purpose would be to support peacekeeping forces in responding to violations of ceasefires and they could be used with the consent of the belligerents. Both recommendations deviated from the norms of traditional peacekeeping. *An Agenda for Peace*, however, was never formally accepted by the UNSC or the General Assembly, and the UNSG himself reneged on his proposed peace enforcement units in favour of standby arrangements.[45]

Urquhart's UN volunteer military force

During the period surrounding the release of *An Agenda for Peace*, the UN deployed multiple complex peace operations which encountered a range of problems. The missions in Cambodia and Angola highlighted the impotence of UN peacekeepers in the face of violent harassment, while the missions in Mozambique and Somalia demonstrated the challenge of convincing governments to contribute troops – because of political, financial or military reasons – resulting in deployment delays or operations with inadequate numbers of personnel.[46]

This led Brian Urquhart, former Under Secretary General for Special Political Affairs and Assistant Secretary-General (to name just two of his UN titles), to write a piece in the *New York Review of Books* in 1993 calling for the creation of a UN Volunteer Military Force that would be directly recruited on an individual basis. Urquhart had previously been opposed to the creation of a permanent international police force because of the cost of setting one up as well as global political and ideological divisions;[47] however, the lessons of post-cold war missions and the optimism of the 1990s led him to change his mind. Cambodia, Angola, Mozambique and Somalia illustrated to Urquhart that the UN was unable to deal promptly, effectively and forcefully with conflict. His small, well-trained UN Volunteer Military Force would have been preventative and able to address situations, such as a humanitarian crisis or ceasefire violations, before the conflict spiralled out of control. Importantly, it would have been willing to take "combat risks" as it would have been trained in the "bloody business of fighting" in low-level but dangerous conflicts and so would not have been limited to the role of traditional peacekeepers. It therefore might have deployed without the consent of one or more of the belligerents provided there was UNSC authorisation. But it would not have replaced preventative diplomacy, traditional peacekeeping or large-scale enforcement under Chapter VII. Commentators, however, argued that practical, political and normative factors would have hindered the realisation of Urquhart's idea.[48]

Calls for changes did not subside, especially in the wake of the Rwandan genocide in 1994.

Rwanda: an impetus for a UN standing force

On 24 September 1993, the UNSG recommended to the UNSC that the United Nations Assistance Mission for Rwanda (UNAMIR) should be established. Its central aim would be to create an environment conducive to implementing the Arusha Peace Accords[49] and, consequently, a functioning transitional Government.[50] UNAMIR was deployed as a neutral intervention force expecting a relatively straightforward mission.[51] It was authorised to contribute to the security of Kigali, monitor the ceasefire, expand the demilitarised zone, demobilise forces, assist with mine clearance, provide humanitarian assistance and monitor security during the period leading up to democratic elections.[52] Because of the lack of intelligence about the underlying political dynamics as well as the challenges faced by the peacekeeping mission, the UN had no contingency plans to respond to an escalation of violence, let alone to the genocide that ensued.

From the beginning, UNAMIR was plagued with an inadequate number of troops and equipment, delays in deployment, a weak mandate and limited political will from UN member states to support the mission.[53] The UN Force Commander in Rwanda, Lieutenant General Romeo Dallaire, estimated after a reconnaissance mission that 4,500 troops would be required, yet only 2,548 of them were approved.[54] It took five months after the UNSC authorised UNAMIR before the force was fully deployed in late March 1994.[55] On the night of 6 April, the Rwandan President's plane was shot down and the systematic killings of Rwandan civilians began in earnest. The subsequent murder of the Rwandan Prime Minister and ten Belgian peacekeepers prompted the governments of Belgium and France to withdraw all their forces,[56] despite the deteriorating security situation and the unfolding genocide. As a result, on 21 April, the UNSC authorised the reduction in UNAMIR force levels from around 2,500 to 270 troops, reflecting the concerns of member states.⁵⁷ The US and UK were reportedly reluctant to move from a Chapter VI consensual peacekeeping operation to the higher risk, Chapter VII confrontational peace enforcement mission.⁵⁸ This meant Dallaire's forces were only mandated to fire when fired upon and not to protect Rwandans from violence.⁵⁹ As a result of the crisis in Rwanda, 800,000 people were killed over the course of approximately 100 days from 6 April through to mid-July 1994.⁶⁰

Similar patterns – no appetite in the UNSC to provide UN peacekeepers with a mandate to protect civilians, and governments' unwillingness to place their citizens in the line of fire because of there being no perceived political, economic or strategic rewards – were played out in Srebrenica, Bosnia two years later with equally devastating consequences. The UN's experiences in Rwanda and Bosnia reignited an interest in standby arrangements and led in 1995 to a resurfacing of proposals for a UN standing force. I have argued together with colleagues elsewhere that a UNEPS could have helped to overcome some of the practical and political obstacles faced by UNAMIR.⁶¹

UN standby arrangements

One step which the international community took to strengthen the UN's capacity to respond rapidly to crises was to establish the UNSAS in 1994. It is still operational today. The arrangement is based on the conditional commitments of participating states to peace operations of, for example, military formations, specialised personnel (civilian and military) and equipment within an agreed timeframe. There is no guarantee, however, that these will be provided to meet the requirements of an operation. Indeed, not one of the participating states agreed to contribute troops to UNAMIR, the peacekeeping operation deployed at the time of the Rwandan genocide, to help avert the atrocities that ensued.⁶² Furthermore, the speed at which national contingents are deployed is left to the discretion of the participating state. It is often based on the perceived risks of a mission and the level of interests at stake. UNSAS also specifies that personnel and resources will only be used for Chapter VI peacekeeping, prohibiting contribution to Chapter VII enforcement operations.⁶³ This is despite the fact that there have been more Chapter VII peace operations from 1993 to 2008 than at any other time in the UN's history.⁶⁴

Notwithstanding the progress on UNSAS and related projects (such as the Standby High-Readiness Brigade) in the latter part of the 1990s, the UN faced difficulties in quickly deploying peace operations in complex and non-permissive environments. This was one of the many factors that led to the publication of the *Report of the Panel on UN Peace Operations*, known as the *Brahimi Report* after the chair of the panel, the former Algerian foreign minister Lakhdar Brahimi.⁶⁵ The Panel reaffirmed the difficulties the UN faced in deploying peace operations; however, it placed renewed emphasis on deployment standards and 'on-call' expertise, particularly through further development of UNSAS, rather than recommending a permanent UN force.

A new interest in a UN legion

Where did this leave ideas for a permanent, individually recruited UN force? The 'high-water mark' of interest in the subject was 1995,[66] and it is here that the roots of the proposed UNEPS can be found, albeit in a tangled form. The Rwanda experience and subsequent 'lessons learned' were catalytic in the emergence of multiple proposals with strikingly similar features during this period. There were several non-government proposals[67] and academic studies on force strengh and design.[68] There were also two prominent national reports published in 1995 by the Netherlands and Canada on options for a UN rapid reaction capability.[69] The Dutch study investigated the possibility of creating a permanent 'rapid deployment brigade' at the service of the UNSC.[70] Its main goal would have been to prevent crises and humanitarian emergencies. But it received no significant international support.[71] The Canadian study, *Towards a Rapid Reaction Capability*, by contrast, focused on improving a broader range of peacekeeping activities and strengthening UN standby arrangements. Peter Langille led a team that developed the standing options in the Canadian report. Contributors to the report also included Sir Brian Urquhart, John Polanyi, Nobel Laureate of the University of Toronto, and the late Sergio Vieira de Mello, who at the time was with the UN High Commission for Refugees.[72]

One of the 26 recommendations of the Canadian study was for the UNSG to examine the technical and political feasibility of a small "UN Standing Emergency Group" that would be under the command and control of the UNSG and the UNSC.[73] It did not, however, explicitly advocate its creation because of the lukewarm reception the proposal was expected to receive following the Dutch study[74] as well as in light of events at the time. As Langille explains:

> the final Canadian report backed away from the more ambitious plans for a standing UN emergency group, largely because the Americans were already signalling a shift back to NATO, away from UN peace operations, a shift strongly favoured by Northern defence establishments.[75]

The US aversion to UN peace operations stemmed in part from their experiences in Somalia. In October 1993, the US-led operation in Somalia suffered serious blows with the violent and very public assassination of 18 US Rangers in Mogadishu which was broadcast by news stations across America and the world. This precipitated the US withdrawal from the mission and dovetailed with the Presidential Policy Directive on peacekeeping in May the following year. Known as the PPD-25, the Clinton administration's directive set forth rigorous standards for US involvement in peace operations, especially those involving combat.[76] Despite the political climate at the time and the cautious tone of the report, the Canadian study noted that:

> UN volunteers offer the best prospect of a completely reliable, well-trained rapid reaction capability. Without the need to consult national authorities,

the UN could cut response times significantly and volunteers could be deployed within hours of a Security Council decision.[77]

The responsibility to protect

Six years later, the Canadian government sponsored the International Commission on Intervention and State Sovereignty (ICISS) which was also partly a reaction to the failures of the international community to prevent the tragedies in Rwanda, Bosnia, East Timor and elsewhere in the 1990s. The ICISS mandate was to develop global political consensus on how to move from 'words to deeds' in the international community, particularly through the UN, on humanitarian intervention or "intervention for human protection purposes", to use the clunky expression that the Commission adopted. Wary that the term 'humanitarian intervention' sounded alarm bells among many in the international community, ICISS coined the term the Responsibility to Protect (R2P). The central tenet of R2P is that sovereignty entails responsibilities as well as rights. ICISS posited that each state has the responsibility to protect its population from "large scale ethnic cleansing" or "large scale loss of life".[78] But if the state is unable or unwilling to do so, it abrogates this responsibility and the R2P shifts to the international community.[79]

The ICISS report achieved three main conceptual shifts that went some way to overcoming the humanitarian intervention deadlock. First, by changing the language of humanitarian intervention to R2P, it divorced the doctrine from the 'right to intervene' debate. R2P advocates that intervention should be designed and undertaken from the perspective of the intervened or those seeking or needing support, not the interveners.[80] Second, it tries to reconcile the tension between human rights and sovereignty by conceiving of sovereignty not only in terms of control but also of responsibility. This language is less confrontational and maximises the doctrine's political saliency.[81] Third, it creates a threshold for humanitarian intervention and presents five criteria based on the just war doctrine for decision-makers to use to assess whether or not to intervene. These are: (1) right authority; (2) just cause; (3) right intention (whether it is primarily to halt or avert the threat); (4) last resort (whether there are reasonable available peaceful alternatives); and (5) proportionality of the response and the 'balance of consequences' (whether overall more good than harm would be done by a military intervention). Finally, because R2P contains a three-layered responsibility – the responsibility to *prevent* large scale loss of life and ethnic cleansing; the responsibility to *react* when these atrocities occur; and the responsibility to *rebuild* after the conflict – "it directs our attention to the costs and results of action".[82]

While ICISS did not call for a standing force, the UNSG's 2009 report on R2P stated that "there are substantial gaps in capacity, imagination and will across the whole spectrum of prevention and protection measures relating to the responsibility to protect". "Nowhere is that gap more pronounced or more damaging than in the realm of forceful and timely response to the most flagrant crimes and violations relating to the responsibility to protect", he wrote.[83] During the General Assembly debate on R2P this same year, South Korea and New Zealand called for the creation of a rapid reaction force.[84] Despite this recognition of a gap in the potential implementation of R2P, the UNSG noted that the UN "is still far from developing the kind of rapid-response military capacity most needed to handle the sort of rapidly unfolding atrocity crimes".[85] As will be seen below, UNEPS is presented by some of its promoters as a tool that would provide the UN with just this kind of capacity.

Langille's UN emergency service

A year after ICISS coined the R2P principle, Peter Langille produced a significant study of his own in 2002 based partly on the idea proposed in the Canadian report, which he helped write, as well as previous papers that he (co-) authored.[86] His study responded to the call to develop the technical properties – and to a lesser extent the political ones – of a UN Standing Emergency Group.[87] It also appeared to respond to the demise of the initiative Friends of Rapid Deployment (FORD), which was developed by Canada and had the support of 27 other states. FORD aimed to provide the UN Department of Peacekeeping Operations with a rapidly deployable headquarters through providing gratis staff but it confronted opposition from some members of the UNGA because most of the staff were from the West. Western governments also expressed a renewed interest in NATO at the time.[88]

Langille proposed a multidimensional and multifunctional UN Emergency Service (UN ES) composed of well-trained and well-equipped military, police and civilian volunteers numbering around 13,200. Personnel would come from all around the world. He envisaged that a UN ES would be based at a static headquarters where training, planning and other activities to prepare the group for deployment would take place.[89] There would also be two mobile field headquarters with identical "deployable military elements" including a military brigade and three companies of police as well as civilians.[90] UN ES would assume a variety of roles, including the prevention of conflict and the protection of civilians. While Langille points out that the UN ES should comprise "combat-capable soldiers", it would focus on defensive, non-provocative interventions as well as peacemaking, peacebuilding and the delivery of humanitarian aid. In certain situations, however, it could manage a Chapter VII operation thanks to its robust and elite military capability, along with its modern, interoperable equipment (or the ability of diverse equipment to work together).[91] Langille's UN ES would have a modular structure in which smaller components could be used in the early stages of a UN operation or to rescue a struggling mission.[92] The start-up cost of a UN ES was projected at US$1.2 billion with around $760 million per year to maintain.[93]

Robert Johansen, Professor of Political Science and Peace Studies at Notre Dame University in the US, noted in 2003 that Langille's proposal for a UN ES was the most sophisticated to date.[94] Indeed, the idea contains detailed and unique information about force structure, basing and equipment. Yet the origins of this proposal can be traced back to earlier initiatives, an observation acknowledged by the author himself.[95] He writes:

> this is not a new idea, but one that draws on earlier and broader initiatives.... A number of the general requirements for such a permanent Standing UN Service have already been identified in related studies conducted by governments, organizations and individuals.[96]

First, it is almost universally recognised that the international community's rapid-response capability ought to be improved.[97] Most if not all major ideas for a permanent force that emerged in the 1990s, but also earlier, criticised the cumbersome peacekeeping system which resulted in slow deploying, and poorly trained and equipped peacekeepers. In response, they called for the establishment of an individually recruited, well-trained and (mostly but not always) well-equipped standing force.[98] Similarly, many previous ideas distinguish between their proposed force or service and a UN army or an Article 43-type arrangement. A much smaller capacity, numbering between 5,000–12,000 personnel, is often advocated instead.[99] Many (with notable exceptions[100]) clarify that their proposed force would fill the gap between UNSC resolution and deployment of peacekeepers, until a larger operation is deployed (if that is deemed necessary) rather than conduct sustained or intense war fighting.[101] In other words, they would be able to manage traditional peacekeeping operations as well as more complex, multidimensional ones that require minimal enforcement. A fairly unusual feature of the UN ES is that it would comprise police, civilians and the military conducting a range of tasks – from providing safe areas for civilians and humanitarian assistance, to low-scale combat – in complex operations.[102] In sum, while certain attributes of the proposed UN ES can be traced back to earlier ideas, Langille's proposal was nevertheless a significant one that triggered a global initiative for a UNEPS.

A nascent transnational advocacy network

In December 2003, Langille presented his idea in a consolidated form at a symposium called "Genocide and Crimes Against Humanity: The Challenge of Prevention and Enforcement" in Santa Barbara, California. Participants included diplomatic and security experts, academics and social activists such as Lloyd Axworthy, former Canadian Foreign Minister; William Pace, Executive Director of the World Federalist Movement-Institute for Global Policy (WFM-IGP) and convener of the International Coalition for the International Criminal Court; Richard Falk, Professor Emeritus of International Law, Princeton University and Chair of the Nuclear Age Peace Foundation; Saul Mendlovitz; Dag Hammarskjøld, Professor of International Law, Rutgers Law School, co-director of the World Order Models Project and co-founder of GAPW; Don Kraus, Executive Vice President of the Citizens for Global Solutions; and Joanna Weschler of the Security Council Report.[103] At this meeting, Langille's proposal was largely endorsed and the word "peace" added to the title – so the UN Emergency Service became the UN Emergency *Peace* Service.

In 2005, 35 experts from around the world met in Cuenca, Spain to examine the "merits of establishing a permanent United Nations emergency capability to protect people from genocide, war crimes, and crimes against humanity".[104] Many of the participants at Santa Barbara – such as Langille, Mendlovitz, Kraus and Pace – were present, along with others,[105] several of whom provided intellectual contribution to the proposed UNEPS and went on to become advocates.[106] Participants at the meeting produced a consensus on the basic principles of the proposal (outlined in the introduction to this book) and unpacked important and complex issues, such as the proposed body to authorise a UNEPS and the question of deployment without the consent of the host state. The momentum for a UNEPS culminated in 2006 in the launch of the publication *A United Nations Emergency Peace Service: to prevent genocide and crimes against humanity* which among other things provided a summary of the 2003 and 2005 meetings. Containing an impassioned preface by Brian Urquhart calling for the establishment of a UNEPS, this booklet was published by the WFM–Institute for Global Policy and edited by Robert Johansen.[107] Saul Mendlovitz, commenting on Johansen's role as rapporteur at the UNEPS meetings, said that he was "assiduous in keeping notes and putting them in a form in which they could be used".[108] The booklet also included various perspectives on the proposal by Satish Nambiar, Lieutenant General (retired) Indian Army and former Commander of UN forces in the former Yugoslavia; Alcides Costa Vaz, Professor of International Relations, University of Brasília; Hussein Solomon, Professor and Director, Centre for International Political Studies, University of Pretoria; and Lois Barber, the director of EarthAction, the Massachusetts-based organisation that focuses on global campaigning. William Pace said of the early meetings on UNEPS, "We had 20 people around a table all with different proposals [for a standing UN capacity] which cancelled each other out".[109] Some people, he explained, only wanted a force that would respond to mass violence and genocide; others, like Pace, were more enthusiastic about a force that would also respond to environmental disasters.

What can we call the association of individuals and organisations dedicated to transforming the UNEPS idea into a reality? It most closely resembles a transnational advocacy network (TAN). According to Keck and Sikkink's classic definition, a TAN is a form of collective action comprising actors – which may include international and domestic NGOs, local social movements, academics and (parts of) states and international governmental organisations – distinguishable largely by the "centrality of principled ideas or values in motivating their formation".[110] Their goal is to change the behaviour of states and international organisations. The essence of a TAN is the exchange of information, personnel and services. Some are formalised but many are based on informal contacts.[111] While this description accurately reflects those involved in the UNEPS initiative, the weak strength and low density of the network along with the fact that no government has expressed enough interest in the proposal to champion it at the international level helps to explain why this TAN has not succeeded in efforts to establish a UNEPS.

The 2006 publication on UNEPS mentioned above, says that the WFM, GAPW, and the Nuclear Age Peace Foundation nominally served as co-secretariats for the global UNEPS project.[112] The following discussion aims to convey a general sense of the geographical scope and nature of the activities of those in the UNEPS network as well as to show who is engaging with the proposal.

GAPW is an NGO based in UN Plaza founded by Saul Mendlovitz, the late Jonathan Dean, a distinguished US career diplomat, and the late Randy Forsberg, prominent academic and peace activist. Among its principal sources of financial support is the Ira Wallach Fund for the Eradication of Genocide and the Simons Foundation. While small in size, it focuses on fostering relationships with UN and government officials in New York and its extended network of partners around the world.[113] GAPW, under the current leadership of Robert Zuber and, to a less extent in recent years, Saul Mendlovitz, has also sought to stimulate interest in and support for the UNEPS proposal by, among other things, hosting workshops and roundtables on UNEPS and UNEPS-related topics. The events were mostly organised in collaboration with local and/or international NGOs, universities and think tanks. They have taken place in various parts of the world including the US (2007, 2010, 2012); Austria (2011); Australia (2008); South Africa (2008); Brazil (2009); Cameroon (2009); Indonesia (2009); Belgium (2012); and the UK (2013).[114] Through a process of outreach and consultation, these meetings were an opportunity for the UNEPS proposal to be discussed and diverse perspectives aired. WFM–IGP has also supported GAPW in their work on UNEPS as well as supporting projects that could contribute to UNEPS' implementation. This includes the so-called Small-5 nations in the General Assembly which sought to make an impact on the working methods of the Security Council, including the use of the veto in situations where atrocity crimes are being committed, as well as monitoring its follow-up project – Accountability, Coherence, and Transparency.[115]

A feature of GAPW's outreach has been to present UNEPS within a wider framework of atrocity prevention and UN-based standing peacekeeping capacities of which UNEPS is merely one proposal.[116] As Bob Zuber remarked:

> Our feeling [at GAPW] was that we had to be able to embed the proposal within a larger series of conversations where we have some resonance. When we talk about UNEPS we talk about it in context. We weren't willing to conduct a UNEPS[-only] campaign. This is not the sense of other people [who were present at the early meetings on UNEPS] and we did take some heat for that.[117]

Such a 'contextualised' approach was also adopted in UNEPS-related studies conducted by others at GAPW. For example, a report written by Kavitha Suthanthiraraj and Mariah Quinn considered the UNEPS proposal in the context of its relationship to R2P, regional peacekeeping and other ideas for UN rapid-reaction capacities.[118] The strategic decision to merge the discussion on the UNEPS proposal with other related capabilities (existing or proposed) may have inadvertently isolated some of the original UNEPS advocates who were interested in supporting a more single-minded campaign.[119] Those who tended to disagree with this strategy favoured "compelling, cost-effective" arguments to retain the integrity of the idea in preparation for a time when the political climate would be more receptive to a UNEPS.[120]

Peter Langille has also done a vast amount of work promoting the proposal. He has addressed diverse audiences including the Global Conference on the Prevention of Genocide in Montreal (2007); Japanese senators and parliamentarians of the new government at the time in Tokyo (2009); the World Peace Forum in Vancouver (2006); the International Peace Research Association in Calgary (2006); and the Military and Police Advisors Community in the Permanent Mission of Austria to the United Nations in New York (2008). Langille has spoken at most of the conferences that GAPW has (co-)organised around the world.[121] He has produced multiple papers and power-point presentations explaining the UNEPS concept, case, model and plans as well as written a number of UNEPS advocacy pieces for the print and online media.[122] He is currently undertaking an updated study on the political and technical feasibility of the proposed UNEPS, commissioned by the German NGO Friedrich-Ebert-Stiftung.[123] Langille has also engaged with the UNEPS proposal through the WFM-Canada, which started promoting the idea of a UN ES in 2000.[124] Recently, Fergus Watt of WFM-Canada has produced a brochure – a "UNEPS backgrounder" – which has been disseminated through the UNEPS network and beyond.[125]

The proposed UNEPS has also gained traction elsewhere. All those mentioned earlier who contributed to the 2006 UNEPS booklet – Nambiar, Costa Vaz, Solomon, and Barber – have gone on, at one point or another, to contribute to the UNEPS network in their own unique way.[126] For example, Hussein Solomon, director of the Centre for International Political Studies, University of Pretoria, has taken the UNEPS proposal to parts of the Middle East, south-east Asia and sub-Saharan Africa. He has conducted several workshops for diplomats based in Pretoria, for African Union (AU) military officials and others.[127] Another contributor from sub-Saharan Africa is Christian Tanyi, President of the Martin Luther King Junior Memorial Foundation, who has advocated the proposal in Cameroon.

In the UK and Europe, Joachim Koops and Daniel Fiott of Vesalius College, Brussels have collaborated with GAPW on UNEPS-related initiatives.[128] In the Asia-Pacific region, former Japanese Senator Tadashi Inuzuka incorporated UNEPS into his policy platform. In 2008, the Upper House of the Japanese Parliament adopted the Terror Elimination Bill which included articles specifically addressing the establishment of a new UN service "capable of immediately taking necessary measures to respond to threats to international peace and security".[129] Another UNEPS contributor in this region is the Centre for Peace and Conflict Studies at the University of Sydney (of which I am a part). Staff members at the Centre have conducted research on the UNEPS proposal in recent years, much of which is used as a basis for this publication, as well as organising events and advocacy for the proposal.

In North America, Pera Wells, the former Secretary-General of the World Federation of United Nations Associations, has contributed to the UNEPS network through, for example, sharing her contacts with diplomats in permanent country missions in New York with those who were actively promoting the idea. Don Kraus and his colleagues at the US-based NGO, Citizens for Global Solutions, were largely responsible for persuading two members of the US Congress to draft a bill in support of UNEPS. In March 2007, Resolution 213 in the House of Representatives addressed the need for a UNEPS to prevent genocide and crimes against humanity and bolster the UN's peacekeeping efforts. It stated that "The United States should use its voice, vote, and influence at the United Nations to facilitate and support the creation of a United Nations Emergency Peace Service". The resolution framed UNEPS as a tool to promote the national security interest of the US. It also highlighted the immense cost of dealing with the aftermath of genocide and identified UNEPS as a critical means of strengthening the UN's preventative capabilities.[130] Kraus, along with other UNEPS supporters, has also produced advocacy material on the proposal.[131] The aim of such pieces is to examine particular cases (Darfur, for example) where UNEPS could have prevented or alleviated widespread suffering among the civilian populations.[132] Recently, Saul Mendlovitz, Melina Lito of GAPW and Captain Ted Westfall of the US Army developed a "Draft Statute for the Formation and Operation of the United Nations Emergency Peace Service for the Prevention of Genocide and Crimes against Humanity" which placed most of the agreed attributes of the proposal into a form that was familiar to UN policymakers and diplomatic missions.

The UNEPS proposal has been presented as a tool to operationalise R2P, especially given the broader attention the doctrine has received since the 2005 World Summit. Reflecting upon the early UNEPS meetings, Saul Mendlovitz explains that "we attempted to sanitise UNEPS from threats to peace, breaches of peace or acts of aggression by a state that are covered in Chapter VII of the UN Charter. We were about genocide and crimes against humanity, and now that R2P has come into being, other forms of mass atrocities".[133] This focus has gone on to define certain UNEPS advocacy initiatives. For example, Christian Tanyi in Cameroon conducted a four-day event on UNEPS and R2P in 2010.[134] In 2011, the WFM-Canada, together with GAPW released a global sign-on letter to UN Country Missions informing them about the UNEPS proposal and encouraging them to support it in the up-coming UN General Assembly meeting on R2P. In this letter, UNEPS was presented as a potential addition to the "R2P toolbox".[135] The International Coalition for the Responsibility to Protect recently provided funding for a UNEPS meeting in Cameroon[136] and in 2010 GAPW along with Austrian civil society organisations hosted a symposium called "The UN's Evolving Responsibility to Protect Civilians from Atrocity Crimes" at which UNEPS was discussed in the context of 'Third Pillar' response capacities.[137]

Conclusion

I have made five basic points in this chapter relating to the history of a standing UN Legion, the development of the UNEPS proposal and its network of supporters. First, the sheer number of proposals for a truly international standing force that have emerged over the last 70 years – and failed – both demonstrates the truly ambitious nature of this task and suggests that such calls are unlikely to subside. Despite evidence that the current system is broken, states cannot agree to implement this idea. Second, proposals for a UN standing force tend to correspond with major global events, changes or failures. Rwanda is a case in point. Third, while I showed that the proposed UNEPS stemmed from Langille's idea of a UN ES, key attributes also echo previous proposals of a similar nature. Fourth, this chapter argues that the UNEPS network has a transnational reach, with people from government, NGO, academic and UN circles in a range of countries engaging with the proposal both intellectually and at the level of advocacy. The network, however, still does not have the requisite strength, density or traction to be a powerful global force for reasons which this research goes on to unpack. Fifth, I reveal that GAPW made a strategic decision to merge UNEPS with other similar proposals – a move that has been unpopular with some UNEPS supporters – and that certain members of this network have framed UNEPS as a tool to operationalise R2P.

In the following chapter, the proposed UNEPS is examined in more detail. I explore the norms and practical ideas underpinning the proposal, the identity and interests of its core promoters and present a framework to consider how it might be re-worked to increase its chances of being implemented.

Notes

1. Lie, *In the Cause of the Peace*.
2. Urquhart, "For a UN Volunteer Military Force".
3. Clark and Sohn, *Introduction to World Peace*, xxi.
4. Langille, *Bridging the Commitment–Capacity Gap*.
5. Frye, *A United Nations Peace Force*, 46.
6. Ibid., 47.
7. Ibid., 51.
8. Pugh, "An International Police Force", 336–7.
9. Kinloch, *A UN 'Legion'*, 15.
10. Stassen, "Blueprint for a World Government".
11. United Nations, *Charter of the United Nations*.
12. Ibid., Articles 43.1 and 43.2.
13. Ibid., Article 43.4.
14. Roberts, "Proposals for UN Standing Forces", 100–1.
15. Kinloch, *A UN 'Legion'*, 28–9; Miller, "Universal Soldiers".
16. Sohn, "The Authority of the United Nations", 229.
17. United Nations, *Charter of the United Nations*.
18. Sohn, "The Authority of the United Nations", 229.
19. Bowett, *United Nations Forces*.
20. Lie, *In the Cause of the Peace*, 98–9.
21. Roberts, "Proposals for UN Standing Forces", 101.

22 Lie, *In the Cause of the Peace*, 99, 192.
23 Bellamy, Williams, and Griffin, *Understanding Peacekeeping*, 176–7, 179.
24 Kinloch, *A UN 'Legion'*, 73, 88–92.
25 Roberts, "Proposals for UN Standing Forces", 104; Kinloch, *A UN 'Legion'*, 76.
26 Kinloch, *A UN 'Legion'*, 80–1.
27 Clark and Sohn, *Introduction to World Peace*, 300.
28 Ibid., xxii.
29 Ibid., 300.
30 Ibid.
31 Such as Bowett, *United Nations Forces*.
32 Frye, *A United Nations Peace Force*; U Thant, "United Nations Peace Force"; Bloomfield, *International Military Forces*.
33 Frye, *A United Nations Peace Force*.
34 Johansen and Mendlovitz, "The Role of Enforcement of Law".
35 Ibid., 324.
36 Ibid., 312.
37 Ibid., 309.
38 Ibid., 320.
39 Roberts, "Proposals for UN Standing Forces".
40 Cited in Barnett, *Eyewitness to a Genocide*, 28.
41 Boutros-Ghali, *An Agenda for Peace*, para. 43.
42 Ibid.
43 Ibid., para. 44.
44 Ibid.
45 Kinloch, *A UN 'Legion'*, 141; UN General Assembly, *Supplement to an Agenda for Peace*.
46 Urquhart, "For a U.N. Volunteer Military Force".
47 Urquhart, "United Nations Peace Forces", 351.
48 Hamilton *et al.*, "A UN Volunteer Military Force".
49 The Arusha Peace Agreement (the Arusha Peace Accords) was the agreement between the Rwandan Patriotic Front and the Government of Rwanda signed on 4 August 1993. It consisted of five protocols (accords) which ended the civil war in Rwanda and began a peace process. Dallaire, *Shake Hands with the Devil*, 524.
50 Adelman and Suhrke, *The Path of a Genocide*, 275.
51 Jones, "The Arusha Peace Process", 143.
52 UN Security Council, *Resolution 872*.
53 UN Security Council, *Actions of the United Nations During the 1994 Genocide in Rwanda*, 31–41.
54 Ibid., 8, 32.
55 UN Security Council, *Resolution 872*; UN Security Council, *Actions of the United Nations During the 1994 Genocide in Rwanda*, 35.
56 UN Security Council, *Actions of the United Nations During the 1994 Genocide in Rwanda*, 69.
57 Ibid., 22; Feil, "Preventing Genocide", 35–6.
58 Feil, "Preventing Genocide", 97.
59 UN Security Council, *Actions of the United Nations During the 1994 Genocide in Rwanda*, 16–17.
60 Dallaire, *Shake Hands with the Devil*, xvii.
61 Herro, Lambourne, and Penklis, "Peacekeeping and Peace Enforcement in Africa".
62 UN General Assembly, *Supplement to an Agenda for Peace*, para. 43.
63 Langille, *Bridging the Commitment–Capacity Gap*, 40–1.
64 Bellamy, Williams, and Griffin, *Understanding Peacekeeping*, 228.
65 Brahimi, *Report of the Panel on United Nations Peace Operations [Brahimi Report]*.
66 Roberts, "Proposals for UN Standing Forces", 115.

67 Commission on Global Governance, *Our Global Neighborhood*; Independent Working Group on the Future of the United Nations, *The United Nations in Its Second Half-Century*.
68 Conetta and Knight, *Vital Force*.
69 The study "The Netherlands Non-paper: A UN Rapid Deployment Brigade: A preliminary study", revised version, April 1995, is found in Annex II of Leurdijk, *A UN Rapid Deployment Brigade*. Also Government of Canada, *Towards a Rapid Reaction Capability*.
70 Leurdijk, *A UN Rapid Deployment Brigade*.
71 Government of Canada, *Towards a Rapid Reaction Capability*, 60.
72 For a full list of contributors see ibid., 72–4.
73 Ibid., 63.
74 Ibid., 60.
75 Email conversation by author, 1 August 2013.
76 The White House, *Presidential Decision Directive/Nsc-25*.
77 Government of Canada, *Towards a Rapid Reaction Capability*, 62.
78 The circumstances or 'triggers' for military intervention are: "[L]arge scale loss of life, actual or apprehended, with genocidal intent or not, which is the product either of deliberate state action, or state neglect or inability to act, or a failed state situation; or large scale 'ethnic cleansing', actual or apprehended, whether carried out by killing, forced expulsion, acts of terror or rape" [bold in original] (International Commission on Intervention and State Sovereignty, *The Responsibility to Protect*, xii).
79 International Commission on Intervention and State Sovereignty, *The Responsibility to Protect*, xi.
80 Ibid., 17.
81 Ibid., 13, 17.
82 Ibid., 17.
83 UN General Assembly, "Implementing the Responsibility to Protect", para 60.
84 Hehir, *The Responsibility to Protect*, 247.
85 UN General Assembly, *Implementing the Responsibility to Protect*, para. 64.
86 Langille and Faille, "Preliminary Blueprint for Long-Term Options"; Langille, "Conflict Prevention".
87 Langille, *Bridging the Commitment–Capacity Gap*, 89.
88 Langille, "Conflict Prevention", 225–7; Bellamy, Williams, and Griffin, *Understanding Peacekeeping*, 131; Langille, "The Initiative for a UN Emergency Peace Service".
89 Langille, *Bridging the Commitment–Capacity Gap*, 90, 94.
90 Ibid., 95.
91 Ibid., 93, 94, 96.
92 Ibid., 96.
93 Ibid., 98–9.
94 Wang, "A Symposium on Genocide and Crimes against Humanity".
95 Langille, *Bridging the Commitment–Capacity Gap*, 64–5, 89.
96 Ibid., 89.
97 Roberts, "Proposals for UN Standing Forces", 100.
98 Johansen, "UN Peacekeeping"; Haynes and Stanley, "The UN Needs a 'Fire Brigade'"; Heidenrich, *Why US Conservatives Should Support a UN Legion*; Leurdijk, *A UN Rapid Deployment Brigade*; Independent Working Group on the Future of the United Nations, *The United Nations in Its Second Half-Century*.
99 Lie, *In the Cause of the Peace*, 98–9.
100 Conetta and Knight, *Vital Force*.
101 Urquhart, "For a U.N. Volunteer Military Force"; Haynes and Stanley, "The UN Needs a 'Fire Brigade'"; Commission on Global Governance, *Our Global Neighborhood*; Heidenrich, *Why US Conservatives Should Support a UN Legion*;

Independent Working Group on the Future of the United Nations, *The United Nations in Its Second Half-Century*.
102 Only the two following proposals contained this feature: Independent Working Group on the Future of the United Nations, *The United Nations in Its Second Half-Century*; Government of Canada, *Towards a Rapid Reaction Capability*.
103 The meeting was co-sponsored by the Nuclear Age Peace Foundation; the Simons Centre for Peace and Disarmament Studies, Liu Institute for Global Issues, University of British Columbia; GAPW; and the Law and Society Program, University of California, Santa Barbara, 5–6 December 2003.
104 Johansen, "Cuenca Report", 43.
105 These included: Alcides Costa Vaz, Professor of International Relations and Executive Coordinator, Center for Mercosur Studies, Instituto de Relações Internacionais, Universidade de Brasília; Jonathan Dean, Former United States Ambassador; Adviser on Security Issues, Union of Concerned Scientists; Hussein Solomon, Professor and Director, Centre for International Political Studies, University of Pretoria; Stuart Rees, Professor Emeritus, Centre for Peace and Conflict Studies, University of Sydney; Satish Nambiar, Lt. Gen. (retired) Indian Army and former Commander of UN forces in the former Yugoslavia; Director, The United Service Institution of India; Lois Barber, Executive Director, EarthAction North America; Creative Director, the World Future Council Initiative; Detlev Wolter, Head of Division, EU Policy and Law, State Chancellery Brandenburg, Germany.
106 Johansen, *A United Nations Emergency Peace Service*, Appendix B.
107 Ibid.
108 Interview by author with Saul Mendlovitz, 23 August 2013, New York, USA.
109 Phone interview by author with William Pace, 27 August 2013, New York, USA.
110 Keck and Sikkink, *Activists Beyond Borders*, 1.
111 Ibid., 2, 6.
112 Krieger, Mendlovitz and Pace, "Introduction", 16.
113 GAPW, "Partner Organizations".
114 GAPW, "Conference Reports".
115 Email correspondence by author with William Pace, 15 April 2014.
116 See for example Zuber and Curran, "Peacekeeping and Rapid Reaction".
117 Interview by author with Bob Zuber, 23 August 2013, New York, USA.
118 Suthanthiraraj and Quinn, *Standing for Change*.
119 Interview by author with Bob Zuber, 23 August 2013, New York, USA.
120 Anonymous book reviewer, 2013.
121 Global Common Security i3, "Peter Langille: Biography".
122 For a full list of Langille's contribution to the UNEPS initiative see ibid.
123 GAPW, "Timely Response to the Threat of Mass Atrocities".
124 Email correspondence by author with Peter Langille, 1 August 2013. For example, World Federalist Movement-Canada, "Analyst: Create Emergency Peace Service – Save Countless Lives".
125 World Federalist Movement, "UNEPS Backgrounder".
126 Interview by author with Bob Zuber, 23 August 2013, New York, USA.
127 GAPW and University of Pretoria, "UNEPS/GAPW Regional Capacity Building".
128 Interview by author with Bob Zuber, 23 August 2013, New York, USA.
129 Inuzuka, "Terror Elimination Bill".
130 Suthanthiraraj and Quinn, *Standing for Change*, 27.
131 Camilleri, "Why We Need a UN Crisis Team"; Mendez, "The Prevention of Genocide and Its Challenges"; Kraus, "Lebanon, Sudan: Who You Gonna Call?"; Kraus, "Syria: Who You Gonna Call?"
132 As a member of GAPW, my colleagues and I at the Centre for Peace and Conflict Studies at the University of Sydney have also been responsible for producing some advocacy and information articles on UNEPS.

133 Interview by author with Saul Mendlovitz, 23 August 2013, New York, USA.
134 Martin Luther King Jr. Memorial Foundation, "Yaounde Regional Workshop on R2P-UNEPS 2010".
135 World Federalist Movement–Canada and GAPW, "Support for UNEPS at UN GA Interactive Dialogue on R2P".
136 Interview by author with Bob Zuber, 23 August 2013, New York, USA.
137 GAPW and The Project for UNEPS, "UNEPS in Context".

References

Adelman, Howard and Astri Suhrke. *The Path of a Genocide: The Rwanda Crisis from Uganda to Zaire.* New Brunswick, Canada: Transaction Publishers, 2000.

Barnett, Michael N. *Eyewitness to a Genocide: The United Nations and Rwanda.* Ithaca, NY: Cornell University Press, 2002.

Bellamy, Alex J., Paul Williams and Stuart Griffin. *Understanding Peacekeeping.* Second ed. Cambridge: Polity, 2010.

Bloomfield, Lincoln P. *International Military Forces: The Question of Peacekeeping in an Armed and Disarming World.* Boston: Little, Brown and Company, 1964.

Boutros-Ghali, Boutros. *An Agenda for Peace: Preventive Diplomacy, Peacemaking and Peace-Keeping. Report of the Secretary-General Pursuant to the Statement Adopted by the Summit Meeting of the Security Council on 31 January 1992.* United Nations: A/47/277 – S/24111 of 17 June 1992.

Bowett, D.W. *United Nations Forces: A Legal Study.* New York: Praeger, 1964.

Brahimi, Lakhdar. *Report of the Panel on United Nations Peace Operations [Brahimi Report].* New York: United Nations (2000).

Camilleri, Joseph A. "Why We Need a UN Crisis Team". *The Age,* 29 July, 2006. www.theage.com.au/news/letters/why-we-need-a-un-crisis-team/2006/07/28/1153816380099.html.

Clark, Grenville and Louis Sohn. *Introduction to World Peace through World Law.* Cambridge, Mass: Harvard University Press, 1958.

Commission on Global Governance. *Our Global Neighborhood: The Report of the Commission on Global Governance.* Oxford: Oxford University Press, 1995.

Conetta, Carl and Charles Knight. *Vital Force: A Proposal for the Overhaul of the UN Peace Operations System and for the Creation of a UN Legion.* Cambridge, Mass: Commonwealth Institute, 1995.

Dallaire, Romeo. *Shake Hands with the Devil: The Failure of Humanity in Rwanda.* Toronto, Canada: Random House, 2005.

Feil, Scott R. "Preventing Genocide: How the Early Use of Force Might Have Succeeded in Rwanda: A Report to the Carnegie Commission on Preventing Deadly Conflict". New York: Carnegie Commission on Preventing Deadly Conflict, 1998.

Frye, William R. *A United Nations Peace Force.* London: The Carnegie Endowment for International Peace, 1957.

Global Action to Prevent War. "Conference Reports". n.d. www.globalactionpw.org/?page_id=79.

Global Action to Prevent War. "Partner Organizations". n.d. www.globalactionpw.org/?page_id=69.

Global Action to Prevent War. "Timely Response to the Threat of Mass Atrocities: Implementing the Responsibility to Protect". 2012. www.thesimonsfoundation.ca/highlights/conference-report-timely-response-threat-mass-atrocities-implementing-responsibility-prot.

Global Action to Prevent War, and University of Pretoria. "UNEPS/GAPW Regional Capacity Building". Global Action to Prevent War and the University of Pretoria, 2008. www.globalactionpw.org/wp/wp-content/uploads/regional-capacity-building.pdf.

Global Action to Prevent War and The Project for a UN Emergency Peace Service (UNEPS). "UNEPS in Context: Third Pillar Capacities and First Pillar Responses". 7 and 8 December 2010. www.globalactionpw.org/wp/wp-content/uploads/uneps-report1.pdf.

Global Common Security i3. "Peter Langille: Biography". n.d. www.globalcommonsecurity.org/gcs/about/bio/.

Government of Canada. *Towards a Rapid Reaction Capability*. Ottawa: Government of Canada. September 1995.

Hamilton, Lee, Gareth Evans, Stanley Hoffmann and Brian Urquhart. "A UN Volunteer Military Force: Four Views". *New York Review of Books*, 24 June 1993.

Haynes, Lukas and Timothy W. Stanley. "The UN Needs a 'Fire Brigade' to Douse Regional Conflicts". *The Christian Science Monitor*, 5 July 1994.

Hehir, Aidan. *The Responsibility to Protect: Rhetoric, Reality and the Future of Humanitarian Intervention*. Basingstoke, UK: Palgrave Macmillan, 2012.

Heidenrich, John G. *Why US Conservatives Should Support a UN Legion*. Washington DC: Project on Defense Alternatives, Commonwealth Institute, 1995.

Herro, Annie, Wendy Lambourne and David Penklis. "Peacekeeping and Peace Enforcement in Africa: The Potential Contribution of a UN Emergency Peace Service". *African Security Review* 18, no. 1 (2009): 49–62.

Independent Working Group on the Future of the United Nations. *The United Nations in Its Second Half-Century: A Report of the Independent Working Group on the Future of the United Nations*. The Independent Working Group on the Future of the United Nations, 1995. www.library.yale.edu/un/images/un-second-half-century.pdf.

International Commission on Intervention and State Sovereignty. *The Responsibility to Protect*. Ottawa: International Development Research Centre, 2001.

Inuzuka, Tadashi. "From Article 9 to Chapter 6½: Perspectives from the Discussion on the Terror Elimination Bill". Paper submitted at the Workshop on the Eradication of Armed Conflict co-sponsored by the Australian Centre for Peace and Conflict Studies, the World Federation of United Nations Associations, and the project for a United Nations Emergency Peace Service, Brisbane, Australia. 8–10 February 2008.

Johansen, Robert C. "UN Peacekeeping: The Changing Utility of Military Force". *Third World Quarterly* 12, no. 2 (1990): 53–70.

Johansen, Robert C. "Expert Discussion of the United Nations Emergency Peace Service: Cuenca Report". In *A United Nations Emergency Peace Service: To Prevent Genocide and Crimes against Humanity*, edited by Robert C. Johansen, 43–74. New York: World Federalist Movement – Institute for Global Policy, 2006.

Johansen, Robert C., ed. *A United Nations Emergency Peace Service: To Prevent Genocide and Crimes against Humanity*. New York: World Federalist Movement – Institute for Global Policy, 2006.

Johansen, Robert C. and Saul H. Mendlovitz. "The Role of Enforcement of Law in the Establishment of a New International Order: A Proposal for a Transnational Police Force". *Alternatives: Global, Local, Political* 6, no. 2 (1980): 307–37.

Jones, Bruce. "The Arusha Peace Process". In *The Path of a Genocide: The Rwanda Crisis from Uganda to Zaire*, edited by H. Adelman and A. Suhrke, 131–56. New Brunswick, Canada: Transaction Publishers, 1999.

Keck, Margaret E. and Kathryn Sikkink. *Activists Beyond Borders: Advocacy Networks in International Politics*. Ithaca, NY: Cornell University Press, 1998.

Kinloch, Stephen. *A UN 'Legion': Between Utopia and Reality*. Abingdon, UK: Routledge, 2012.

Kraus, Don. "Lebanon, Sudan: Who You Gonna Call?" *Foreign Policy in Focus*, 29 August 2006. www.fpif.org/articles/lebanon_sudan_who_you_gonna_call.

Kraus, Don. "Syria: Who You Gonna Call?" *care2 make a difference*, 18 August 2011. www.care2.com/causes/syria-who-you-gonna-call.html.

Krieger, David, Saul Mendlovitz and William Pace. "Introduction". In *A United Nations Emergency Peace Service: To Prevent Genocide and Crimes against Humanity*, edited by Robert C. Johansen, 11–19. New York: World Federalist Movement – Institute for Global Policy, 2006.

Langille, H. Peter. "Conflict Prevention: Options for Rapid Deployment and UN Standing Forces". *International Peacekeeping* 7, no. 1 (2000): 219–53.

Langille, H. Peter. *Bridging the Commitment–Capacity Gap: A Review of Existing Arrangements and Options for Enhancing UN Rapid Deployment*. New York: Center for UN Reform Education, 2002.

Langille, H. Peter. "The Initiative for a UN Emergency Peace Service". 2013. www.youtube.com/watch?v=ZkyHuSLZ6iY.

Langille, H. Peter and Maxime Faille. "Preliminary Blueprint for Long-Term Options for Enhancing a Rapid Reaction Capability. " In *UN Rapid Reaction Capabilities*, edited by David Cox and Albert Legault, 179–200. Ottawa: Canadian Peacekeeping Press, 1995.

Leurdijk, Dick A., ed. *A UN Rapid Deployment Brigade: Strengthening the Capacity for Quick Response*. The Hague: Netherlands Institute of International Relations, 1995.

Lie, Trygve. *In the Cause of the Peace: Seven Years with the United Nations*. New York: The Macmilliam Company, 1954.

Martin Luther King Jr. Memorial Foundation. "Yaounde Regional Workshop on R2P-UNEPS 2010". n.d. www.lukmefcameroon.org/yaounde2010/conferenceorganizers.html.

Mendez, Juan. "The Prevention of Genocide and Its Challenges". In *Standing for Change in Peacekeeping Operations: Project for a United Nations Emergency Peace Service (UNEPS)*, 43–9. New York: Global Action to Prevent War, 2009.

Miller, Andrew S. "Universal Soldiers: UN Standing Armies and the Legal Alternatives". *Georgetown Law Journal* 81 (1992): 773–828.

Pugh, Michael C. "An International Police Force: Lord Davies and the British Debate in the 1930s". *International Relations* 9, no. 4 (1988): 335–51.

Roberts, Adam. "Proposals for UN Standing Forces: A Critical History". In *The United Nations Security Council and War: The Evolution of Thought and Practice since 1945*, edited by Vaughan Lowe, Adam Roberts, Jennifer Welsh and Dominik Zaum, 99–130. New York: Oxford University Press, 2008.

Sohn, Louis B. "The Authority of the United Nations to Establish and Maintain a Permanent United Nations Force". *American Journal of International Law* 52, no. 2 (1958): 229–40.

Stassen, Harold. "Blueprint for a World Government". *New York Times Magazine*, 23 May, 1943.

Suthanthiraraj, Kavitha and Mariah Quinn. *Standing for Change in Peacekeeping Operations: Project for a United Nations Emergency Peace Service (UNEPS)*. New York: Global Action to Prevent War, 2009.

Thant, U. "United Nations Peace Force". In *International Military Forces*, edited by Lincoln Bloomfield, 259–67. New York: Little, Brown and Company, 1964.

The White House. *Presidential Decision Directive/Nsc-25* 20482 of 1 May 1994. www.fas.org/irp/offdocs/pdd/pdd-25.pdf.

United Nations. *Charter of the United Nations*. New York: United Nations, 1945.
UN General Assembly. *Supplement to an Agenda for Peace: Position Paper of the Secretary-General on the Occasion of the Fiftieth Anniversary of the United Nations*. A/50/60 of 25 January 1995.
UN General Assembly. *Implementing the Responsibility to Protect: Report of the Secretary-General*. A/63/677 of 12 January 2009. New York: United Nations
UN Security Council. *Resolution 872*. S/RES/872 of 5 October 1993. New York: United Nations.
UN Security Council. *Report of the Independent Inquiry into the Actions of the United Nations During the 1994 Genocide in Rwanda*. S/1999/1257 of 16 December 1999. New York: United Nations.
Urquhart, Brian. "For a U.N. Volunteer Military Force". *New York Review of Books*, 10 June 1993, 3–4.
Urquhart, Brian E. "United Nations Peace Forces and the Changing United Nations". *International Organization* 17, no. 2 (1963).
Wang, Justine. "A Symposium on Genocide and Crimes against Humanity: The Challenge of Prevention and Enforcement". Convened by the Nuclear Age Peace Foundation and the Simons Centre for Peace and Disarmament Studies, University of Santa Barbara, California, 5–6 December 2003. www.wagingpeace.org/tag/genocide/.
World Federalist Movement–Canada. "Analyst: Create Emergency Peace Service – Save Countless Lives". 2009. www.worldfederalistscanada.org/pressreleases/pressreleases-091209.html.
World Federalist Movement – Canada, and Global Action to Prevent War. "Support for UNEPS at UN GA Interactive Dialogue on R2P" 2011. www.worldfederalistscanada.org/0611%20UNEPS%20&%20R2P%20sign-on%20Ltr%20%20(1).pdf.
World Federalist Movement. "UNEPS Backgrounder". n.d. www.worldfederalistscanada.org/uneps%20backgrounder.pdf.
Zuber, Robert and David Curran. "Peacekeeping and Rapid Reaction: Towards the Establishment of Cosmopolitan Capacities for Rapid Deployment". Division of Peace Studies at the University of Bradford, Global Action to Prevent War and Armed Conflict, the World Federalist Movement Canada, 8 July 2013. www.bradford.ac.uk/ssis/media/ssis/peacestudies/Bradford-Write-Up-Sept.pdf

3 Normative and problem-solving ideas

Introduction

The term 'norm' often makes people's eyes glaze over when they hear it. It has several meanings, and is seldom used in everyday nomenclature. This chapter attempts to demystify this concept and the theories surrounding it, and explains in simple terms what norms are and why they are a useful tool when investigating attitudes towards the UNEPS proposal.

I argue that the UNEPS proposal is constituted by both normative ideas, broadly understood as ethical claims, and problem-solving or technical ideas that prescribe a precise course of policy action in response to a particular problem. Several of the normative ideas are aligned to R2P and the protection of civilians from violence in armed conflict, ideas which have their roots in human rights and international humanitarian law. The UNEPS proposal is also constituted by other cosmopolitan norms which reinforce the role of the UN in conflict prevention and response as well as the authorisation of the proposed service. Where relevant, I discuss the operational implications of certain norms or how these norms translate into what UNEPS would actually *do* in a mission.

The problem-solving ideas relate to filling a gap in the UN's capacity to respond rapidly and effectively to (imminent) atrocities; the provision of multidimensional personnel of police, troops and civilians performing a range of tasks that would not only stop the violence but also contribute to sustainable peace; and the cost and size of the service which, according to UNEPS' proponents, would save the international community funds in post-conflict reconstruction and be sufficiently large to carry out its mandate.

This chapter ends with a discussion on how norms are transmitted, 'imported' or 'diffused' and introduces Amitav Acharya's theory of localisation as the primary analytical framework for this book. Stages of the localisation process, such as framing a norm in a particular way or 'grafting' it onto a similar, 'local' norm, supply valuable conceptual tools that help explain how respondents (could) adapt the UNEPS proposal into a more acceptable form.

Norms

Norms enjoy a central place within constructivism, which is the philosophical lens through which I approach this research. There are several interconnecting definitions of norms, which come from different philosophical traditions and theoretical approaches. Norms are ethical in nature, referring to a standard of behaviour that should be followed in accordance with a particular value system – what 'ought' to be.[1] Crawford calls these "prescriptive" norms.[2] A norm can also be described statistically as a widely prevalent pattern of behaviour – what is "normal".[3] Describing the transition from prescriptive norms to norms in practice, Khagram, Riker and Sikkink propose as a working definition that about one-quarter to one-third of states must support and accept a new standard of behaviour in order to identify a new global norm in a statistical sense.[4] But there is no agreement on who can legitimately claim to pinpoint "global norms".[5] For example, some, such as Bellamy, have referred to R2P as a "principle" which is understood as "a fundamental truth or proposition which serves as the basis for belief leading to action".[6] Others, such as Badescu and Weiss, have called R2P an "emerging norm".[7] They claim that while R2P "has moved from the prose and passion of an international commission" it also has "substantial potential to evolve further in customary international law".[8] Others still, such as Gareth Evans, insist that R2P has well and truly emerged as an international norm.[9] This is the expected approach of a norm entrepreneur – to insist on a prescriptive norm's status as an accepted norm, perhaps before others do so.[10]

Finnemore and Sikkink's broad and classic definition of a norm is a "standard of appropriate behavior for actors with a given identity".[11] This combines the ethical or prescriptive dimension of a norm by defining it as "appropriate" as well as its descriptive sense by defining it as a "standard" which depends on a certain amount of regular behaviour. Finnemore and Sikkink's definition of a norm contains a third meaning which points to a norm's *constitutive* function. Specifically, the "standard of appropriate behaviour" to which they refer is only followed by those with "a given identity". In other words, what is appropriate is known only by reference to a social community. For constructivists, not only do norms matter, they are seen to constitute (read 'form') agents' identities and interests.[12] In fact, identity, interests and norms are "mutually constitutive" – so while norms and ideas constitute agents' identities and interests, these ideational structures would not exist if it were not for agents' identities and interests, not to mention their corresponding actions.[13]

Contested claims about the normative status of R2P – and, as will be seen, other norms relating to the protection of civilians in conflict and the international society of states – indicate that it is likely that the normative ideas I identify in the UNEPS proposal would be debatable in a statistical sense. I therefore do not make such claims. I argue, however, that these norms have an ethical character as well as constitutive one. Human rights norms have a special status, according to Risse, Ropp and Sikkink, because they both prescribe rules for appropriate behaviour and help define identities of liberal states.[14] This suggests that the

40 *Normative and problem-solving ideas*

norms I identify below both constitute the moral claims embedded within the UNEPS proposal as well as the identity and interests of individuals and organisations supporting the proposal, many of whom are mentioned in the previous chapter. Importantly, however, these norms may also be shared by others with similar identities and interests outside the UNEPS network.[15] One of the central goals of this book is to explore the extent to which such norms are indeed shared and how support for norms related to (not strictly constituting) the proposed UNEPS might be leveraged.

I understand the relationship between the norms and ideas constituting the UNEPS proposal, agents' identities and interests, and the ideational structures (norms and ideas) that reflect and constitute those identities and interests, to be mutually constitutive. This dynamic is illustrated in Figure 3.1 below. It means, firstly, that norms and ideas are important in understanding agents' attitudes towards the proposed UNEPS. As Kratochwil writes, "not only must an actor refer to rules and norms when he/she wants to make a choice, but the observer, as well, must understand the normative structure underlying the action in order to interpret and appraise choice".[16] Indeed, as observer and analyst, I try to understand the norms informing the views on the proposed UNEPS among those I consult for this research. Second, agents' perceptions on a UNEPS can, in turn, influence the norms constituting the proposal – or what the proposal "looks like" – as well as how it is advocated. Considering opportunities for the idea to be recalibrated in ways that are consistent with agents' identities and interests could help to understand how it might enjoy greater support and carve out a path towards its implementation.

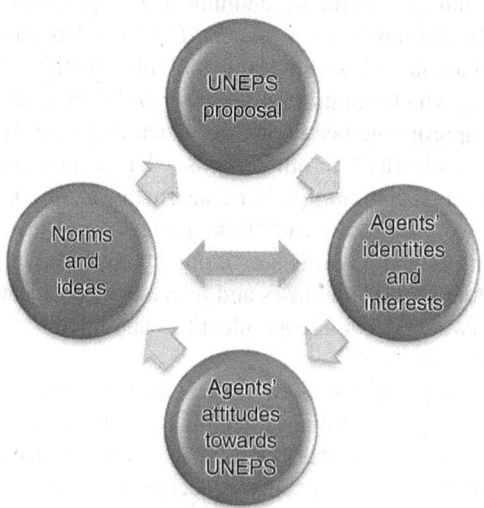

Figure 3.1 Relationship between the norms and ideas constituting the UNEPS proposal, agents' identities and interests, and the ideational structures that reflect and constitute those identities and interests.

Normative and problem-solving ideas

A principal factor influencing interest in the UNEPS proposal is the attributes of the proposal itself. Theorists suggest that an idea's attributes contribute to its level of international support and are a powerful force in effecting normative change.[17] According to Cooper and English, policy proposals are inspired by two interconnected ideas: one normative, the other problem-solving.[18] Unpacking the UNEPS proposal in such a way indicates that there are ethical issues that resonate with respondents as well as technical or practical ones. This chapter uses this analytical framework to understand UNEPS explain respondents' views on UNEPS and consider ways to increase support of the proposal.

Broadly speaking, normative ideas identify criteria for distinguishing right from wrong,[19] although, as I have just discussed, norms encompass more than this. Problem-solving ideas, on the other hand, relate to a cause-and-effect relationship. Selling his proposed reforms to boost immigration to the USA, US President Barack Obama combined the two types of ideas, saying: "...immigration is not just the right thing to do. It's smart for our economy".[20] While problem-solving ideas are supported by evidence, normative ideas may be connected to problem-solving ideas but are not as easily understood by appeals to evidence.

Norms constituting the UNEPS proposal and their operational implications

According to my analysis, the UNEPS proposal is based on six norms.[21] While I have categorised these separately, and explore some of them in different chapters of this book, many of them are interconnected. These ideas are taken from an examination of the proposal agreed upon at the meeting of peace and security scholars, activists and practitioners in Cuenca, Spain, in 2005 and supplemented by other sources from the UNEPS network. As I unpack these norms, I also touch on their implications for the goals of the proposed UNEPS and the tasks that it would perform. In other words, not only does the UNEPS literature contain normative claims but – through describing how the service could realise these norms – it can be read as translating them into operational language.

The first two normative ideas mentioned below resemble, but are not identical to, the first two pillars of R2P.[22] The pillars were famously enunciated by UNSG Ban Ki-moon in 2009 (elaborating on the paragraphs addressing R2P in the World Summit Outcome Document from 2005), which was several years after the meetings at which agreement on the UNEPS proposal was reached. Therefore, the early UNEPS literature does not use the language of "pillars". The political, ethical and legal dimensions of these pillars, however, are central to understanding the normative foundations of UNEPS.

The first norm is that states have a responsibility to protect their population from atrocity crimes,[23] which is referred to as Pillar One. Johansen notes that the:

prospects for UNEPS to be established ... are enormously increased by the international community's recent acceptance of the idea that sovereignty carries responsibilities for every government to protect its own citizens from victimization by acts of genocide and crimes against humanity.[24]

The legal instruments which most directly shape R2P are those defining atrocity crimes, including the Genocide Convention, the Rome Statute, and the statutes of the International Criminal Tribunal for Rwanda and the International Criminal Tribunal for the former Yugoslavia,[25] all of which are referenced in the 2006 UNEPS publication to illustrate that no one is allowed to commit mass atrocities.

The second norm constituting a proposed UNEPS is that the international community has a responsibility to prevent genocide and crimes against humanity, using both military and non-military means. The cover of the first significant UNEPS publication, edited by Robert Johansen and published with the support of GAPW, the Nuclear Age Peace Foundation and the WFM-IGP, reads "A UN Emergency Peace Service: To prevent Genocide and Crimes against Humanity".[26] At first glance, therefore, those behind the UNEPS transnational activist network viewed it principally as a tool to prevent these two crimes. Yet, as mentioned in the previous chapter, some of the later UNEPS events and literature use the terms "atrocity crimes" or R2P – which also invokes war crimes and crimes against humanity – more generally as a framework in which to discuss the proposal.[27]

The prevention of atrocities is referred to as Pillar Two in Ban Ki-moon's nomenclature. It is distinct from Pillar One because it focuses on the *international community's* role in building peace and preventing war, rather than that of the government in whose territory atrocity crimes could occur. Let us first deal with the relatively uncontroversial aspects of Pillar two that relate to the proposed UNEPS – those not requiring the use of force. Ban Ki-moon argues that Pillar Two involves helping states to exercise their responsibility to prevent R2P crimes through, for example, security sector reforms aimed at building and sustaining legitimate and effective security forces which contributes to stability and provides states with the capacity to respond rapidly to crises.[28] Ban also argues that it involves helping states through, for example, targeted economic assistance which would reduce inequalities, improve education and increase political participation among other goods. These measures relate to structural and direct prevention norms and reflect many of the tasks that UNEPS would perform (albeit restricted to the duration of its deployment). Structural prevention is based on the premise that the root causes of violent conflict are structural and long-term.[29] Non-military direct prevention, on the other hand, tackles more immediate causes of conflict.[30] UNEPS would undertake a mix of structural prevention, such as human rights monitoring and education, reconstruction, and reintegration and reconciliation programmes, as well as measures directly aimed at preventing atrocities, such as on-site fact-finding and data-gathering for war crimes investigations and conflict resolution.[31]

Normative and problem-solving ideas   43

The more controversial aspects of Pillar Two deal with the use of force, and include preventative deployments or an international military presence to help prevent the escalation of armed conflict.[32] Breakey has labelled operations whose primary objective is to avert R2P crimes "R2P Pillar Two Missions".[33] UNEPS' primary goal would be to prevent atrocities and the Cuenca report stresses that coercive, preventative deployments are potentially part of this. As Johansen notes, "the international community's goal presumably should be to address the crisis at a moment *early* enough to avoid mass murder" (italics in original).[34]

There are specific operational features that Breakey ascribes to R2P Pillar Two Missions. They use a systematic strategy and the robust use of force under Chapter VII. Because resistance to such operations is anticipated, the mission must be sufficiently resourced. Host-state consent (even begrudgingly given) is necessary for logistical and political reasons, and the perception of the mission's neutrality is helpful but not essential.[35] There is significant overlap, however, between Pillar Two and Pillar Three Missions – or those that *react* to atrocities. UNSG himself acknowledges this overlap, writing "pillar two ... can also comprise elements of prevention and response, sometimes even at the same time".[36] So while a UNEPS would be focused in theory on prevention, it probably would undertake some reactive measures, as noted in the Cuenca report.[37]

The norms constituting the UNEPS proposal are different from those constituting Pillar Two in two ways: they include criteria for deployment and the proposed body to authorise a UNEPS operation extends beyond the UN Security Council. According to UNEPS' promoters, "the Security Council is the first, the most legitimate, and the most likely body to authorize UNEPS and to clarify the threshold criteria that would justify deploying it".[38] But what if the UNSC is paralysed because of a veto by one of the P-5 members?

On the one hand, Langille restricts the proposed authorisation body to the Security Council.[39] On the other hand, participants at Cuenca agreed that "UNEPS also could be authorized for use by the General Assembly, following processes similar to those used under Uniting for Peace procedures".[40] Others have also considered[41] and advocated[42] additional means of authorisation, such as regional organisations and the UNSG, some of which are also canvassed by the ICISS.[43] Johansen, for example, suggests that a regional organisation might be able to authorise intervention in a state that is not a member of the organisation, though he recognises that this is not widely viewed as legitimate.[44] Mendlovitz proposes that the UN could authorise the UNSG to deploy UNEPS under carefully specified conditions defined in advance by the Security Council or General Assembly. The authority of the Secretary-General to call out this proposed force would be based on the condition that, if the Security Council agrees at the end of 60 days that UNEPS should be brought back, then the UNSG could authorise this provided he or she has the support of two-thirds of the members of the Security Council.[45] Such proposals to bestow responsibility on the UNSG for direction and control of a UNEPS are very ambitious as, legally, the only security function the Charter confers on the UNSG is to "bring to the attention of the Security Council any matter which in his opinion may threaten the maintenance of international peace and security".[46]

On the issue of the use of force criteria, UNEPS' advocates (echoing the ICISS report) argue that six conditions should govern such an intervention: (1) a legitimate authority must authorize deployment; (2) there must be a just cause; (3) intervention must be undertaken with a right intention; (4) intervention should occur only when there is an immediate and evident threat of gross violations of international humanitarian and human rights law; (5) the means employed must be proportional to and consistent with the ends sought; and (6) a reasonable prospect of success must exist.[47] The criteria explicated by ICISS were rejected by states at the World Summit in 2005. Indeed, on both the issue of authorisation and the use of force, the UNEPS principles are closest to those agreed to by ICISS members in their 2001 report.

The role envisaged for a proposed UNEPS in preventing and perhaps even reacting to atrocity crimes is thus more ambitious in some areas than the coverage of Pillar Two and, indeed, what several scholars have argued is permissible under international law. Simon Chesterman, J.L Holzgrefe and Olivier Corten, for example, maintain that there is no legal foundation – neither in the UN Charter, nor state practice, nor *opinio juris* – for war waged for a humanitarian cause without the UNSC's endorsement.[48] Moreover, an evaluation of states' responses to recent history's most prominent 'humanitarian intervention' without the consent of the UNSC – the 1999 NATO bombing of Kosovo – reveals that it was almost universally condemned by member states.[49] The World Summit Outcome Document (WSOD), moreover, specifically identified the Council as the sole source of authority for Chapter VII operations.[50]

The third norm constituting the UNEPS proposal is the protection of civilians in armed conflict or Protection of Civilians (POC). While this norm is not singled out in the Cuenca principles, it is nevertheless mentioned by other UNEPS promoters. The task of "[p]rotecting civilians at extreme risk" is central to the proposed UNEPS, says a UNEPS factsheet released by the World Federalist Movement-Canada.[51] Juan Mendez also writes in his contribution to the GAPW publication *Standing for Change*, that UNEPS' "main objective [is]: the *protection of the civilian population*" (italics in original).[52] POC and R2P share a normative base. They are both rooted in notions of empathy and humanity, and reflect lengthy attempts to ensure states protect their populations and that the international community ensures this responsibility.[53] Operationally, however, they are distinct. As noted by Francis and Breakey, in R2P situations, there is the threat of atrocity crimes, meaning that violence against civilians is not peripheral to the armed conflict or symptoms of the conflict. Rather, the threat against civilians posed by one or both sides is large-scale, deliberate and systematic, and might take place in times of war or peace. This type of threat must be dealt with quite differently to instances of small-scale, localised and opportunistic violence against civilians.[54]

Breakey describes the concept of "Peacekeeping POC" which refers to the responsibility some (in fact, most nowadays) peace operations have through their Security Council mandate to protect civilians. Specifically, they have a duty to provide a certain level of basic security to the local civilians – conditional on the operation's mandate and capacity – and to work with the host state towards a more peaceful environment. Peacekeepers in POC missions are charged with protecting civilians as one of many potential roles within a Chapter VII operation. Robust military action to protect civilians is anticipated, but is generally responsive and reactive. Consent of the state is crucial and the mission is committed to being perceived as neutral by both sides.[55] The UN peace operation in Liberia (UNMIL) is an example of a POC mission as the mandate of civilian protection is coupled with other tasks, including monitoring the ceasefire, disarmament, security reform and more. A proposed UNEPS would secure safe havens, guard humanitarian corridors and counter 'spoilers' (or those seeking to derail a peace agreement), which are typical tasks of POC missions.[56]

The forth norm constituting the proposal resembles what has been called "Humanitarian POC".[57] This norm relates to how civilians should be protected from a range of threats to rights, such as large-scale personal violence, through exclusively non-military measures undertaken by humanitarian actors.[58] These threats may arise in various contexts, including situations of armed conflict, post-conflict, natural disasters and famine.[59] Johansen notes that, "most participants [at Cuenca] support UNEPS authorization to address natural or environmental disasters ... [and] such a deployment would usually not be a coercive intervention".[60] The Cuenca proceedings mentioned that UNEPS would include a diversity of professionals covering areas such as "humanitarian assistance", and Langille has since noted that UNEPS would address "human needs in areas where others could not".[61] While Humanitarian POC is related to the work of mandated organisations that have a particular legal role, such as the International Committee of the Red Cross, and the jobs undertaken by UN bodies, such as the UN High Commission for Refugees, it is also foundational to the spirit and goals of UNEPS.

The fifth norm (arguably) underpinning UNEPS is the prevention of armed conflict. The prevention of armed conflict is enshrined in the UN Charter as well as multiple UN resolutions and reports.[62] It is not, however, a norm which all UNEPS proponents ascribe to the proposal. As noted in the introduction to this book, participants at the 2005 Cuenca meeting framed the proposal solely in terms of responding to mass atrocities and natural disasters. Indeed, Johansen, the rapporteur of the meeting, even posed the question: "Should UNEPS be deployed in some circumstances for the purpose of preventing armed conflict as well as for preventing violations of laws prohibiting genocide, crimes against humanity, and war crimes?", indicating that consensus on this subject was lacking among the 35 participants.[63] On the other hand, Peter Langille has argued on numerous occasions that the prevention of conflict would be among the central goals of a proposed UNEPS.[64] Operationally, this means that a UNEPS would initiate, among other things, the prompt start-up of peace operations and begin tasks necessary to help to prevent armed conflict.

While this norm is not universally used to frame the proposal, it is closely intertwined with norms previously mentioned such as POC and R2P. For instance, the prevention of armed conflict is the best way to protect civilians.

46 *Normative and problem-solving ideas*

Delaying the deployment of peacekeepers often prolongs the suffering endured by civilians and increases the risks that atrocities will break out. We see these kinds of fears being anticipated with the recent events in the Central African Republic (CAR). In April 2014, the UN Security Council approved the creation of a UN peacekeeping force in the CAR to try to stop violence between Christians and Muslims. The operation, however, will not assume control until the middle of September the same year. A representative of Amnesty International responded to this announcement by saying "the big issue is how to fit the gap between now and September", while a citizen of the CAR cried "Until then, lots of Central Africans will continue to die, so who are they coming to save?"[65]

The sixth and final norm constituting the proposed UNEPS is the belief that the UN ought to be strengthened as the principal institution for conflict prevention and response,[66] and that UNEPS would be a means through which to achieve this. Peace operations are one of the most high profile demonstrations of the UN's contribution to international peace and security and their conduct has implications for the organisation as whole. The inability of UN peacekeeping operations to protect civilians, deploy on time and possess the necessary police, troops and civilians called for by the UNSC mandate authorising the operations damages the standing of the UN and contributes to discrediting peacekeeping in general.[67] Langille writes that the UNEPS proposal "represents the higher ideal of a universal system for preventing armed conflict, protecting civilians and enforcing international law. In this respect, it is seen as a potentially critical step towards an effective and empowered UN".[68] Further reinforcing the UN's importance, staff from GAPW, a central hub of activities related to the UNEPS, wrote in a publication on the proposal that their intention is "to initiate a conversation we believe to be essential to the continued health and viability of the UN".[69] This theme extends throughout the network of UNEPS' supporters, with Brian Urquhart, former UN Under-Secretary-General of Special Political Affairs, arguing that the UN is a "driving force for human progress" and declaring his intention to strengthen the collective interests it represents through advocating UNEPS.[70] Such cosmopolitan norms constitute the identity of most UNEPS' advocates.[71]

Problem-solving ideas

According to John Campbell, problem-solving ideas can "facilitate action among elites by specifying how to solve specific policy problems".[72] Campbell explains that they are often "technical and professional ideas that specify cause-and-effect relationships and prescribe a precise course of policy action".[73] He argues that actors use these ideas self-consciously and deliberately to attract support for their policy proposal.[74] This strategy applies to UNEPS' advocates in the way they talk and write about the proposal and the arguments they use to justify its creation.

My analysis indicates that the UNEPS proposal is based on four problem-solving ideas that resonated with respondents. The first is that a permanent, directly recruited UN peacekeeping service would address the lack of rapidly deployable peacekeepers available to avert or respond to a humanitarian crisis.

As mentioned previously, this same logic has been cited by proponents of a standing force in the past. The second idea is that a multidimensional and multifunctional service would address the problem of an inadequate number of troops, police and civilians and overcome the challenge they face in working together cohesively in peace operations.[75]

The third and fourth problem-solving ideas on which UNEPS is based relate to the size and cost of the service, respectively. Advocates argue that a permanent UN service comprising up to 18,000 personnel (around 10,000 of whom would be troops) would be capable of preventing the outbreak, or lessening the severity, of instances of genocide and crimes against humanity, which the UN has struggled to deal with in an effective and timely manner. The latter relates to the idea that the cost of the service – US$2.5 billion to create and under US$1 billion per year to maintain – is a feasible and ultimately cost-saving investment for the international community in the area of post-conflict reconstruction.[76]

There are different theoretical claims surrounding the function of problem-solving ideas. Rationalists Goldstein and Keohane maintain that, under conditions of uncertainty or incomplete information, actors can use causal ideas as "roadmaps" or "signposts" guiding them on how best to realise their interests through stipulating causal patterns or providing moral motivations for action.[77] Acharya touches on this same concept from a constructivist perspective. As part of his theory of localisation on which I elaborate below, he argues that local actors might resist new external norms because of "doubts about the norms' utility and applicability".[78] Kratochwil likewise gives norms a problem-solving (or rational-choice) dimension, saying that they simplify choices and "impart 'rationality'" to situations by identifying factors that decision makers must consider.[79]

Critical theorist Robert Cox argues that problem-solving theories are concerned only with taking the world as given and attempting to understand its operation.[80] Consequently, such theories are often said to be concerned with improving the world within clearly defined and limited parameters.[81] He writes that a problem-solving approach thus fails to reflect upon the constitutive role of "the social and power relationships and the institutions into which they are organised, as the framework for action".[82] Along the same lines as Cox's critique of problem-solving ideas, the conventional constructivist John Ruggie criticises problem-solving theorists because they treat ideas as causal factors that are exchanged by fully formed individuals.[83] He writes that such theorists believe that individuals "are not born into any system of social relationships that helps shape who they become. When we first encounter them, they are already fully constituted and poised in problem-solving mode".[84] I take heed of this critique by considering in Chapter 7 the normative underpinnings of respondents' perspectives on the problem-solving attributes of the UNEPS proposal.

Theorising the evolution of the UNEPS proposal

The literature on norms adopts various models to explain norm displacement and diffusion and to understand why some norms matter more than others. Do certain norms have particular endogenous characteristics that give them an edge above the rest? Some would argue, yes. Theorists have highlighted several attributes that have been shown to influence the success that a norm enjoys internationally. These include norms that are clear, specific and exhibit longevity[85] (that is, they have been around for a while); norms that make universal claims about what is good for all people, such as many liberal norms; norms that are buttressed by certain principles that are dominant in the modern world, such as universalism, individualism, voluntaristic authority, rational progress and world citizenship; and norms that try to humanise the "other" or represent "moral progress".[86] Furthermore, Keck and Sikkink argue that norms involving "bodily integrity and prevention of bodily harm for vulnerable or 'innocent' groups, especially when a short causal chain exists between cause and effect", are more likely to receive support over other norms.[87]

By contrast, Krook and True counter the argument that certain norms gain support over others based on their attributes.[88] They maintain that constructivist scholars studying the creation and diffusion of norms are susceptible to treating norms as static "things" rather than "processes". They argue that, in each stage of the development of a norm, its content may be substantially changed by local interpretations, moving it onto a new trajectory altogether.[89] In the context of UNEPS, while many of the norms on which the proposal is based are supported by a wide network, I explore whether these same norms are viewed as legitimate and influential among those consulted for this research. The exercise of understanding attitudes towards the UNEPS proposal is important if UNEPS is to gain the support of a range of constituencies.

Literature on the processes of norm diffusion in international relations suggests that "universal norms" do not automatically become embedded in communities. Some theorists suggest that the success of norm diffusion processes depends on the extent to which there are opportunities for "localization". Amitav Acharya defines localisation as "the active construction (through discourse, framing, grafting, and cultural selection) of foreign ideas by local actors, which results in the former developing significant congruence with local beliefs and practices".[90] Elements of Acharya's thesis supply useful heuristic tools that help to investigate how a proposed UNEPS might gain the support of political, military and non-state actors in diverse communities. Localisation involves reconstituting an outside norm to harmonise it with a local normative order. It is also a process in which the role of local actors is more crucial than that of actors importing the outside norm.[91] Acharya broadly argues that new international norms such as R2P are more likely to spread if the responsibility for their creation and diffusion is seen to be widely shared rather than being credited to a particular group.[92]

How exactly could the theory of localisation help us find a path towards UNEPS' acceptance and implementation? First, Acharya's theory of localisation is built upon a regional analysis of two transnational norms in South East Asia – cooperative security and flexible engagement. While my primary research comprises interviews with individuals from South East Asia, it also includes those from other regions as detailed in the introduction to this book. This means that I apply localisation transnationally rather than regionally. Consequently, when Acharya refers to "local actors", in reference to South East Asian actors, I refer simply to 'actors', 'agents' or 'respondents', which encompasses individuals, organisations and states with different identities and interests. I am therefore not simply using the category of regional affiliations to explain perspectives on UNEPS but also other aspects of respondents' identities, as mentioned previously in this chapter. I also suggest alternatives to designing and promoting the UNEPS proposal based on the findings from this research. The process of localisation has certain dimensions which I will now discuss.

First, as mentioned above, Acharya writes that local actors might resist a new norm because they question whether it would apply to their regional context and effectively address the "problems" to which it purports to respond.[93] Thus, while Acharya does not explicitly recognise it, his theory of localisation encompasses problems-solving ideas. In the context of my research, I explore the extent to which respondents' views on the utility of UNEPS (views which, themselves, reflect and reinforce certain normative orders) challenge the technical attributes of the proposal.

Second, Acharya writes that opportunities to localise arise when actors begin to view the external norm as having a potential to contribute to the legitimacy and efficacy of existing institutions and practices without undermining them significantly or drastically altering their existing identity. The important condition for localisation to take place is that some aspects of the existing normative order must already be discredited from within.[94] In the context of this book, I explore ways in which actors identify problems or gaps within their existing normative orders or institutions and the dimensions of the UNEPS proposal (both normative and problem-solving) which potentially address these shortcomings.

A third factor in the localisation process involves framing, which is a way of representing a norm. Framing establishes links between existing and new norms that are sometimes not obvious.[95] Norm advocates draw attention to issues using language that "names, interprets, and dramatizes them".[96] In this sense, it can make a global norm *appear* local.[97] A fourth factor involves the adaptation of new ideas through "grafting" and "pruning". These are two similar strategies that actors use to ensure that a new norm fits with their own beliefs and practices. Acharya writes that the relative scope that a new idea offers for grafting and pruning contributes to the norm-taker's interest in its localisation and is critical to its success.[98] Grafting or "incremental norm transplantation" involves associating a new norm with a pre-existing credible and popular norm, which makes a similar (behavioural) claim. Pruning involves selecting the elements of the new norm that fit the pre-existing normative structure and rejecting those that do not. It is more "invasive" than framing and grafting (which are essentially forms of representing a norm) because it alters the substance of the new norm. I explore ways in which actors frame, graft and prune the UNEPS proposal as a condition of their interest in and support for the idea. I also make suggestions on ways to adjust the proposal so that it is more compatible with respondents' perspectives.[99]

Conclusion

This chapter identified six normative ideas constituting the proposal. These are: (1) the responsibility of governments to protect their populations from atrocity crimes; (2) the responsibility of the international community to prevent atrocities, using military and non-military means. This also includes a criteria for intervention and the potential for a proposed UNEPS to be authorised by the UNSC, General Assembly or UNSG; (3) the responsibility to protect civilians in armed conflict when the threat to civilians is a symptom of the conflict rather than deliberate and systematic; (4) the responsibility to protect populations from a range of threats to rights through exclusively non-military measures and in contexts such as armed conflict and natural disasters; (5) the duty to prevent armed conflict; and (6) the imperative of upholding and strengthening the UN as the principal institution for conflict prevention and resolution and ensuring that it is the institution in which UNEPS is housed.

Next, I identified four interconnecting problem-solving ideas that resonated with respondents: (1) a permanent service would 'plug' a systemic 'hole' in the UN in terms of the provision of available well-trained and equipped peacekeepers at short notice; (2) a multidimensional and multifunctional service would address the deficiencies in the peacekeeping system caused by an inadequate number of troops, police and civilians who struggle to work as a cohesive unit; (3) a proposed UNEPS of 18,000 personnel would be capable of preventing the outbreak, or lessening the severity, of instances of atrocities and other threats to civilians which the UN has struggled to address adequately; and (4) the cost of the service is feasible and would save the international community money in the long run in the area of post-conflict reconstruction.

Finally, this chapter argued that the conditions for localisation, such as pruning the original idea and grafting it on to a norm that possesses greater resonance in a particular context, provide useful heuristic tools to understand how to increase support for the UNEPS proposal and ultimately pave the way towards its implementation.

Having situated the place this book takes in the norms debate and articulated the nuts and bolts of a proposed UNEPS and the theoretical framework used to examine it, I now explore attitudes on two principal norms constituting the proposal: sovereign responsibility and preventing R2P crimes without the use of force.

Notes

1 Krasner, "Structural Causes and Regime Consequences"; Axelrod, "An Evolutionary Approach to Norms"; Goldstein and Keohane, *Ideas and Foreign Policy*.
2 Crawford, *Argument and Change in World Politics*, 24, 40, 86–8, 106–9.
3 Ibid., 41, 99.
4 Khagram, Riker and Sikkink, *Restructuring World Politics*.
5 Thakur, *The Responsibility to Protect*, 5.
6 Bellamy, *Responsibility to Protect*, 6.

7 Badescu and Weiss, "Misrepresenting R2P and Advancing Norms", 354.
8 Ibid., 356.
9 Evans, "Healing Injustices by Preventing Future Atrocities".
10 Thank you to Matthew Evangelista for alerting me to this point.
11 Finnemore and Sikkink, "International Norm Dynamics and Political Change", 891.
12 Wendt, *Social Theory of International Politics*, 272–3, 289.
13 Kratochwil, *Rules, Norms, and Decisions*; Wendt, "Anarchy Is What States Make of It"; Wendt, "Constructing International Politics".
14 Risse-Kappen, Ropp and Sikkink, *The Power of Human Rights*, 8.
15 See Wendt, "Anarchy Is What States Make of It", 406–7.
16 Kratochwil, *Rules, Norms, and Decisions*, 11.
17 Price, "Reversing the Gun Sights"; Nadelmann, "Global Prohibition Regimes"; Carpenter, "Setting the Advocacy Agenda".
18 Cooper and English, "International Commissions", 7. The language of "normative" and "problem-solving" that Cooper and English use corresponds to the language of "principled" ideas and "causal" ideas, respectively, which Goldstein and Keohane use. See Goldstein and Keohane, *Ideas and Foreign Policy*.
19 Goldstein and Keohane, *Ideas and Foreign Policy*, 3, 9–10.
20 *Wall Street Journal* 10 May, 2011.
21 There are other norms constituting the UNEPS proposal, such as the claim that the full representation of women ought to be given but, because these did not resonate with respondents, they will not be explored.
22 This is notwithstanding the fact that the UN ES proposal on which UNEPS was based was released before the ICISS enunciated the R2P doctrine.
23 Atrocity crimes refer to genocide, ethnic cleansing, war crimes and crimes against humanity. Scheffer, "Genocide and Atrocity Crimes", 247. They are also referred to as R2P crimes.
24 Johansen, "Cuenca Report", 52.
25 Breakey and Francis, "Points of Convergence and Divergence".
26 Johansen, *A United Nations Emergency Peace Service*.
27 For example, GAPW and UNEPS, "UNEPS in Context",
28 UN General Assembly, *2005 World Summit Outcome*, paras 138–9; UN General Assembly *Implementing the Responsibility to Protect*, paras 43, 46.
29 ICISS, *The Responsibility to Protect*, 23–6; Carnegie Commission on Preventing Deadly Conflict, *Preventing Deadly Conflict*; Ackermann, "The Idea and Practice of Conflict Prevention".
30 Ackermann, "The Idea and Practice of Conflict Prevention", 341.
31 Langille, "Preventing Genocide", 302; Johansen, "Cuenca Report", 49; UN General Assembly, *2005 World Summit Outcome*, para. 25.
32 UN General Assembly *Implementing the Responsibility to Protect*, paras 41–2.
33 Breakey takes pains to explain that this is not a norm but a "principle" though I remind the reader how I treat the term "norm" in this book.
34 Johansen, "Cuenca Report", 48. See also Langille, *Preparing for a UN Emergency Peace Service*.
35 Breakey, "The Responsibility to Protect", 77.
36 UN General Assembly, *Timely and Decisive Response*, para. 12.
37 Johansen, "Cuenca Report", 62.
38 Johansen, "Proposal for a United Nations Emergency Peace Service", 28.
39 For example, Langille, "The Initiative for a UN Emergency Peace Service"; "Fixing Darfur", 301; "Preventing Genocide".
40 Johansen, "Cuenca Report", 63.
41 Suthanthiraraj and Quinn, *Standing for Change*, 29; Johansen, "Proposal for a United Nations Emergency Peace Service", 28.
42 Mendlovitz, "Interview with Professor Saul Mendlovitz".

52 *Normative and problem-solving ideas*

43 ICISS, *The Responsibility to Protect*.
44 Johansen, "Proposal for a United Nations Emergency Peace Service".
45 Mendlovitz, "Interview with Professor Saul Mendlovitz".
46 United Nations, *Charter of the United Nations*, Article 99.
47 Johansen, "Cuenca Report", 47; ICISS, *The Responsibility to Protect*, xii; Langille, "The Initiative for a UN Emergency Peace Service".
48 Chesterman, *Just War or Just Peace?*, 45–87; Holzgrefe, "The Humanitarian Intervention Debate", 36–49; Corten, "Human Rights and Collective Security", 116–17.
49 In response to NATO's bombing of the Federal Republic of Yugoslavia, only Belgium and the UK made reference to the right of humanitarian intervention – that is, without UNSC approval – and argued in support of the bombing. Belgium defended the intervention stating that "NATO intervened to protect fundamental values enshrined in the *jus cogens*", such as the right to life and the prohibition of torture, and "to prevent an impending catastrophe recognized as such by the Security Council". International Court of Justice, *Legality of Use of Force Case*.
50 UN General Assembly, *2005 World Summit Outcome*, para. 139.
51 World Federalist Movement, "UNEPS Backgrounder".
52 Mendez, "The Prevention of Genocide", 47.
53 Breakey and Francis, "Points of Convergence and Divergence".
54 Ibid.
55 Breakey, "The Responsibility to Protect", 63, 74–7; "The Protection of Civilians in Armed Conflict", 40–1.
56 Langille, "A UN Emergency Peace Service".
57 Breakey, "The Protection of Civilians in Armed Conflict", 54.
58 Ibid., 55; Slim and Bonwick, *Protection: An Alnap Guide*.
59 Breakey, "The Protection of Civilians in Armed Conflict", 55.
60 Johansen, "Cuenca Report", 60.
61 Langille, *Linking UNEPS to Responsibility to Protect*.
62 For example: UN General Assembly, *Prevention of Armed Conflict*; UN Security Council, *Resolution 1366*; United Nations, *Charter of the United Nations*, for example, Articles 1.1 and 2.5; UN General Assembly, *A More Secure World*.
63 Johansen, "Cuenca Report", 65.
64 Langille, "Preventing Genocide", 301; "Fixing Darfur"; "The Initiative for a UN Emergency Peace Service"; "A UN Emergency Peace Service".
65 "UN Approves Peacekeepers for CAR", *Al Jazeera*, 10 April, 2014.
66 Johansen, "Proposal for a United Nations Emergency Peace Service", 25.
67 Holt, Taylor and Kelly, "Protecting Civilians", 4.
68 Langille, *Bridging the Commitment–Capacity Gap*, 65.
69 Suthanthiraraj and Quinn, *Standing for Change*, 5; See also Langille, *Bridging the Commitment–Capacity Gap*, 65.
70 Urquhart, "For a U.N. Volunteer Military Force"; "Finding the Hidden UN".
71 GAPW, "To Prevent Genocide".
72 Campbell, "Institutional Analysis", 385–6.
73 Ibid., 386.
74 Ibid.
75 UN General Assembly, *Report of the Panel on United Nations Peace Operations*, para. 108; Durch, "United Nations Police Evolution", 15; Chandran *et al.*, "Rapid Deployment of Civilians for Peace Operations", para. 9a.
76 Johansen, "Proposal for a United Nations Emergency Peace Service", 30; Langille, *Preparing for a UN Emergency Peace Service*. Back in 2006, it was estimated at $2 billion to set up but this has been increased to $2.5 billion in recent years.
77 Goldstein and Keohane, *Ideas and Foreign Policy*, 12; Risse, "'Let's Argue!': Communicative Action in World Politics", 4; McNamara, *The Currency of Ideas*.
78 Acharya, "How Ideas Spread", 251.

79 Kratochwil, *Rules, Norms, and Decisions*, 10.
80 Cox, "Social Forces, States, and World Orders", 128–30.
81 Ibid.
82 Ibid., 128.
83 Ruggie, "What Makes the World Hang Together?"
84 Ibid.
85 Chayes and Chayes, "On Compliance"; Legro, "Which Norms Matter?"
86 Meyer *et al.*, "World Society and the Nation-State".
87 Keck and Sikkink, *Activists Beyond Borders*, 27.
88 Krook and True, "Rethinking the Life Cycles of International Norms".
89 Ibid., 104, 123.
90 Acharya, "How Ideas Spread", 245.
91 Ibid., 244.
92 Acharya, "The R2P and Norm Diffusion".
93 Acharya, "How Ideas Spread", 251.
94 Ibid., 248, 251.
95 Ibid., 243.
96 Finnemore and Sikkink, "International Norm Dynamics and Political Change", 268.
97 Ibid., 244; Acharya, "How Ideas Spread".
98 Acharya, "How Ideas Spread", 250.
99 Acharya also argued that norm entrepreneurs are important in the localisation process. I have written a chapter on norm entrepreneurs and a proposed UNEPS in a forthcoming edited collection and so it will not be included in this book. See Herro, "Norm Entrepreneurs and the UN Emergency Peace Service".

References

Acharya, Amitav. "How Ideas Spread: Whose Norms Matter? Norm Localization and Institutional Change in Asian Regionalism". *International Organization* 58, Spring 2004 (2004): 239–75.
Acharya, Amitav. "The R2P and Norm Diffusion: Towards a Framework of Norm Circulation". *Global Responsibility to Protect* 5, no. 4 (2013): 466–79.
Ackermann, Alice. "The Idea and Practice of Conflict Prevention". *Journal of Peace Research* 40, no. 3 (2003): 339.
Axelrod, Robert. "An Evolutionary Approach to Norms". *American political science review* 80, no. 4 (1986): 1095–111.
Badescu, Cristina G., and Thomas G. Weiss. "Misrepresenting R2P and Advancing Norms: An Alternative Spiral?" *International Studies Perspectives* 11, no. 4 (2010): 354–74.
Bellamy, Alex. *Responsibility to Protect: The Global Effort to End Mass Atrocities*. Cambridge: Polity, 2009.
Breakey, Hugh. "The Protection of Civilians in Armed Conflict: Four Concepts". In *Norms of Protection: Responsibility to Protect, Protection of Civilians and Their Interaction*, edited by Angus Francis, Vesselin Popovski and Charles Sampford, 40–61. Tokyo: United Nations University Press, 2012.
Breakey, Hugh. "The Responsibility to Protect and the Protection of Civilians in Armed Conflict: Overlap and Contrast". In *Norms of Protection: Responsibility to Protect, Protection of Civilians and Their Interaction*, edited by Angus Francis, Vesselin Popovski and Charles Stampford, 62–81. Tokyo: United Nations University Press, 2012.
Breakey, Hugh, and Angus J. Francis. "Points of Convergence and Divergence: Normative, Institutional and Operational Relationships between R2P and POC". *Security Challenges* 7, no. 4 (2011): 39–50.

Campbell, John L. "Institutional Analysis and the Role of Ideas in Political Economy". *Theory and Society* 27, no. 3 (1998): 377–409.

Carnegie Commission on Preventing Deadly Conflict. *Preventing Deadly Conflict*. New York: Carnegie Corporation of New York, 1997.

Carpenter, R. Charli. "Setting the Advocacy Agenda: Theorizing Issue Emergence and Nonemergence in Transnational Advocacy Networks". *International Studies Quarterly* 51, no. 1 (2007): 99–120.

Chandran, Rahul, Jake Sherman, Bruce Jones with Shepard Forman, Anne le More, Yoshino Funaki and Andrew Hart. "Rapid Deployment of Civilians for Peace Operations: Status, Gaps, and Options". NYU Center on International Cooperation, April 2009. www.cic.nyu.edu/peacebuilding/docs/Deployment_annex_links.pdf.

Chayes, Abram and Antonia Handler Chayes. "On Compliance". *International Organization* 47, no. 2 (1993): 175–205.

Chesterman, Simon. *Just War or Just Peace?: Humanitarian Intervention and International Law*. Oxford: Oxford University Press, 2001.

Cooper, Andrew F. and John English. "International Commissions and the Mind of Global Governance". In *International Commissions and the Power of Ideas*, edited by Ramesh. C. Thakur, Andrew F. Cooper and John English, 1–26. Tokyo: United Nations University Press, 2005.

Corten, Oliver. "Human Rights and Collective Security". In *Human Rights, Intervention and the Use of Force*, edited by Philip Alston and Euan MacDonald, 87–138. Oxford: Oxford University Press, 2008.

Cox, Robert. "Social Forces, States, and World Orders: Beyond International Relations Theory". *Millennium: Journal of International Studies* 10, no. 2 (1981): 126–55.

Crawford, Neta. *Argument and Change in World Politics: Ethics, Decolonization, and Humanitarian Intervention*. Cambridge: Cambridge University Press, 2002.

Durch, William J. "United Nations Police Evolution, Present Capacity and Future Tasks". Prepared for the GRIPS State-Building workshop: 'Organizing police forces in post-conflict peace-support operations' of 27–28 January 2010. National Graduate Institute for Policy Studies, 2010. www3.grips.ac.jp/~pinc/data/10-03.pdf.

Evans, Gareth. "Healing Injustices by Preventing Future Atrocities". Rama Mani in conversation with Gareth Evans, Public Lecture Theatre, University of Melbourne, 15 February 2012.

Finnemore, Martha and Kathryn Sikkink. "International Norm Dynamics and Political Change". *International Organization* 52, no. 4 (1998): 887–917.

Global Action to Prevent War. "To Prevent Genocide and Crimes against Humanity: Diverse Perspectives on a Standing, Rapid-Reaction UN Emergency Peace Service". Symposium Report on the United Nations Emergency Peace Service Initiative. Convened at Rutgers Law School, Rutgers University, NJ, 29 March 2007. www.globalactionpw.org/wp/wp-content/uploads/rutgers_uneps_conference_report_2007.pdf.

Global Action to Prevent War and The Project for a UN Emergency Peace Service (UNEPS). *UNEPS in Context: Third Pillar Capacities and First Pillar Responses*. 7 and 8 December 2010. www.globalactionpw.org/wp/wp-content/uploads/uneps-report1.pdf.

Goldstein, Judith and Robert O. Keohane, eds. *Ideas and Foreign Policy: Beliefs, Institutions, and Political Change*. Ithaca, NY: Cornell University Press, 1993.

Herro, Annie. "Norm Entrepreneurs and the UN Emergency Peace Service". In *Perspectives on Peacekeeping and Atrocity Prevention: Expanding Stakeholders and Regional Arrangements*, edited by Robert Zuber and Larry Roeder David Curran. New York: Springer, forthcoming.

Holt, Victoria, Glyn Taylor and Max Kelly. "Protecting Civilians in the Context of UN Peacekeeping Operations: Successes, Setbacks and Remaining Challenges". Independent study jointly commissioned by the United Nations Department of Peacekeeping Operations and the Office for the Coordination of Humanitarian Affairs, 2009. www.peacekeepingbestpractices.unlb.org/pbps/Library/Protecting%20Civilians%20in%20the%20Context%20of%20UN%20PKO.pdf

Holzgrefe, J.L. "The Humanitarian Intervention Debate". In *Humanitarian Intervention: Ethical, Legal and Political Dilemmas*, edited by J.L. Holzgrefe and Robert O. Keohane, 15–52. Cambridge: Cambridge University Press, 2003.

International Commission on Intervention and State Sovereignty. *The Responsibility to Protect*. Ottawa: International Development Research Centre, 2001.

International Court of Justice. *Legality of Use of Force Case (Provisional Measures), Pleadings of Belgium*. CR 99/15 of 10 May 1999.

Johansen, Robert C. "Expert Discussion of the United Nations Emergency Peace Service: Cuenca Report". In *A United Nations Emergency Peace Service: To Prevent Genocide and Crimes against Humanity*, edited by Robert C. Johansen, 43–74. New York World Federalist Movement – Institute for Global Policy, 2006.

Johansen, Robert C. "Proposal for a United Nations Emergency Peace Service to Prevent Genocide and Crimes against Humanity". In *A United Nations Emergency Peace Service: To Prevent Genocide and Crimes against Humanity*, edited by Robert C. Johansen, 23–41. New York: World Federalist Movement–Institute for Global Policy, 2006.

Johansen, Robert C., ed. *A United Nations Emergency Peace Service: To Prevent Genocide and Crimes against Humanity*. New York: World Federalist Movement–Institute for Global Policy, 2006.

Keck, Margaret E. and Kathryn Sikkink. *Activists Beyond Borders: Advocacy Networks in International Politics*. Ithaca, NY: Cornell University Press, 1998.

Khagram, Sangeev, James V. Riker and Kathryn Sikkink. *Restructuring World Politics: Transnational Social Movements, Networks, and Norms*. Minneapolis: University of Minnesota Press, 2002.

Krasner, Stephen D. "Structural Causes and Regime Consequences: Regimes as Intervening Variables". *International Organization* 36, no. 2 (1982): 185–205.

Kratochwil, Friedrich V. *Rules, Norms, and Decisions*. Cambridge: Cambridge University Press, 1989.

Krook, Mona L. and Jacqui True. "Rethinking the Life Cycles of International Norms: The United Nations and the Global Promotion of Gender Equality". *European Journal of International Relations* 18, no. 1 (2012): 103–27.

Langille, H. Peter. *Bridging the Commitment–Capacity Gap: A Review of Existing Arrangements and Options for Enhancing UN Rapid Deployment*. New York: Center for UN Reform Education, 2002.

Langille, H. Peter. "Fixing Darfur". *The Globe and Mail*, 29 April, 2009.

Langille, H. Peter. "Preventing Genocide". In *The World and Darfur: International Response to Crimes against Humanity in Western Sudan*, edited by Amanda Grzyb, 281–327. Montreal: McGill Queens University Press, 2009.

Langille, H. Peter. *Linking UNEPS to Responsibility to Protect* 2010. www.worldfederalistscanada.org/mondial1210/p13%20UNEPS%20%28Mondial%20Dec%2010%29.pdf.

Langille, H. Peter. *Preparing for a UN Emergency Peace Service*. Friedrich Ebert Stiftung, August, 2012. http://library.fes.de/pdf-files/iez/09282.pdf.

Langille, H. Peter. "A UN Emergency Peace Service". openDemocracy, 2012. www.opendemocracy.net/opensecurity/h-peter-langille/un-emergency-peace-service.

Langille, H. Peter. "The Initiative for a UN Emergency Peace Service". 2013. www.youtube.com/watch?v=ZkyHuSLZ6iY.

Legro, Jeffery W. "Which Norms Matter? Revisiting the 'Failure' of Internationalism". *International Organization* 51, no. 1 (1997): 31–63.

McNamara, Kathleen R. *The Currency of Ideas: Monetary Politics in the European Union*. Ithaca, NY: Cornell University Press, 1998.

Mendez, Juan. "The Prevention of Genocide and its Challenges". In *Standing for Change in Peacekeeping Operations: Project for a United Nations Emergency Peace Service (UNEPS)*, 43–9. New York: GAPW, 2009.

Mendlovitz, Saul. *Interview with Professor Saul Mendlovitz – Part 2*. School of Law, Rutgers-Newark University, NJ, 2010. www.youtube.com/watch?v=SOAXvRwgbMg.

Meyer, John W., John Boli Boli, George M. Thomas and Francisco O. Ramirez. "World Society and the Nation-State". *American Journal of Sociology* 103, no. 1 (1997): 144–81.

Nadelmann, Ethan A. "Global Prohibition Regimes: The Evolution of Norms in International Society". *International Organization* 44, no. 4 (1990): 479–526.

Price, Richard. "Reversing the Gun Sights: Transnational Civil Society Targets Land Mines". *International Organization* 52, no. 3 (1998): 613–44.

Risse, Thomas. "'Let's Argue!': Communicative Action in World Politics". *International Organization* 54, no. 1 (2000): 1–39.

Risse-Kappen, Thomas, Stephen C. Ropp and Kathryn Sikkink. *The Power of Human Rights: International Norms and Domestic Change*. Cambridge: Cambridge University Press 1999.

Ruggie, John G. "What Makes the World Hang Together? Neo-Utilitarianism and the Social Constructivist Challenge". *International Organization* 52, no. 4 (1998): 855–85.

Scheffer, David. "Genocide and Atrocity Crimes". *Genocide Studies and Prevention* 1, no. 3 (2006): 229–50.

Slim, Hugo and Andrew Bonwick. *Protection: An Alnap Guide for Humanitarian Agencies*. Oxford: Oxfam, 2006.

Suthanthiraraj, Kavitha and Mariah Quinn. *Standing for Change in Peacekeeping Operations: Project for a United Nations Emergency Peace Service (UNEPS)*. New York: GAPW, 2009.

Thakur, Ramesh. *The Responsibility to Protect: Norms, Laws and the Use of Force in International Politics*. London: Routledge, 2011.

United Nations. *Charter of the United Nations*. New York: United Nations, 1945.

UN General Assembly. *Report of the Panel on United Nations Peace Operations*. A/55/305 of 21 August 2000. New York: United Nations.

UN General Assembly. *Resolution Adopted by the General Assembly: 57/337. Prevention of Armed Conflict*. A/RES/57/337 of 3 July 2002. New York: United Nations.

UN General Assembly. *A More Secure World: Our Shared Responsibility. Report of the Secretary-General's High-Level Panel on Threats, Challenges and Change*. A/59/565 of 2 December 2004. New York: United Nations.

UN General Assembly. *Resolution Adopted by the General Assembly: 60/1. 2005 World Summit Outcome*. A/RES/60/1 of 24 October 2005. New York: United Nations.

UN General Assembly. *Implementing the Responsibility to Protect: Report of the Secretary-General*. A/63/677 of 12 January 2009.

UN General Assembly. *Report of the Secretary-General on the Responsibility to Protect: Timely and Decisive Response*. A/66/874–S/2012/578 of 25 July 2012. New York: United Nations.

UN Security Council. *Resolution 1366*. S/RES/1366 of 30 August 2001. New York: United Nations.
Urquhart, Brian. "For a UN Volunteer Military Force". *New York Review of Books*, 10 June 1993, 3–4.
Urquhart, Brian. "Finding the Hidden UN". *New York Review of Books*, 27 May 2010.
Wendt, A. "Anarchy is What States Make of It: The Social Construction of Power Politics". *International Organization* 46, no. 2 (1992): 391–425.
Wendt, Alexander. "Constructing International Politics". *International Security* (1995): 71–81.
Wendt, Alexander. *Social Theory of International Politics*. Cambridge: Cambridge University Press, 1999.
World Federalist Movement. "UNEPS Backgrounder". n.d. www.worldfederalistscanada.org/uneps%20backgrounder.pdf.

4 An un-armed UNEPS

Introduction

As we have just seen, a defining feature of the UNEPS proposal is the range of norms with which it is underpinned. Two of these norms are Pillar One – each state's responsibility to protect its populations from atrocities – and Pillar Two – the international community's responsibility to assist states in preventing atrocities from breaking out. Operationally, Pillar Two translates into an integrated service comprising police, civilians and the military performing a range of tasks that contribute to averting conflict and building sustainable peace. Yet the proposition that a UNEPS would possess troops capable of using force at the permanent disposal of the UN hindered the support the proposal has received. This begs the question whether the proposed UNEPS should possess a coercive military component at all.

This chapter examines perspectives on both the normative and operational attributes of the UNEPS proposal related to the non-use of force. It shows how respondents use localisation strategies by pruning, grafting and framing the proposal in ways that eliminate parts of R2P and the protection of civilians in conflict (POC) linked to the use of force, while emphasising other norms that are not. There is a connection between the aversion to incorporating a military component in previous proposals for a UN Legion and some responses to the UNEPS proposal and this also supports omitting the coercive capacity of such a service. Pillar One was, by contrast, largely supported by respondents as well as by UNEPS' advocates.

This research suggests three alternative versions of the UNEPS proposal which avoid the use of force and reflect each of the following three norms, respectively: (1) peacebuilding; (2) Pillar Two (sans force); and (3) a version of R2P called "R2P-plus". In relation to the third option, this chapter argues that a service comprising military personnel that would respond to natural disasters could be a viable and valuable tool in the international community's toolbox and a first step towards the establishment of a service that prevents or responds to manmade humanitarian crises. It concludes with a pragmatic question surrounding the extent to which a standing civilian service charged with peacebuilding or preventing R2P crimes would be a constructive contribution to the UN's efforts to prevent war and atrocities.

Historical aversion to force

History has shown – through the experiences of the first UNSG, Trygve Lie, in his efforts to establish a UN standing capacity – that removing the military component from this earlier proposal was instrumental in securing the idea's acceptance.[1] The "UN Guard Force" proposed by Lie in 1948 would have comprised 800 men, 500 of whom would be held in reserve in their respective home countries to support United Nations Missions in the provided, provide limited protection to UN personnel and property, and conducted plebiscites, among other duties.[2] While the officers would have been uniformed and armed with light defence weapons, it would have been "entirely non-military in character", according to Lie.[3] In other words, Lie's idea was to create a tool for peaceful settlement of disputes under Chapter VI of the UN Charter.[4]

A small Special Committee was set up to debate Lie's proposal. The Americans labelled it "too ambitious" and claimed that it encroached too closely on a "military theme"[5] while the Soviets argued that a force with automatic weapons and armoured vehicles would transform the Guard into a genuine armed force. The South African delegate was also worried that the Guard might generate a "paramilitary character".[6] Lie's proposal was only successful when it was stripped of its truce and plebiscite functions and, importantly, its arms.[7] It thus bore little resemblance to his original idea. Between 1958 and 1960, almost a decade after Lie proposed his UN Guard, the International Law Association, which is mandated to study, clarify and develop public and private international law, looked into establishing a permanent UN Force for peacekeeping operations. Concerns about military capability proved, again, to be a stumbling block.[8]

The question of removing the coercive component from the UNEPS proposal to increase its political salience was raised at the 2005 conference in Cuenca, Spain. Participants discussed a phased implementation in which the least controversial dimensions – the humanitarian assistance, civilian police, judicial and conflict resolution functions – could be established without the armed security service. Johansen noted that "if the most contested element of UNEPS is its permanent military capability, then should UNEPS be implemented in a first phase without that robust enforcement element?"[9] The question was eventually answered in the negative, with most participants agreeing that the entire proposal should be kept as an inseparable package so that the UNEPS could effectively provide the comprehensive services – especially robust security – needed to meet the demands likely to be placed on it.[10]

Yet the issue of separating the military component from its civilian counterparts has not disappeared. One of the authors of the ICISS report who was consulted about his views on the UNEPS proposal believes that the idea of an integrated, multidimensional service ought to be rethought. He argued that given the "huge sensitivity of a military body of this kind", it is important to disassociate any proposal for a military force from a standing civilian capacity.[11] Furthermore, a representative from the UN's Department of Peacekeeping Operations suggests that "it is best to progress where inroads have already been made, such as civilians and police, especially in areas such as gender-based violence". He is referring to the United Nations Team of Experts on the Rule of Law and Sexual Violence in Conflict (who focus on strengthening the capacity of national rule of law and justice actors) and the Standing Police Capacity, respectively.[12] This respondent was explicitly suggesting avoiding proposals that possess a military component: "rapid deployment in other areas [military] is more politically tricky. Currently the political environment is risk averse and it will be hard".[13]

Given the sensitivity around the use of force and the UNEPS proposal, what alternatives are there for a non-violent iteration of the proposal? Before answering this question, I briefly consider respondents' perspectives on Pillar One – a central norm underpinning the proposed UNEPS.

Consensus on Pillar One

Pillar One or the responsibility of the state to protect its population from atrocity crimes is codified in international humanitarian and human rights law[14] and has been described by UNSG Ban Ki-moon as the "bedrock" of R2P.[15] Given that there was consensus among states at the 2009 UN General Assembly meeting on the importance of "sovereignty as responsibility" it is unsurprising that the respondents in this study either implicitly or explicitly endorsed this norm.[16] *Implicitly*, respondents supported this norm by championing Pillar Two measures. For example, a representative from the Ugandan Mission to the UN reinforced the importance of peacekeeping forces protecting civilians, "especially if you are talking about R2P crimes".[17] This shows his support for the principle that if a government fails to protect its civilians, it is the responsibility of the international community to step in. Respondents also expressed support for this idea by showing interest (albeit often qualified) in the proposed UNEPS and providing suggestions on ways of increasing its political acceptance. Such views are discussed further later in this chapter and in subsequent chapters. Among those who *explicitly* supported the principle of sovereign responsibility was a former Secretary-General of the Association of South East Asian Nations (ASEAN) who said, "I think most politicians in South East Asia can understand that they must act in a disaster situation. If they don't care about their population, there will still be an adverse reaction outside their country".[18]

While Pillar One is relatively uncontroversial, what happens when a state is expected to fail in its duty to protect? Do respondents believe that a UNEPS might strengthen the existing non-violent capacities available to the international community in implementing Pillar Two? And, if so, how?

Structural prevention – a peacebuilding service

As mentioned in the previous chapter, UNEPS is conceived as a service that would prevent genocide and crimes against humanity, among other humanitarian catastrophes, and as such is underpinned by norms of both direct and structural prevention. Stuart Rees of the University of Sydney, however, who was present during an early meeting on the proposed UNEPS and subsequently became an advocate, suggested that the service should be solely committed to structural prevention.[19] While he was a lone voice in these meetings, I include him in this discussion because some of his views were shared by respondents in my research.

Rees, who was a social worker before he became an academic, has a commitment to non-violence. He believes that non-violence not only is an effective means of preventing atrocities (and thereby valid from a practical perspective), but also is ethically the most appropriate means of intervention. Non-violence, as understood by Rees, reflects elements of (liberal) democratic peacebuilding because it involves a commitment to human rights, strengthening democratic structures and social justice.[20]

When speaking to a Shadow Minister in the Australian Labor Party about UNEPS, Rees remarked that "in every field of policy – social or foreign policy – we're not giving enough attention to the philosophy, language and practice of non-violence...". Articulating the activities that UNEPS members *ought* to perform, he said:

> the focus [of the UNEPS proposal] is on short-term prevention, but my experience with the War Against Poverty programme in the United States was that you couldn't see the relationship between what you did and the consequences in under three years ...[21]

Rees is implying that the proposed UNEPS should provide countries at risk of genocidal or other types of violence with a long-term presence that would undertake structural preventative activities. This is at odds with UNEPS' 'first-in, first-out' deployment philosophy advocated by most of its core promoters.[22] Reinforcing this view, Rees said, and has repeated since, that UNEPS' personnel would comprise "civilian police, experts in the administration of justice, community development workers, human rights practitioners" which is more suited to structural prevention, rather than direct prevention.

The Director of an Indonesian peacebuilding NGO supported a similar incarnation of the UNEPS proposal to that espoused by Rees, by prioritising structural prevention for normative and problem-solving reasons. The respondent argued for the need to empower civil society to conduct so-called civilian peacekeeping.[23] Having worked in conflicts in Ambon and West Kalimantan in Indonesia, he suggested downplaying the emphasis on the military elements of the proposal because of the limitations of what armed force can achieve.

The perspectives of a former ASEAN Secretary-General on UNEPS were also helpful in considering how the proposal could be localised to increase the support it received.[24] This respondent announced his commitment to a range of norms from the Treaty of Amity and Cooperation – a peace treaty among South East Asian and other states – such as non-interference in the internal affairs of one another, mutual respect for sovereignty, independence and national identity, and the renunciation of the use of force. He explained his commitment to these norms because they "contribute to stability, make economic development possible and this means jobs and better standards of living". Consequently, he (implicitly) grafted norms of structural prevention on to the proposal. The respondent argued, using the example of the devastating 2008 cyclone in Myanmar, that the international community should be limited to offering impartial and neutral assistance to the government and the population, such as "delivering relief goods and building the economy". "Let us not expect it to go in there with armed force", he remarked. His views were corroborated by a representative of the Bangladeshi Permanent Mission to the UN who suggested incorporating human security and economic development into the UNEPS proposal because such ideas "are more common in Asia and could be a means of stimulating debate".[25]

Some South East Asian states have taken a similar approach to the R2P doctrine by emphasising "root cause" prevention, such as economic development and democratisation. They argue that root causes should be prioritised as a central part of the R2P agenda, in particular as part of the "responsibility to prevent". Statements from Brunei, Cambodia, Laos, the Philippines and Vietnam on R2P, for example, illustrate states' interest in strengthening efforts to protect relating to economic development, not the use of force.[26] Generally, states from the global South claim that the root causes of conflict and atrocity crimes are found in poverty and underdevelopment.[27] The literature linking poverty and violent conflict supports this view. For example, the well-known economist Paul Collier argues that there is a greater risk of conflict breaking out in poor countries, and that conflict-affected countries generally have higher levels of poverty and lower growth rates.[28]

Fikry Cassidy, Deputy Director for International Security and Disarmament in the Indonesian Department of Foreign Affairs, suggested that support for a standing civilian capacity might be found among countries in the UN Peacebuilding Commission (UNPBC).[29] Another respondent who served in several high ranking UN peacekeeping appointments and is currently an international consultant on peace and security issues also suggested that UNEPS might, "find a home within the Peacebuilding Commission".[30] While neither elaborated on what this would mean – operationally – for a UNEPS, their preferences reinforce the normative value of grafting the peacebuilding norm on to the UNEPS proposal.

A further advocate for establishing a service that would solely undertake peacebuilding activities was more specific about the tasks a recalibrated UNEPS would perform. This senior figure in Amnesty International's (UK) legal team argued that proponents should "pitch UNEPS to countries as a service that would ensure a country's systems are made as strong and effective as possible".[31] Focusing on strengthening "systems" encompasses certain economic, political, legal, social and cultural measures that can create the conditions of sustainable peace in countries at risk of armed conflict, and are part of the peacebuilding package.[32] The respondent went on to say, "don't sell it to some countries as conflict prevention because it's too sensitive". He is therefore highlighting the importance of framing the proposal using non-confrontational language and, like those previously mentioned, pruning its coercive elements.

A representative from the UN Office for the Special Advisor on Genocide Prevention also argued that UNEPS should support "states to abide by minimal standards". This respondent claimed that "you won't move forward if you only focus on intervention – it is needed but I have attended a number of meetings with states and there is no appetite to talk about Pillar Three...".[33] She is indicating that ideas about direct military responses to threats of atrocity crimes might jar with some states' normative orders. This respondent suggested orienting the UNEPS proposal towards "early peacebuilding elements which many current missions are trying to perform. Weak institutions often facilitate genocide, for example security institutions". She suggested taking the case of Liberia as an example of the kind of activities to which UNEPS might contribute.

The UN Mission in Liberia (UNMIL), which was authorised from 2003 until 2012, is a large, multidimensional operation composed of political, military, civilian police, criminal justice, civil affairs, human rights, gender, child protection, disarmament, demobilisation and reintegration, public information and support components.[34] UNMIL's activities included bridging the gap of structural inequality and poverty eradication; re-establishing democratic government or institutions, such as the independent judiciary and electoral commission; security reforms such as training of the military, police and other security organs; re-establishing the rule of law and respect of human rights, such as support for the establishment of the independent human rights commission and training of journalists; and revamping the economy including the provision of micro-financing to the poor.[35] The respondent recognised that peacebuilding activities like these might, in practice, contribute to prevention. A UNEPS might contribute to such a UN mission, by commencing such tasks or supplementing activities that are not being carried out effectively.

If respondents' interest in a peacebuilding service or one that would conduct structural prevention were to shape the form, composition and function of the proposed UNEPS, it would end up looking more like a unit that supports existing peacebuilding efforts in countries that have experienced conflict or are at risk of conflict breaking out. This would thus have a transformative effect on the proposal to the point where it bears little resemblance to the original idea.

Structural prevention measures are often incorporated into developmental assistance programmes which are presently being carried out by a number of international and governmental agencies.[36] This point raises a question which I discuss further in Chapters 7 and 8 of this book: if such work is already being done by existing agencies, what added-value would a standing service that conducts peacebuilding activities actually have?

A non-violent R2P prevention service

The second incarnation of the proposed UNEPS is based on respondents' attempts to recalibrate or localise the proposal so that it would focus solely on non-military elements of Pillar Two or other measures that directly and immediately prevent conflict. The direct prevention approach is attractive because of its potential to achieve results fairly quickly and because of the short chain of logic between specific actions and the prevention of an atrocity. Such actions include offering incentives for good behaviour, fact-finding or monitoring missions and restricting the flow of arms and other assets that might lead to violence.[37] But the relationship between direct and structural prevention is complicated because they do not always take place in a linear fashion. Direct prevention may run parallel to structural prevention, or the two may support each other.[38] Indeed, peacebuilding or structural prevention measures fall within the ambit of preventing mass atrocities.[39] Respondents mentioned below highlight the normative value of creating a service that would be devoted to directly preventing atrocities or other forms of disasters through non-violent means.

One such advocate was Alex Bellamy, then Executive Director of the Asia-Pacific Centre for the Responsibility to Protect. Bellamy suggested at a symposium on UNEPS the creation of a standing civilian capacity to prevent R2P crimes because (1) of the political sensitivity surrounding cross-border military intervention and (2) such a service could be one means of operationalising Pillar Two. The aim of his proposed civilian service would be to help states strengthen their capacity to prevent crimes occurring in the first place. Bellamy noted that there are three things that need to exist in the lead up to genocide in particular: economic or political grievances, radical ideology and capability to commit mass murder. UNEPS, he argued, could play an important role in mitigating these factors.[40] While defining the preconditions of genocide is too difficult and controversial to capture in a short sentence and includes more than is cited above,[41] Bellamy's suggestion is important because it points to a potential role for UNEPS in addressing some of the direct causes of certain R2P crimes.

First, it could respond to the causes of breakdown of governance and economy, for example, by assisting in rule of law and security sector reform; strengthening the resilience of national economies to make them crisis proof; developing local conflict resolution capacities; and addressing the question of how to resolve issues such as land rights and water usage. Second, highlighting the 2005 World Summit Outcome Document's reference to states' responsibility to prevent the incitement of R2P crimes, it could prevent radical ideology from evolving by tackling hate media and promoting moderate views. Third, it could prevent rogue regimes from acquiring the capacity for mass killings by supplying early warning information to the Security Council and advocating arms embargoes.[42] Bellamy's proposed target areas for a UNEPS encompass therefore both structural and direct preventative measures.

Also endorsing similar direct preventative measures was the former Secretary-General of ASEAN.[43] He stated that:

> we should try to prevent the need to mobilise a force [in response to conflict].... Given our globalised world, we should bring certain serious situations to the global community and say 'look this is threatening to develop into scenario a, b, c all of which would not be good for the community ... it is necessary

for us to take action now'.... You can study the trends of some governments that might lead to disasters. From there we should apply the corrective measures to minimise the potential. This would be a more cost effective way to go forward. We need to say: what is the decent thing to do for the population in the affected area? We should be preventing right from the outset.

While the former Secretary-General does not explicitly conceive of a role for a UNEPS, his comments suggest that, should a mechanism like UNEPS be created, it might receive his support if it addressed the causes of conflict and other disasters. His aversion to the cross-border use of force is unsurprising given two of the central norms of ASEAN are non-interference in the domestic affairs of other states and the non-use of force to settle disputes. These are discussed in further detail below and in the following chapter. Similar preferences for direct preventative measures have been expressed by certain states in debates about R2P. At the 2009 General Assembly plenary debates on the doctrine, Japan argued that R2P applies to the four crimes only (genocide, ethnic cleansing, war crimes and crimes against humanity) and that:

> what we should do is to implement and consolidate properly this agreement and focus on issues which have direct links with those four most serious crimes ... not to enlarge the scope of R2P to overall threats to humanities such as poverty, pandemics, climate change, natural disasters, etc.[44]

In sum, from a normative perspective it is clear that there is a preference for non-violent Pillar Two measures which a standing civilian UNEPS might help address. The question remains whether such a service would be a valuable contribution to the UN's capacity to prevent atrocities. Answering this question requires a broader discussion on the coordination within, and potential overlaps between, UN field operations, so will not be dealt with until the last two chapters of this book.

Responding to natural disasters and "R2P-plus"

The final iteration of the proposed UNEPS that appeared to increase the support it received was the idea of a unit that would respond to natural disasters. It would include troops but – importantly – preclude the use of force. As mentioned in Chapter 3, while some of UNEPS' architects suggested that the service might respond to natural disasters as *one* of the situations that it would be mandated to address, none envisaged a service that would be solely devoted to such a goal. The scope of civilian protection is broad enough to encompass populations displaced or at risk as a result of natural disasters, which suggests that altering the UNEPS mandate in this way would not compromise the norms on which it is based – the need to save lives and alleviate human suffering in humanitarian crises.[45]

Natural disaster response is an area where the civilian-military-police relationships tend to be less contentious. In a natural disaster environment, the aid community and other civilian actors recognise the capacity of the military to provide medical, logistical and engineering capabilities. In the Asia-Pacific region specifically, militaries (both domestic and those of other countries) are often the first principal responders, even though at first sight such a response appears to violate regional norms such as sovereignty and territorial integrity.

But natural disasters can also be political, especially when they take place in conflict zones, such as in the Philippines, Iraq, Somalia and Haiti. The Government of Myanmar, for example, when faced with the destruction caused by Cyclone Nargis in 2008, rejected offers of international assistance, which some commentators labelled crimes against humanity.[46] These politicised contexts did not seem to influence respondents' interest in a localised version of the proposal, with some expressing their general support for interventions responding to natural disasters in places where there was ongoing conflict (such as Aceh, Indonesia) and which would have otherwise been highly controversial.

Several respondents agreed that interventions after natural disasters are an area in which respect for state sovereignty is of less importance – "it's about human beings against nature", as one prominent Indonesian journalist puts it – suggesting such interventions could be an important gateway to broader international cooperation in response to more sensitive crises like atrocity crimes.[47] Specifically, some respondents argued that, for political reasons, a proposal for a standing service that focused on natural disasters would be an effective entry point to start a conversation about a UNEPS. For example, sensitivities about discussing human rights violations in Asia, such as in Mindanao and Myanmar, convinced a Bangladeshi diplomat that UNEPS could be a means of responding to large-scale natural disasters and other "less politicised" tasks.[48] Others, including a senior Australian Defence Force (ADF) figure and a prominent Indonesian political and defence analyst, argued that creating a regional mechanism in the Asia-Pacific capable of responding to natural disasters might build the necessary trust between states to create a service with an accepted mandate to prevent mass human rights abuses also.[49] For example, the respondent from the ADF, who was impressed with the skills of certain South East Asian neighbours in responding to recent tsunamis and earthquakes in the region, argued that:

> if you start with genocide, you probably won't do it; but if you start with humanitarian aid, it could go a long way towards establishing the trust that could flow into the other ... it's not about security, it's not about who's superior ... [it is] a recognition that working together is a smart thing to do that doesn't cause ... the loss of face.[50]

Those who suggested that re-designing the UNEPS proposal to respond to natural disasters could be a precursor to the establishment of a service that prevents manmade humanitarian crises seemed to be distinguishing between a vision of a UNEPS and the strategy to achieve it. The appeal of a service that could respond to natural disasters was also influenced by a normative commitment to protect people who are neglected by their governments and an interest in strengthening the capacity of their various regions to respond to crises.

In the same spirit of this localised UNEPS, South East Asian scholars Mely Cabarello-Anthony and Belinda Chng suggest creating a variation of R2P, called "R2P-Plus", tailored to a South East Asian context. R2P-Plus would be devoid of coercive measures and could help to advance the application of R2P by concentrating on natural catastrophes (as well as conflict situations that are on a lighter scale in terms of widespread and deliberate physical violence).[51] Consequently, they argue, R2P-Plus "which focuses only on addressing natural catastrophes and preventing conflicts in a non-coercive manner and with the co-operation of the states involved, could fill the void in R2P"[52] and "blunt the arguments of those who accuse R2P of being a neo-imperialist instrument".[53] Aspects of R2P-plus echo the principles that emerged from the Shangri-La Dialogue of 2008, which is a non-official annual forum for senior defence officials and intellectuals from Asia-Pacific and Europe. Officials agreed that multilateral cooperation in humanitarian assistance within situations of disaster could be guided by three principles: (1) the responsibility of disaster-hit countries to bring humanitarian relief quickly and effectively to their people; (2) where necessary, affected countries should facilitate the entry of external assistance; and, (3) any external help should have the consent of the affected countries and fall under their control.[54] The same logic that Caballero-Anthony and Chng apply to increasing support for R2P might also be applied to UNEPS. Indeed, R2P-Plus could be grafted on to the proposed UNEPS and used as the normative bedrock of a localised idea.

From a practical perspective, does the international community need a more effective mechanism to respond to natural catastrophes? On the one hand, there are a number of services already provided by UN agencies and coordinated by the Office of the Coordination of Humanitarian Affairs. These include: a permanent stand-by Disaster Assessment and Coordination Team, On-Site Operations Coordination Centre and the coordination of civil-military assets, and the management of a Central Emergency Response Fund. On the other hand, Caballero-Anthony and Chng argue that responses to natural disasters over the last decade do indeed suggest that the international community needs to be better equipped.[55] An Oxfam report builds on their assertion. It states that UN agencies, donors, and international NGOs struggled to cope with the vast number of humanitarian crises from natural disasters in Haiti, Pakistan, Somalia and elsewhere, producing responses that were "too little and too late".[56]

The UN Economic and Social Council adopted a resolution after the 2004 tsunami recommending that more must be done to develop and improve emergency standby capacities.[57] Then, following the March 2011 deadly earthquake and tsunami in Japan, the UN reiterated calls for the world to respond quickly to current natural disasters and streamline efforts to tackle their inevitable impacts.[58] Reacting to such calls, the NGO Forced Migration has argued that the creation of a "[a] standing global response mechanism under the auspices of the UN, with immediate authority to launch the initial response and build on available local and regional capacities, would lead to prompter dispatch of relief teams and supplies".[59] In sum, the international community's response to natural disasters suggests that a proposal for a standing UN capacity tailored to such situations could be both viable and valuable.

Since Asia was the continent that experienced the greatest number of natural disasters and the highest death toll in 2012,[60] the idea of establishing a permanent regional arrangement, as suggested by one respondent, makes good sense. A model for such an arrangement could be Greece and Turkey's response following the devastating earthquakes that hit the two countries in 1999. These governments signed a bilateral agreement in 2001 to establish a joint standby disaster response unit comprising personnel drawn from governments and NGOs of both countries to facilitate timely humanitarian assistance to populations affected by sudden natural disasters. The UN Office for the Coordination of Humanitarian Affairs assisted in working out the arrangements for how this joint unit would operate.[61] In the case of the Asia-Pacific region, a standing capacity could be established at a sub-regional level (instead of bilaterally), provided the political appetite for such a unit exists. A more in-depth discussion on regional and sub-regional arrangements, and on the potential for the UN to be involved in such initiatives, is conducted in Chapters 6 and 8.

Conclusion

This chapter has illustrated the greater comfort surrounding non-violent responses to conflict and suggests that support for the UNEPS proposal might increase if it were transformed into a standing service without a military capacity to use force. Consequently, I have considered what UNEPS would need to look like to increase support for the idea based on what respondents explicitly suggested as well as their preferences for, or aversion to, certain norms. This would involve pruning aspects of Pillar Two that relate to the use of force, and grafting norms of peacebuilding and R2P-plus onto the proposal. Respondents supported such norms for reasons relating to ethics (it is the right response), pragmatism (it is the most effective response and it is the only response that would receive support). A UNEPS modeled on the norm R2P-Plus especially pertains to those interested in restructuring the proposal into a mechanism that would respond to natural disasters. This would be a valuable contribution to the international community's efforts to respond rapidly and effectively to catastrophes of this kind.

There is clearly a tension here between retaining the purity of the UNEPS proposal – as agreed upon by UNEPS' advocates – and localising it so that it is consistent with respondents' normative orders. I suggest that the creation of a service that would respond to natural disasters might be a pragmatic way of arriving at the point where states could accept the UNEPS proposal as we know it today. In other words, reworking the UNEPS proposal as a mechanism to respond to natural disasters could result in incremental reform that could eventually build the momentum to create a service with a mandate to prevent atrocity crimes. This chapter also raises the questions: to what extent are the civilian activities relating to peacebuilding and direct prevention of R2P crimes that the respondents suggest already being undertaken by other UN agencies? I explore these questions in Chapters 7 and 8 of this book.

Building on this discussion, the following chapter explores perspectives on the proposed UNEPS that relate to the use of force to prevent atrocities and protect civilians.

Notes

1. Schwebel, *Justice in International Law*, 317.
2. Ibid., 309; Roberts, "Proposals for UN Standing Forces", 101–2.
3. United Nations Guard Report: Report of the Secretary-General to the General Assembly.
4. Schwebel, *Justice in International Law*, 309.
5. Public Papers of the Secretaries-General of the United Nations, vol. 1, Trygve Lie.
6. Schwebel, *Justice in International Law*, 313.
7. Ibid., 317.
8. Bowett, *United Nations Forces*, 326.
9. Johansen, "Cuenca Report", 61.
10. Ibid., 62.
11. Phone interview by author and Stuart Rees, 18 July 2007.
12. UN General Assembly and UN Security Council, *Sexual Violence in Conflict*, para. 119; Le Roy, "Remarks of the under Secretary-General for Peacekeeping Operations".
13. Interview by Kavitha Suthanthiraraj, 16 November 2010, New York, USA.
14. Gierycz, "International Law and the Responsibility to Protect".
15. UN General Assembly, *Implementing the Responsibility to Protect*, para. 11(a).
16. International Coalition for the Responsibility to Protect, "Report on the General Assembly Plenary Debate", 4.
17. Interview by Kavitha Suthanthiraraj, 21 December 2010, New York, USA.
18. Interview by author, 16 June 2009, Singapore.
19. Rees was present at the Cuenca meeting on UNEPS in 2005. Johansen, *A United Nations Emergency Peace Service*, 95.
20. Rees, *Passion for Peace*, 194–5, 230–1, 271.
21. Interview by Herro and Stuart Rees, 27 June 2007, Sydney, Australia.
22. Global Action to Prevent War, "To Prevent Genocide and Crimes against Humanity".
23. Interview by author, 8 May 2008, Jakarta, Indonesia.
24. Interview by author, 16 June 2009, Singapore.
25. Interview by Kavitha Suthanthiraraj, 18 June 2010, New York, USA.
26. Asia-Pacific Centre for the Responsibility to Protect, *The Responsibility to Protect in Southeast Asia*, 13, 15, 30, 42, 67.
27. Bellamy, *Global Politics and the Responsibility to Protect*, 94; Asia-Pacific Centre for the Responsibility to Protect, "Implementing the Responsibility to Protect", 15.
28. Collier, *Breaking the Conflict Trap*; Collier, "On the Economic Consequences of Civil War".
29. Global Action to Prevent War, Centre for Peace and Conflict Studies, and Centre for Strategic and International Studies, "Peacekeeping and Civilian Protection: Asia-Pacific Perspectives", 13.
30. Interview by author, 14 November 2007, Sydney, Australia.
31. Phone interview by author, 21 May 2007.
32. Lambourne and Herro, "Peacebuilding Theory and the United Nations Peacebuilding Commission".
33. Interview by Kavitha Suthanthiraraj, 10 June 2010, New York, USA.

34 UN Security Council, *Resolution 872*; *Resolution 2008*.
35 UN Mission in Liberia, "United Nations Mission in Liberia".
36 Ackermann, "The Idea and Practice of Conflict Prevention", 341.
37 Woocher, "The Responsibility to Prevent".
38 Ackermann, "The Idea and Practice of Conflict Prevention", 341.
39 International Commission on Intervention and State Sovereignty, *The Responsibility to Protect*, 19, 23.
40 Caritas Australia, Global Action to Prevent War, Centre for Peace and Conflict Studies, "Right to Protection", 8.
41 Chalk and Jonassohn, *The History and Sociology of Genocide*; Fein, *Genocide*; Harff and Gurr, "Toward Empirical Theory of Genocides and Politicides"; Staub, *The Roots of Evil*.
42 Caritas Australia, Global Action to Prevent War, Centre for Peace and Conflict Studies, "Right to Protection".
43 Interview by author, 16 June 2009, Singapore.
44 International Coalition for the Responsibility to Protect, "Report on the General Assembly Plenary Debate on the Responsibility to Protect", 8.
45 O'Callaghan and Pantuliano, "Protective Action", 2.
46 Evans, "Facing up to Our Responsibilities".
47 Interview by author, 30 April 2008, Jakarta, Indonesia.
48 Interview by Kavitha Suthanthiraraj, 18 June 2010, New York, USA.
49 Interview by author, 13 December 2007, Canberra, Australia; Interview by author, 7 May 2008, Jakarta, Indonesia.
50 Interview by author, 13 December 2007, Canberra, Australia.
51 Caballero-Anthony and Chng, "Cyclones and Humanitarian Crises".
52 Ibid., 148.
53 Ibid., 145.
54 See Seng Tan, "Towards a 'Responsibility to Provide,'" 256–7.
55 Caballero-Anthony and Chng, "Cyclones and Humanitarian Crises", 147.
56 Oxfam, "Crisis in a New World Order".
57 UN Economic and Social Council, *Resolution 2004/5: Strengthening of the Coordination of Emergency Humanitarian Assistance of the United Nations*, para. 10.
58 Musthofid, "UN Calls for Quicker Responses".
59 Couldrey and Morris, "Tsunami", 7.
60 UN General Assembly, *Strengthening of Coordination of Emergency Humanitarian Assistance*, para. 16.
61 UN General Assembly, *Emergency Response to Disasters*.

References

Ackermann, Alice. "The Idea and Practice of Conflict Prevention". *Journal of Peace Research* 40, no. 3 (2003): 339.

Asia-Pacific Centre for the Responsibility to Protect. "Implementing the Responsibility to Protect: Asia-Pacific in the 2009 General Assembly Dialogue". Asia-Pacific Centre for the Responsibility to Protect, October 2009. www.r2pasiapacific.org/documents/final_un_ga_debate_july_2009.pdf.

Asia-Pacific Centre for the Responsibility to Protect. *The Responsibility to Protect in Southeast Asia*. Brisbane: The Asia-Pacific Centre for the Responsibility to Protect, 2009.

Bellamy, Alex. *Global Politics and the Responsibility to Protect: From Words to Deeds*. London: Routledge, 2011.

Bowett, D.W. *United Nations Forces: A Legal Study*. New York: Praeger, 1964.

Caballero-Anthony, Mely and Belinda Chng. "Cyclones and Humanitarian Crises: Pushing the Limits of R2P in Southeast Asia". *Global Responsibility to Protect* 1, no. 2 (2009): 135–55.

Caritas Australia, Global Action to Prevent War, Centre for Peace and Conflict Studies. "Right to Protection: Whose Responsibility and How? Summary Report". Caritas Australia, Global Action to Prevent War, Centre for Peace and Conflict Studies, 4 September 2008. http://sydney.edu.au/arts/peace_conflict/research/AH_Conference%20report%202.pdf.

Chalk, Frank Robert and Kurt Jonassohn. *The History and Sociology of Genocide: Analyses and Case Studies*. New Haven, Conn: Yale University Press, 1990.

Collier, Paul. "On the Economic Consequences of Civil War". *Oxford Economic Papers* 51, no. 1 (1999): 168–83.

Collier, Paul *Breaking the Conflict Trap: Civil War and Development Policy*. Washington DC: World Bank and Oxford University Press, 2003.

Couldrey, Marion and Tim Morris. "Tsunami: Learning from the Humanitarian Response". *Forced Migration Review*. Special Issue, July 2005. www.fmreview.org/FMRpdfs/Tsunami/full.pdf.

Evans, Gareth. "Facing up to our Responsibilities". *Guardian* 12 May, 2008. www.guardian.co.uk/commentisfree/2008/may/12/facinguptoourresponsbilities.

Fein, Helen. *Genocide: A Sociological Perspective*. London: Sage Publications, 1993.

Ferris, Elizabeth G. *The Politics of Protection: The Limits of Humanitarian Action*. Washington, DC: Brookings Institution Press, 2011.

Gierycz, Dorota. "International Law and the Responsibility to Protect: Clarifying or Expanding States' Responsibilities?" In *The Responsibility to Protect and International Law*, edited by Alex J. Bellamy, Sara Davies and Luke Glanville. Leiden, the Netherlands: Martinus Nijhoff Publisher, 2011.

Global Action to Prevent War. "To Prevent Genocide and Crimes against Humanity: Diverse Perspectives on a Standing, Rapid-Reaction UN Emergency Peace Service". Symposium Report on the United Nations Emergency Peace Service Initiative. Convened at Rutgers Law School, Rutgers University, New Jersey, 29 March, 2007. www.globalactionpw.org/wp/wp-content/uploads/rutgers_uneps_conference_report_2007.pdf.

Global Action to Prevent War, Centre for Peace and Conflict Studies, and Centre for Strategic and International Studies. "Peacekeeping and Civilian Protection: Asia-Pacific Perspectives". Convened by Global Action to Prevent War, Centre for Peace and Conflict Studies, Centre for Strategic and International Studies, 11 June 2009. www.globalactionpw.org/wp/wp-content/uploads/jakarta-full-reportv6.pdf.

Harff, Barbara and Ted Robert Gurr. "Toward Empirical Theory of Genocides and Politicides: Identification and Measurement of Cases since 1945". *International Studies Quarterly* (1988): 359–71.

International Coalition for the Responsibility to Protect. "Report on the General Assembly Plenary Debate on the Responsibility to Protect". International Coalition for the Responsibility to Protect, 15 September 2009. www.responsibilitytoprotect.org/ICRtoP%20Report-General_Assembly_Debate_on_the_Responsibility_to_Protect%20FINAL%209_22_09.pdf.

International Commission on Intervention and State Sovereignty. *The Responsibility to Protect*. Ottawa: International Development Research Centre, 2001.

Johansen, Robert C. "Expert Discussion of the United Nations Emergency Peace Service: Cuenca Report". In *A United Nations Emergency Peace Service: To Prevent Genocide and Crimes against Humanity*, edited by Robert C. Johansen, 43–74. New York: World Federalist Movement – Institute for Global Policy, 2006.

Johansen, Robert C., ed. *A United Nations Emergency Peace Service: To Prevent Genocide and Crimes against Humanity*. New York: World Federalist Movement–Institute for Global Policy, 2006.

Lambourne, Wendy and Annie Herro. "Peacebuilding Theory and the United Nations Peacebuilding Commission: Implications for Non-UN Interventions". *Global Change, Peace & Security* 20, no. 3 (2008): 275–89.

Le Roy, Alain. "Remarks of the under Secretary-General for Peacekeeping Operations, Mr Alain Le Roy, to the Special Committee on Peacekeeping Operations". United Nations, 23 February 2009. www.un.org/en/peacekeeping/articles/article230209.htm.

Musthofid. "UN Calls for Quicker Responses to Reduce Impacts of Disasters". *Jakarta Post*, 11 May, 2011. www.thejakartapost.com/news/2011/05/11/un-calls-quicker-responses-reduce-impacts-disasters.html.

O'Callaghan, Sorcha and Sara Pantuliano. "Protective Action: Incorporating Civilian Protection into Humanitarian Response". Overseas Development Institute, 2007. www.humanitarianreform.org/humanitarianreform/Portals/1/cluster%20approach%20page/clusters%20pages/Protection/hpgreport26.pdf.

Oxfam. "Crisis in a New World Order: Challenging the Humanitarian Project". 7 February Oxfam, 2012. www.oxfam.org/sites/www.oxfam.org/files/bp158-crises-in-a-new-world-order-humanitarianism-070212-summ-en.pdf.

Public Papers of the Secretaries-General of the United Nations, vol. 1, Trygve Lie 1946–53. New York: Columbia University Press, 1969.

Rees, Stuart. *Passion for Peace: Exercising Power Creatively*. Sydney: UNSW Press, 2003.

Roberts, Adam. "Proposals for UN Standing Forces: A Critical History". In *The United Nations Security Council and War: The Evolution of Thought and Practice since 1945*, edited by Vaughan Lowe, Adam Roberts, Jennifer Welsh and Dominik Zaum, 99–130. New York: Oxford University Press, 2008.

Schwebel, Stephen M. *Justice in International Law*. Cambridge: Cambridge University Press, 1994.

Staub, Ervin. *The Roots of Evil: The Origins of Genocide and Other Group Violence*. Cambridge: Cambridge University Press, 1989.

Tan, See Seng. "Towards a 'Responsibility to Provide': Cultivating an Ethic of Responsible Sovereignty in Southeast Asia". In *The Norms of Protection: Protection of Civilians and the Responsibility to Protect*, edited by Angus Francis, Vesselin Popovski and Charles Sampford, 249–67. Tokyo: United Nations University Press, 2012.

United Nations Guard Report: Report of the Secretary-General to the General Assembly, 1948. Cited in Adam Roberts, "Proposals for UN Standing Forces: A Critical History", 102.

UN Economic and Social Council. *Resolution 2004/5: Strengthening of the Coordination of Emergency Humanitarian Assistance of the United Nations*. 2005/4 of 15 July 2005.

UN General Assembly. *Emergency Response to Disasters: Report of the Secretary-General*. A/57/320 of 16 August 2002.

UN General Assembly. *Implementing the Responsibility to Protect: Report of the Secretary-General*. A/63/677 of 12 January 2009.

UN General Assembly and UN Security Council. *Sexual Violence in Conflict*. A/67/792–S/2013/149 of 14 March 2013.

UN General Assembly. *Strengthening of the Coordination of Emergency Humanitarian Assistance of the United Nations: Report of the Secretary-General*. A/68/84–E/2013/77 of 20 May 2013.

UN Mission in Liberia. "United Nations Mission in Liberia". n.d. www.un.org/en/peace-keeping/missions/unmil/mandate.shtml.
UN Security Council. *Resolution 872.* S/RES/872 of 5 October 1993.
UN Security Council. *Resolution 2008* S/RES/2008 of 16 September 2011.
Woocher, Lawrence. "The Responsibility to Prevent: Towards a Strategy". In *The Routledge Handbook of the Responsibility to Protect*, edited by Frazer Egerton and Andy Knight. Abingdon, UK: Routledge, 2012.

5   The use of force

Introduction

Twenty-six years ago, Fernando Teson encapsulated the tensions between sovereignty and human rights. Teson said that while military intervention opened the door "to unpredictable and serious undermining of world order", non-intervention was the predicator of impotence – that the international community would be powerless to "combat massacres, acts of genocide, mass murder and widespread torture".[1] His thoughts are just as applicable today as when they were written.

There is an ongoing dilemma about what outsiders ought legally and morally to do when mass human rights violations are perpetrated. Scholars, politicians and human rights activists perennially debate the appropriate course of action when a state is unable or unwilling to protect its population, or when the state itself becomes the perpetrator of violence against its own people. Should the responsibility fall on the world at large? And if so, who has the right and authority to intervene and under what circumstances? Responses to these questions are intrinsically linked to generating support for the UNEPS proposal and answers to them become all the more pronounced when the object of intervention is a permanent UN capacity.

This chapter examines respondents' attitudes towards the norms constituting the UNEPS proposal that relate to the use of force in the face of atrocities and to protect civilians from violence in armed conflict. It also considers the implications of these attitudes for increasing support for the proposal.

Broadly speaking there are two kinds of responses to a UNEPS that has the capacity to use force. The first reflects a cautious response. Respondents hold such views for three principal reasons: (1) a commitment to non-intervention and territorial integrity; (2) a belief in (the strength of) patriotic norms and difficultly accepting that an entity such as UNEPS would be truly independent of the interests of powerful states; and (3) the view that such interventions would do more harm than good.

The second type of responders comprised those who believed the UNEPS proposal has potential, but these also had their reservations. There were two reasons for this schizophrenic response: (1) a tension between, on the one hand, an interest in Pillar Two and other cosmopolitanism norms that put human beings ahead of states and, on the other, an attachment to non-intervention and sovereignty; and (2) a reluctance to support an R2P Pillar Two capacity, which is how the UNEPS proposal is often framed, and a preference for the POC peacekeeping norm.

I suggest that the creation of an independent funding structure could placate fears that UNEPS would be co-opted by powerful states. I further suggest that incorporating a higher litmus test for those wishing to intervene – with more detailed precautionary principles attached – would help those intervening to make a reasonable judgment about the long-term consequences of their actions. Emphasising that UNEPS would only be deployed with the consent of the host state and the endorsement of the UNSC could also go some way towards allaying the concerns of those who seemed torn between supporting the proposal and rejecting it.

Finally, I argue that foregrounding or grafting the POC norm onto the proposal and using it to frame UNEPS might be a fruitful way of localising the proposal. In other words, this would mean designing and promoting UNEPS as a tool to protect civilians in violent conflict – either to kick-start a mission or to support existing missions.[2]

A cautious approach towards the use of force

To understand why the UNEPS proposal as it stands is rejected or challenged, we must understand the norms that underlie the respondents' antipathy. This section explores three types of cautious responses to the proposal.

Non-intervention and territorial integrity: "many countries ... will not be comfortable giving the UN an independent force that they fear may be used against them!"

Non-intervention and territorial integrity are perhaps the most obvious obstacles confronting the proposal. They are often referred to as the doctrine of Westphalian sovereignty (based on the 1648 Peace of Westphalia, even though this took place over a hundred years *before* non-intervention was first clearly articulated).[3] Krasner makes the point that the norms associated with sovereignty have always been violated, through both coercive and non-coercive means,[4] which renders the Westphalian principles redundant. Some scholars even refer to the "myth of Westphalian absolutism".[5] Furthermore, Luke Glanville argues that the basic tenet of R2P – that sovereignty entails rights as well as responsibilities – was first articulated in the sixteenth and seventeenth centuries.[6] This implies that the so-called inviolability status of sovereignty is possibly overstated given how countries have behaved in the international sphere.

Despite such contradictions, the norms of Westphalian sovereignty are still constitutively powerful and clearly play a role in shaping respondents' interests and, by extension, their views on UNEPS.

76 *The use of force*

A former Indonesian ambassador, who is an influential member of a prominent Jakarta-based think tank, was opposed to peace enforcement operations – that is, international peacekeepers using force, for whatever reason within a sovereign's territory. He said, "a peacekeeping force is ... not a war fighting machine...". He further stated that "when we were fighting the Dutch, there were only military observers".[7] He is expressing his support for traditional peacekeeping missions that are deployed at the point between a ceasefire and a political settlement. Such missions do not propose or enforce solutions between states but rather try to build confidence between belligerents in an attempt to facilitate political dialogue.[8] The ambassador's response is both a testimony to the strength of non-intervention and a reflection of his expectations of the UN's role in managing international conflict. This is the system that Beck calls "schizophrenic" because it is mandated to function as an impartial as well as a partisan organisation.[9] This point is elaborated upon in the following chapter.

Non-intervention is also central to the political culture of South East Asia of which Indonesia is a part. The ASEAN embodies a set of regional principles put forward in the 1990s by former Prime Ministers Lee Kuan Yew of Singapore and Mahathir bin Mohamad of Malaysia. At heart they advocate non-interference in the domestic affairs of other states and promote a consensus-based style of decision-making. Since the organisation's birth, during the conflict between Indonesia and Malaysia from 1962 to 1966 and many other civil wars in South East Asia it has renounced the threat or use of force to settle international disputes. Indeed, the ASEAN Charter calls for "respect for the independence, sovereignty, equality, territorial integrity and national identity of all ASEAN member states".[10]

Having said this, UN peace operations were in fact deployed in Cambodia in the early 1990s and East Timor from 1999. These interventions had tenuous consent from the host states though they violated the norms of both Westphalian sovereignty and the ASEAN Way. Some have argued that the ASEAN Way has evolved its thinking since Lee and Mahathir held sway. The so-called post-Westphalian ideas, which put human rights at the centre of the agenda, have resulted in – among other things – the creation of the ASEAN Intergovernmental Commission on Human Rights. So while the views of the Indonesian ambassador might reflect the 'old' ASEAN and the traditional narrative of Westphalian sovereignty, others also share his views.[11]

Non-intervention as a guiding tenet is guarded for a variety of reasons. It tends to be the view taken up by states that are conscious of their own frailty and have experienced colonisation in their history. It is often espoused by tyrants who seek cover for human rights violations and also by people with humane values unwilling to create opportunities for oppression.[12] But what reasons did respondents cite? A representative of the Permanent Mission of Australia to the UN who also sits on the UN Special Committee on Peacekeeping Operations said in relation to UNEPS that many countries in the UN General Assembly (UNGA) would not be comfortable giving the UN "an independent force that they fear may be used against them!"[13] As an Indonesian scholar candidly noted: "That's why the idea isn't going to fly. Because it is against the sovereignty of the state. While everyone agrees that we don't want Rwanda to happen, but what happens to you [the "intervened"] can happen to us!"[14] She is recognising that despite the moral imperative to prevent atrocities, she would be reluctant to permit an intervention force like UNEPS into her country if such crimes took place there because it would violate their territorial integrity, and domestic authority and control. In the lead up to the 2005 World Summit, ministers of the so-called Non-Aligned Movement – traditionally strong advocates of non-intervention, sovereignty and mutual non-aggression – were of the same view. They requested clarification on how these norms would be reconciled with R2P.[15]

In sum, the views of those in this category suggest that the fear of being the target of a UNEPS intervention is a significant obstacle to the proposal receiving support. On the one hand, this fixation with the norms of Westphalia may be the usual antipathy to establishing any kind of supra-national arrangement. Indeed, nurturing strong states is the bedrock of R2P because it guards against imperialism among other positive qualities. On the other hand, it invites UNEPS advocates to consider what safeguards might be built into the idea to placate such fears. These ideas are explored further below.

Patriotic norms: "how can the troops be independent if the money comes from states?"

Some respondents were cautious about a permanent, supra-national UN service that would have the capacity to use force because they insisted, as realists do, that states are at the centre of the international system and that the pursuit of morality in the international sphere will never be possible because states are driven by power. All politics, wrote the classical realist Hans Morgenthau, is a struggle for power.[16] Some respondents hold such views because they believed that states *do* behave like this, while others thought that states *should* behave like this. Because of these beliefs, respondents could not accept that a mechanism like UNEPS would ever be created for purely for cosmopolitan reasons – that it would have its own *esprit de corps* and be independent of states' narrowly defined interests. As a senior representative of the Australian Department of Foreign Affairs and Trade put it: "with a UN mission [like UNEPS].... Who do you serve? Not national interests ... Australians fight for national interest".[17] Like Kenneth Waltz, for this respondent national interests were viewed in fairly limited terms such as increasing military power, economic growth and security.[18] They did not include the protection of civilians "in a faraway country of which we know little".[19]

His perspective was likely to have been influenced by the statecraft of former conservative Australian Prime Minister John Howard under whom this senior bureaucrat was serving at the time of the interview. Howard's conception of foreign policy was anchored in state-to-state relations, witnessed by his preference for bilateralism and scepticism about multilateral institutions.[20] He was criticised for giving insufficient weight to principle and morality – a core attribute of realism – and he was unconvinced about the norms of "global citizenship".[21] By contrast, cosmopolitans (an identity that reflects most UNEPS' advocates) maintain that we are all facing collective problems such as poverty, genocide, nuclear proliferation and so a universal belief in a globally shared future, free of national, religious or ideological divisions, is both politically and socially necessary.[22]

Echoing classical realist arguments, other respondents claimed that the legitimacy of interventions will always be questionable because the powerful set the agenda. Morgenthau writes that, whenever possible, people and states attempt to convince those who must submit to their will that they are acting in their interests or those of the wider community.[23] He insists that "universal moral principles cannot be applied to the actions of states".[24] Respondents' concerns specifically related to the funding of the proposed UNEPS and the potential for it to be manipulated by Western states.

A representative at the Permanent Mission of Croatia to the UN, who had experience working with Security Council members during Croatia's tenure on the Council, said "money is a big question – whoever gives the money wants to have control – how can the troops be independent if the money comes from states?"[25] Despite being a supporter of R2P capacities such as UNEPS, he went on to comment that "if UNEPS is influenced by the 'white' states how will it not be perceived as imperial?" He is arguing that all interventions have an imperialist agenda even though the aim of UNEPS is to maintain a degree of autonomy from member states. As Noam Chomsky has argued, throughout history the most violent and destructive interventions, including Japan's attack on Manchuria, Mussolini's invasion of Abyssinia (Ethiopia) and Hitler's occupation of parts of Czechoslovakia (Czech Republic), have been justified in the name of a humanitarian imperative.[26] More recently we see the language of civilian protection used by Russian President Vladimir Putin to justify the intervention in the Crimea. Putin announced that Russia had "the right to use all available means" to protect the Russian-speaking population in the eastern and southern regions of Ukraine.[27]

Patriotic norms are also apparent in the response of an influential Indonesian journalist who worked closely with a former Indonesia President.[28] She claimed that interveners "always end up taking sides" and implied that UNEPS could only be trusted if it were neutral which, she also argued, is impossible. She goes on to say that:

> It all comes down to interest … in the end, we are all nationalistic.… Someone is going to pay the bulk of the fees for UNEPS and the country that does will end up calling the shots and that will cause problems.

The Indonesian ambassador (cited above) supported this view saying: "In the end, we are all nationalistic. Maybe when there is an attack from Mars then we will become more united".[29]

Similar concerns were raised in 1948 when a small committee was set up to debate UN Secretary-General Lie's proposal for a permanent UN Guard. The representative from South Africa questioned whether it would be possible for the UN Guard to be impartial and neutral.[30] The same issues were raised a decade later when Georg Schwarzenberger, the Rapporteur of the Committee on the Charter of the UN, argued for a study to investigate a proposal to establish a permanent Peace Force of between two and ten thousand personnel to assist the organisation in maintaining international peace and security. Concerns about military capability and interference by the powerful in states' affairs proved, again, to be a stumbling block. The representatives from the USSR, Ceylon (Sri Lanka) and Poland argued that they were cautious about the idea because, among other reasons, they feared the force might be used to interfere with state sovereignty or used by a group or bloc of states to advance their own interests rather than the interests of the UN.[31]

More harm than good

One respondent – a former Secretary-General of ASEAN – opposed the idea of a UNEPS that would have the capacity to use force based on the view that military interventions cause more harm than good.[32] He gives the example of 2008 when many in the international community accused the leader of Myanmar, General Than Shwe, and his military junta of committing crimes against humanity when they resisted relief efforts for the millions affected by Cyclone Nargis. Coercive measures would have made "the situation worse", he says. While he is mounting a practical argument on the negative consequences of intervention, his views are likely informed by the widespread suspicions in the ASEAN community which were mentioned earlier. Nevertheless, there are valid practical concerns about the disadvantages of a UNEPS-type capacity. In 1963 Brian Urquhart, who is now a strong advocate of a permanent UN force, argued that a "permanent international police force ... might, by its very existence or through precipitate and inappropriate use, complicate the very situation it was designed to solve".[33]

Alan Kuperman has mounted a similar argument with regard to NATO's 2011 humanitarian military intervention in Libya. He writes that the intervention extended the war's duration about six fold; increased its death toll approximately seven to ten times; and exacerbated human rights abuses, humanitarian suffering, Islamic radicalism and weapons proliferation in Libya and its neighbours.[34] He has also argued with regard to Libya and Kosovo that an R2P military intervention, even if mounted for the 'right' reasons, can exacerbate a conflict because of what he labels "the moral hazard of humanitarian intervention". He believes that some groups, for example the Kosovo Liberation Army, were encouraged by the possibility of humanitarian intervention "to launch armed challenges against the state, provoking genocidal retaliations".[35] Notwithstanding Bellamy's argument that claims made by Kuperman and others about moral hazard and R2P have no empirical basis, such perceptions are worth taking seriously as they are an obstacle to UNEPS' creation.[36]

80   *The use of force*

Similar concerns were identified – but not resolved – by participants at the Cuenca conference on UNEPS in 2005, with Johansen noting that it is "important to have developed and publicised ways to discourage people from instigating violence deliberately in the hope of triggering UNEPS intervention".[37] This issue is further discussed later in this chapter.

Interested but with reservations

Respondents in this category comprised those who were interested in the proposed UNEPS' military capability but had certain reservations relating to its mandate and modes of authorisation. Respondents are shown localising the proposal – explicitly and implicitly – through the techniques of pruning, grafting and framing.

Cosmopolitanism vs. non-intervention and sovereignty

Those in this category can be seen weighing up the validity of Pillar Two and other cosmopolitanism norms against the strength of Westphalian norms like non-intervention and sovereignty. I explore how these norms might be reconciled through a recalibration of the UNEPS proposal.

On the one hand, a respondent who was a scholar from an Indonesian political science think tank and had once served the government of Indonesia in the area of foreign affairs was cautious about the supranational dimension of UNEPS and worried that it would circumvent the collective will of states by intervening in countries without the UNSC's agreement to do so.[38] She said:

> What stops countries from intervening in a country like Myanmar is the fear of fallout in countries concerned. China or India don't want the economic fallouts of intervention, Myanmar might leak too heavily. A standing UNEPS would not have this fear because they are not [reliant on contributions from] member states – there is less hesitancy to upset countries …
>
> So you are going to see a more proactive UN and one that will be more intrusive into the affairs of Member States. If there is a need for rapid deployment, New York can say we will send troops to Aceh and it doesn't matter what Indonesia has to say about it.

She is concerned that a proposed UNEPS might compromise the material benefits states gain from bilateral relationships with countries that could be the target of a UNEPS intervention (even if such governments are illegitimate). Some have argued that a principal reason that Russia failed to support a UNSC resolution authorising the use of force against the Assad regime in Syria is because it is the main supplier of arms to Syria, accounting for approximately ten per cent of Russia's arms sales. In the wake of the significant financial losses in cancelled arms sales after the UN imposed an arms embargo on Libya, a further loss could be damaging to the Russian economy.[39] The respondent is also concerned that if a UNEPS were established there would be more coercive interventions, which would erode the norms of Westphalia including a state's territorial integrity. Therefore, unlike those in the cautious group above, her reluctance to support a truly cosmopolitan peacekeeping service is not because of a concern about certain states controlling UNEPS but rather because of a concern that states connected to the intervened *will not have enough* control.

On the other hand, this same respondent was also prepared to accept that, in some instances, there is a moral imperative to use force to protect civilians from mass violence. She said:

> You are not neutral in term of the crimes. You don't accept atrocities.... You have to bring certain values [to an intervention] ... there are often clear victims and perpetrators of a crime ... in Kosovo you had Serbs killing Muslims.[40]

She seems to be expressing her support for the 1999 NATO-led airstrikes over Kosovo, ostensibly conducted to stop Serbian ethnic cleansing in Kosovo.[41] While most states opposed this intervention (as mentioned in Chapter 3), Malaysia – a predominately Muslim state and Indonesia's neighbour – supported it, stating that it "was necessary to prevent genocide in Kosovo".[42] Indeed, many in the Arab and Islamic world were in 'two minds' about the intervention. Some supported it out of an emotional solidarity with other Muslims, but from a political viewpoint it was seen to set a dangerous precedent.[43] In sum, this respondent is showing some interest in applying R2P norms in certain circumstances but falls short of expressing support for a permanent UN standing capacity.

POC vs R2P

While R2P received unanimous support at the World Summit in 2005, the doctrine has faced serious obstacles within the international community. This has been labelled the post-2005 'revolt' against R2P in which a number of states expressed scepticism about the norm and how it is used in different contexts.[44] The revolt, Bellamy argues, was largely due to the continuing association between R2P and humanitarian intervention – an issue which is reflected in respondents' attitudes towards the UNEPS proposal.

Thinking about UNEPS as a tool to support POC Missions in their efforts to protect civilians appeared to increase respondents' interest in the initiative. As mentioned in Chapter 3, a POC Mission refers to peacekeepers who are tasked with protecting civilians as one of the many potential roles within a Chapter VII operation. The threats to civilians are viewed as symptoms of the conflict rather than a strategy of the warring parties (as in R2P situations). Robust military action to protect civilians is likely but is generally reactive (rather than preventative). Consent of the state is essential and the mission is committed to being perceived as neutral by conflicting parties.[45] R2P Pillar Two missions, by contrast, have the primary goal of preventing mass atrocities through a systematic strategy and the robust use of force. The perception of the mission's neutrality is helpful but not essential.

Despite the similarities between POC Missions and R2P Missions, a representative of the Permanent Mission of Uruguay to the UN illustrates the different reaction each concept invokes:

> There is still much friction being caused by the confusion between POC and R2P. These concepts overlap but one is more toxic than the other. This is why it's important to focus on pragmatic components like timing of deployment and training – this stops member states from focusing on words and to take action![46]

While some in recent years have associated POC with regime change,[47] there was an overwhelmingly negative response directed at R2P. Confirming the latter's 'toxicity', an Indonesia ambassador said: "R2P means a developing country getting intervened by a developed country. No credibility because of Mr Bush. What we see is the US is using force to introduce democracy".[48] He is referring to the persistent accusation that the 2003 US-led invasion of Iraq was an example of the (mis)application of R2P.[49] In 2008, Hilary Charlesworth also predicted that R2P (read Pillar Three) would be likely to be used by powerful states against the less powerful ones, running the risk of self-serving conflict assessments masquerading as humanitarian.[50] The NATO-led intervention in Libya has further strengthened claims that R2P is a tool for Western states to overthrow the regimes of weaker ones, even though Pillars Two and Three were not mentioned in the Security Council Resolution.[51]

Other respondents cited the difficulties peacekeepers acting under a Chapter VII mandate face in protecting civilians from conflict. They complained about the absence of uniform training among peacekeepers, their lack of understanding about how to protect civilians on the ground as well as the meagre resources available to them.[52] Some respondents directly and indirectly mounted a case for using POC to frame UNEPS based on the argument that POC (implying POC Missions) commands greater legitimacy within and outside the UN. According to a representative of the Permanent Mission of Australia to the United Nations, POC is winning more acceptance in the UNGA partly because it is seen as less threatening than R2P.[53]

Applying this 'softly-softly' approach to R2P, Tang Siew Mun, director of foreign policy and security studies at the Institute of Strategic and International Studies in Malaysia, said that selling R2P directly may not work in his country. However, he said advocates could build on Malaysia's support for, and contribution to, UNSC-endorsed peace operations as a strategy to acclimatise his government to the idea.[54] The POC Mission norm has also proven to be a helpful framework when hosting regional events on UNEPS. A central component of UNEPS' advocacy campaign is the development of a series of workshops and/or roundtables in regional centres like Indonesia, Brazil and Cameroon to further interest in, and support for, the proposal. Those involved in organising these events discovered that using the POC norm as a 'drawcard' attracted more participation and provided a useful and familiar framework in which discussions on UNEPS could be pursued.[55]

Increasing support for the UNEPS proposal

What opportunities for localisation can be gleaned from this analysis of the use of force and the UNEPS proposal? First, there is a strong belief that any kind of permanent UN force could be misappropriated by the most powerful states and a suspicion that such a cosmopolitan *esprit de corps* would be an impossible goal. These two beliefs may come to be insurmountable hurdles in building a viable UNEPS proposal. Such concerns are real – we have seen the effects of domestic politics interfering with the funding of a UN body when the US government cut off tens of millions of dollars in annual support to the UN Educational, Scientific and Cultural Organisation after it voted to admit Palestine as a full member.[56] Yet these fears also point to a possible solution: the creation of an alternative funding structure that does not (solely) rely on contributions from member states. The tasks of making a standing UN force financially independent is an old debate.[57] The essence of the argument is that a fund would be established from sources such as a tax on tobacco so that a UNEPS would not be held hostage to the interests of individual donor states. I will return to this subject in Chapter 7 because it relates to the respondents' misgivings about the cost of the proposed service.

Second, the issue of a coercive UNEPS intervention causing more harm than good is important to address both in the context of increasing support for the proposal and in light of practical and ethical considerations of a UNEPS deployment. The ICISS report provides some suggestions on how to respond to such concerns. The report adopts the principle, based on the just war doctrine, that military action can only be justified if it is likely to halt or avert the atrocities that triggered the intervention in the first place.[58] In other words, military intervention is unjustified if actual protection cannot be achieved, or if the consequences of an intervention are likely to be worse than if there is no action at all. UNEPS' supporters have also adopted this same precautionary principle.[59] The question, of course, is how do you know if coercive action is likely to do more harm than good?

Kuperman has provided two suggestions on preventing interventions from doing more harm than good that pertain to a proposed UNEPS and might respond to concerns about the ability of such a service to achieve its ends: to alleviate suffering and save lives. The first is that the potential interveners should be aware of misinformation – resulting from inaccurate reporting or their own biased perceptions – and disinformation from concerted propaganda campaigns.[60] Pattison also highlights the importance of having the correct information to allow interveners to make a reasonable judgment about the long-term consequences of any intervention. His focus, however, is on whether the interveners are capable of, and have a clear strategy to carry out, their mission as well as having sufficient local and global support for an intervention.[61] While this list is far from exhaustive, it identifies some principles for UNEPS' advocates to consider in response to accusations that the proposed service would make an already volatile situation worse. This discussion also highlights the value of other criteria identified in the ICISS report (and in the UNEPS literature) that guide decision-makers on whether or not to take robust action in the face of extreme violence against civilians.

Third, what can we make of the tension between, on the one hand, cosmopolitan norms such as those pertaining to R2P Pillar Two and the supra-national dimension of UNEPS with, on the other hand, commitments to Westphalian norms? Given that a major concern was the ability of a permanent service to intervene in situations where vital national interests are at stake, the UNEPS proposal could contain clearer safeguards indicating that it would only be able to deploy with UNSC authorisation and the consent of the state in question. Indeed, the veto ensures that the UN will not identify a global interest that is inconsistent with the national interests of the P5. Expressing a preference for a UNSC authorisation was a prominent Australian scholar in international relations.[62] He said, "As flawed as the Council is, it is the right body [to authorise UNEPS]. [You need a] body of international law with experience in [this sort of] decision making".[63] Similarly, an influential European scholar in genocide studies said:

> Going outside the UNSC would not be productive – it is dangerous to move outside the UNSC regarding the use of force. The danger of relaxing the rules is worse than the benefits – ultimately [it means] letting any country intervene when they feel like it, using R2P as justification.[64]

A representative of the Jakarta office of a prominent international NGO that deals with preventing and resolving violent conflict (who was formerly a British diplomat) cited the importance of securing the consent of the government into whose territory UNEPS would intervene. He said:

> The more you flag this as a force that could get sent in regardless of the wishes of the local government, the harder I'd imagine it would be in more benign circumstances to invite them in. The UN is normally careful to badge its interventions in the most un-confrontational way possible because that maximises the chances of them being invited in.[65]

A respondent from the Australian Department of Foreign Affairs and Trade who served in senior positions in the Bougainville Truce and Peace Monitoring Groups and the Regional Assistance Mission to Solomon Islands, also highlighted the importance of obtaining government consent before intervening. He remarked, "[When Australia] intervenes in the region – in East Timor, Tonga, the Solomon Islands – we've sought government approval".[66]

In fact, with the exception of the 2011 peace enforcement operation in Libya, full-scale military interventions to protect civilians have only been undertaken with host country consent or when there is no functioning government to consult such as in Somalia and Rwanda.[67] Furthermore, the modest British-led intervention force in Sierra Leone (2000) and the European Union-led Operation Artemis in the Democratic Republic of the Congo (2003) are just two examples that illustrate the potential value of the consent-based, short-term deployment of an international military presence to help prevent the escalation of armed conflict.[68] Consent, however, is not always static, and can also be the result of coercion. For example, former Indonesian President B.J. Habibie, and his minister for defence and security (and commander-in-chief of Indonesian armed forces or TNI), General Wiranto, agreed to the peace enforcement operation, the International Force for East Timor (INTERFET), partly because of pressure from the international community.[69] But even nominal consent of the host-state can serve as a safeguard against attacks on the interveners. Scholars have argued that the cooperation of the TNI with INTERFET was a major reason behind the very low number of casualties of Australian and other foreign forces.[70]

This discussion highlights one of the paradoxes of a localised UNEPS proposal. The logic behind UNEPS is to create a service that would not be held hostage to the interests of member states; however, in order for UNEPS to achieve support, it might need to be contingent on UNSC authorisation. A similar process occurred when the R2P doctrine was transitioning from the ICISS report to the World Summit Outcome Document (WSOD). The ICISS report's suggestion – that a military intervention to protect civilians might be deployed under a UNGA's "Uniting for Peace Resolution" if the six criteria for intervention were addressed – was omitted from the WSOD and the final wording on the authority placed R2P's coercive components firmly within the ambit of the UNSC.[71]

The creation of an independent funding structure for the proposed UNEPS to increase the autonomy of such a service is not necessarily incommensurable with adding safeguards, such as UNSC authorisation. The former may address concerns about the domination of one state, while the latter might provide comfort to those who fear that a UNEPS intervention could comprise the strategic and economic interests of states that have alliances with the intervened. This might exclude situations where the state is the perpetrator of the atrocities; however, as the deployment of INTERFET in East Timor suggests, a peace enforcement operation can still be deployed with the consent of the host even when an arm of the state – the Indonesian military in this case – is committing the atrocities.

Finally, the discussion on the comfort surrounding the POC norm highlights the value of grafting this norm onto the proposal. This means emphasising the neutrality of a UNEPS and conditioning its deployments upon the consent of the host state. It also means highlighting the 'problem-solving' properties of the proposed UNEPS, specifically its capacity to respond to the challenges faced by POC Missions, which is discussed further in Chapter 8. Finally, the interest in the POC norm suggest that framing UNEPS as a POC service or a service that would protect civilians against violence in conflict as opposed to a tool to operationalise R2P might be a helpful strategy to increase support for the proposal.

Conclusion

This chapter has examined attitudes towards the norms constituting the UNEPS proposal that relate to the use of force. It revealed respondents and other actors citing multiple norms that, on the one hand, were potentially incompatible with UNEPS but, on the other, provided an opportunity to localise the proposal. First, we can understand respondents' cautious approach to UNEPS based on their commitment to the norm of non-intervention. This was partly because of the concern (or an awareness of the concerns of others) that their country might be the recipient of a UNEPS intervention and a belief that such a permanent force might compromise economic relations between the intervened and those with which it has bilateral ties. A cautious approach to UNEPS was also informed by respondents' scepticism that the cosmopolitan nature of the intervention was false and that, indeed, funding would rely on member states with an agenda. Finally, a cautious response to the UNEPS proposal was taken based on the belief that such interventions would do more harm than good.

Despite these objections, some respondents expressed an interest in the cosmopolitan precepts, including R2P, acknowledging the moral imperative to use force to respond to mass atrocities where there are clear victims and perpetrators. Respondents also found comfort in the POC peacekeeping norm, in particular the practical obstacles facing peace operations when called upon to protect civilians from violence in conflict.

Caution surrounding the use of force when a government fails to protect its population must be taken into consideration and it is integral to the R2P doctrine. It is therefore essential that any capacity like a UNEPS does not compromise these virtues and ensures that states retain meaningful independence. How can we preserve the almost sacrosanct sovereign equality of states but still edge towards the creation of a supra-national capacity like UNEPS?

I argued that creating an alternative funding structure could partly reduce the reliance on member states' contributions and, by proxy, their influence. This might go some way towards placating fears that UNEPS would be used for purposes other than those intended. I further argued that the development of certain principles would demonstrate that a UNEPS intervention would not cause more harm than good. I suggest other opportunities for localisation including that the proposed UNEPS might be recalibrated so that it would only deploy with UNSC authorisation. This research finally illustrates the value of grafting the pre-existing norm of POC Mission on to the proposal as a means of increasing the support it enjoys. Concerns about the capacity of peace operations to protect civilians piqued respondents' interest in UNEPS, which suggests that framing UNEPS as a service that would buttress POC Missions might attract more interest in the proposal. It is important for POC Missions to be perceived as neutral and to secure the initial and ongoing host state consent which suggests that these are two important features to integrate into the UNEPS proposal. The contribution a UNEPS could make to the UN's capacity to protect civilians from violence in conflict is discussed in the conclusion to this book.

This analysis raises another question: to what extent is the reform to the voting procedures and the composition of the UNSC integral to the success of the UNEPS campaign? This and other issues related to the UN are explored in the following chapter.

Notes

1. Teson, *Humanitarian Intervention*, 4.
2. At times, I explore interviewees' perceptions on military intervention and R2P in a general sense without always addressing UNEPS specifically. In these instances, respondents did not always cite UNEPS in their comments on military intervention and R2P; however, the implication is that their views on the latter would necessarily affect their support for the former.
3. Krasner, *Sovereignty*, 20.
4. Ibid., 22, 24.
5. Hehir, *The Responsibility to Protect*.
6. Glanville, "Christianity and the Responsibility to Protect".
7. Interview by author, 7 May 2008, Jakarta, Indonesia.
8. Bellamy, Williams, and Griffin, *Understanding Peacekeeping*, 8.
9. Cited in Kinloch, *A UN 'Legion'*, 225.
10. ASEAN Secretariat, *The Asean Charter*, Article 2, 2a.
11. Global Action to Prevent War, Centre for Peace and Conflict Studies, and Centre for Strategic and International Studies, "Peacekeeping and Civilian Protection".
12. Bellamy, *Responsibility to Protect*, 16, 18–19.
13. Interview with Kavitha Suthanthiraraj, 30 June 2010, New York, USA.
14. Interview with author, 8 May 2008, Jakarta, Indonesia.
15. Bellamy, *Responsibility to Protect*, 88.
16. Morgenthau, *Politics among Nations*.
17. Interview with author, 11 July 2007, Canberra, Australia.
18. Waltz, *Theory of International Relations*.
19. International Commission on Intervention and State Sovereignty, *The Responsibility to Protect*, 5.
20. Kelly, "Howard's Decade", 3.
21. Ibid., 13, 15.
22. Beck, "The Cosmopolitan Manifesto".
23. Morgenthau, *The Decline of Domestic Politics*, 59.
24. Morgenthau, *Politics among Nations*, 10.
25. Interview by Kavitha Suthanthiraraj, 25 June 2010, New York, USA.
26. Chomsky, "Statement by Professor Noam Chomsky", 1.
27. Lally and Englund, "Putin Defends Ukraine Stance".
28. Interview by author, 30 April 2008, Jakarta, Indonesia.
29. Interview by author, 7 May 2008, Jakarta, Indonesia.
30. Schwebel, *Justice in International Law*, 313.
31. Bowett, *United Nations Forces*, 326.
32. Interview by author, 16 June 2009, Singapore.
33. Urquhart, "United Nations Peace Forces", 351.
34. Kuperman, "A Model Humanitarian Intervention?"
35. Kuperman, "Humanitarian Hazard", 66.
36. Bellamy, *Global Politics and the Responsibility to Protect*, 71–80.
37. Johansen, "Cuenca Report", 54.
38. Interview by author, 8 May 2008, Jakarta, Indonesia.
39. Gifkins, "The UN Security Council Divided", 391.
40. Ibid.

41 Wheeler, *Saving Strangers*, 259.
42 "World: Europe Mixed Asian Reaction to NATO Strikes". *BBC News*, 25 March, 1999. http://news.bbc.co.uk/2/hi/europe/303671.stm.
43 Curtiss, "Kosovo Tragedy Contains Hard Lessons".
44 Bellamy, *Responsibility to Protect*, 111.
45 Breakey, "The Responsibility to Protect and the Protection of Civilians in Armed Conflict".
46 Interview by Kavitha Suthanthiraraj, 2010, New York, USA.
47 Prizeman, "Cross-Cutting Discussion in Unsc".
48 Interview by author, 7 May 2008, Jakarta, Indonesia.
49 Evans, *The Responsibility to Protect*, 69.
50 Caritas Australia, Global Action to Prevent War, Centre for Peace and Conflict Studies, "Right to Protection".
51 UN Security Council, *Resolution 1973*; Boreham, "Libya and R2P".
52 Interview by Kavitha Suthanthiraraj, 30 June 2010, New York; Interview by Kavitha Suthanthiraraj, 2 December 2010, New York, USA.
53 Interview by Kavitha Suthanthiraraj, 30 June 2010, New York, USA.
54 Tang Siew Mun, "Challenges and Opportunities".
55 See the following reports: Global Action to Prevent War and University of Brasilia Institute of International Relations, "Peacekeeping and Civilian Protection"; Global Action to Prevent War, Centre for Peace and Conflict Studies, and Centre for Strategic and International Studies, "Peacekeeping and Civilian Protection"; Global Action to Prevent War, Martin Luther King Jr. Memorial Foundation, and International Coalition for the Responsibility to Protect, "Civilian Protection, UN Peacekeeping and Human Security".
56 Carlstrom, "US Condemns Unesco over Palestine Vote".
57 Kinloch, *A UN 'Legion'*, 210.
58 International Commission on Intervention and State Sovereignty, *The Responsibility to Protect*, 37; Elbe, "The Evolution of the Concept of the Just War".
59 Johansen, "Proposal for a United Nations Emergency Peace Service", 29.
60 Kuperman, "A Model Humanitarian Intervention?".
61 Pattison, "The Ethics of Humanitarian Intervention in Libya".
62 Interview by author, 2 August 2007, Sydney, Australia.
63 Ibid.
64 Interview by Kavitha Suthanthiraraj, 30 September 2008, unknown location.
65 Interview by author, 9 May 2008, Jakarta, Indonesia.
66 Phone interview by author, 15 November 2007.
67 Bellamy, "We Can't Dodge the Hard Part Stabilising Libya".
68 UN General Assembly, *Implementing the Responsibility to Protect*, para. 42.
69 Wheeler and Dunne, "East Timor and the New Humanitarian Interventionism", 818–20.
70 Ibid., 825.
71 International Commission on Intervention and State Sovereignty, *The Responsibility to Protect*, xiii; UN General Assembly, *2005 World Summit Outcome*.

References

ASEAN Secretariat. *The Asean Charter*. Jakarta: ASEAN Secretariat, 2008.
Beck, Ulrich. "The Cosmopolitan Manifesto". In *The Cosmopolitanism Reader*, edited by Garrett W Brown and David Held, 217–28. Cambridge: Polity, 2010.
Bellamy, Alex. *Responsibility to Protect: The Global Effort to End Mass Atrocities*. Cambridge: Polity, 2009.

Bellamy, Alex. *Global Politics and the Responsibility to Protect: From Words to Deeds.* London: Routledge, 2011.

Bellamy, Alex. "We Can't Dodge the Hard Part Stabilising Libya". *The Australian*, 21 March 2011. www.theaustralian.com.au/news/opinion/we-cant-dodge-the-hard-part-stabilising-libya/story-e6frg6zo-1226025034896.

Bellamy, Alex J., Paul Williams and Stuart Griffin. *Understanding Peacekeeping.* Second ed. Cambridge: Polity, 2010.

Boreham, Kevin. "Libya and R2P: The Limits of Responsibility". *East Asian Forum* 31 March, 2011. www.eastasiaforum.org/2011/03/31/libya-and-r2p-the-limits-of-responsibility/.

Bowett, D.W. *United Nations Forces: A Legal Study.* New York: Praeger, 1964.

Breakey, Hugh. "The Responsibility to Protect and the Protection of Civilians in Armed Conflict: Overlap and Contrast". In *Norms of Protection: Responsibility to Protect, Protection of Civilians and Their Interaction*, edited by Angus Francis, Vesselin Popovski and Charles Sampford, 62–81. Tokyo: United Nations University Press, 2012.

Caritas Australia, Global Action to Prevent War, Centre for Peace and Conflict Studies. "Right to Protection: Whose Responsibility and How? Summary Report". Caritas Australia, Global Action to Prevent War, Centre for Peace and Conflict Studies, 4 September 2008. http://sydney.edu.au/arts/peace_conflict/research/AH_Conference%20report%202.pdf.

Carlstrom, Gregg. "US Condemns Unesco over Palestine Vote". *Al Jazeera*, 1 November, 2011. www.aljazeera.com/news/middleeast/2011/10/2011103172551498181.html.

Chomsky, Noam. "Statement by Professor Noam Chomsky to the United Nations General Assembly Thematic Dialogue on the Responsibility to Protect". United Nations, 2009. www.un.org/ga/president/63/interactive/protect/noam.pdf.

Curtiss, Richard H. "Kosovo Tragedy Contains Hard Lessons". *The Daily Star*, 30 May, 1999. www.dailystar.com.lb/Opinion/Commentary/1999/Apr-30/108392-kosovo-tragedy-contains-hard-lessons.ashx#axzz2zQ1YG0Ek.

Elbe, Joachim von. "The Evolution of the Concept of the Just War in International Law". *American Journal of International Law* 33, no. 4 (1939): 665–88.

Evans, Gareth. *The Responsibility to Protect: Ending Mass Atrocity Crimes Once and for All.* Washington DC: Brookings Institution Press, 2008.

Gifkins, Jess. "The UN Security Council Divided: Syria in Crisis". *Global Responsibility to Protect* 4, no. 3 (2012): 377–93.

Glanville, Luke. "Christianity and the Responsibility to Protect". *Studies in Christian Ethics* 25, no. 3 (2012): 312–26.

Global Action to Prevent War, Centre for Peace and Conflict Studies, and Centre for Strategic and International Studies. "Peacekeeping and Civilian Protection: Asia-Pacific Perspectives". Convened by Global Action to Prevent War, Centre for Peace and Conflict Studies, Centre for Strategic and International Studies, 11 June 2009. www.globalactionpw.org/wp/wp-content/uploads/jakarta-full-reportv6.pdf.

Global Action to Prevent War, and University of Brasilia Institute of International Relations. "Peacekeeping and Civilian Protection: Perspectives from Latin America". Convened by Global Action to Prevent War and Institute of International Relations, University of Brasilia, 29 September 2009. www.globalactionpw.org/wp/wp-content/uploads/brazil-outcome-report.pdf.

Global Action to Prevent War, Martin Luther King Jr. Memorial Foundation, and International Coalition for the Responsibility to Protect. "Civilian Protection, UN Peacekeeping and Human Security: Perspectives from the Central African Region".

Convened by Global Action to Prevent War, Martin Luther King Jr. Memorial Foundation, International Coalition for the Responsibility to Protect, 18, 20 February 2010. www.globalactionpw.org/wp/wp-content/uploads/cameroon2.pdf.

Hehir, Aidan. *The Responsibility to Protect: Rhetoric, Reality and the Future of Humanitarian Intervention*. Basingstoke, UK: Palgrave Macmillan, 2012.

International Commission on Intervention and State Sovereignty. *The Responsibility to Protect*. Ottawa: International Development Research Centre, 2001.

Johansen, Robert C. "Expert Discussion of the United Nations Emergency Peace Service: Cuenca Report". In *A United Nations Emergency Peace Service: To Prevent Genocide and Crimes against Humanity*, edited by Robert C. Johansen, 43–74. New York: World Federalist Movement – Institute for Global Policy, 2006.

Johansen, Robert C. "Proposal for a United Nations Emergency Peace Service to Prevent Genocide and Crimes against Humanity". In *A United Nations Emergency Peace Service: To Prevent Genocide and Crimes against Humanity*, edited by Robert C. Johansen, 23–41. New York: World Federalist Movement – Institute for Global Policy, 2006.

Kelly, Paul. "Howard's Decade: An Australian Foreign Policy Reappraisal". Lowy Institute Paper 15. Lowy Institute for International Policy, 2006. www.lowyinstitute.org/Publication.asp?pid=522.

Kinloch, Stephen. *A UN 'Legion': Between Utopia and Reality*. Abingdon, UK: Routledge, 2012.

Krasner, Stephen. *Sovereignty: Organized Hypocrisy*. Princeton, NJ: Princeton University Press, 1999.

Kuperman, Alan J. "Humanitarian Hazard: Revisiting Doctrines of Intervention". *Harvard International Review* 26, no. 1 (2004): 64–9.

Kuperman, Alan J. "A Model Humanitarian Intervention? Reassessing Nato's Libya Campaign". *International Security* 38, no. 1 (2013): 105–36.

Lally, Kathy and Will Englund. "Putin Defends Ukraine Stance, Cites Lawlessness". *Washington Post*, 4 March, 2014. www.washingtonpost.com/world/putin-reserves-the-right-to-use-force-in-ukraine/2014/03/04/92d4ca70-a389-11e3-a5fa-55f0c77bf39c_story.html.

Morgenthau, Hans J. *Politics among Nations: The Struggle for Power and Peace*. Fourth ed. New York: Knopf, 1948.

Morgenthau, Hans J. *The Decline of Domestic Politics*. Chicago: University of Chicago Press, 1958.

Pattison, James. "The Ethics of Humanitarian Intervention in Libya". *Ethics & International Affairs* 25, no. 3 (2011): 271–7.

Prizeman, Katherine. "Cross-Cutting Discussion in Unsc on Protection of Civilians". 2013. http://gapwblog.wordpress.com/tag/rtop/.

Schwebel, Stephen M. *Justice in International Law*. Cambridge: Cambridge University Press, 1994.

Siew Mun, Tang. "Challenges and Opportunities of Translating Rtop into Action in Southeast Asia: A Malaysian Perspective". Paper read at Responsibility to Protect and the Protection of Civilians in Armed Conflicts: Academic-Practitioner International Workshop Program. 17 and 18 November 2010.

Teson, Fernando R. *Humanitarian Intervention: An Inquiry into Law and Morality*. Dobbs Ferry, NY: Transnational Publishers, 1988.

UN General Assembly. *Resolution Adopted by the General Assembly: 60/1. 2005 World Summit Outcome*. A/RES/60/1 of 24 October 2005.

UN General Assembly. *Implementing the Responsibility to Protect: Report of the Secretary-General*. A/63/677 of 12 January 2009.
UN Security Council. *Resolution 1973* S/RES/1973 of 17 March 2011.
Urquhart, Brian E. "United Nations Peace Forces and the Changing United Nations". *International Organization* 17, no. 2 (1963).
Waltz, Kenneth. *Theory of International Relations*. Reading, Mass: Addison-Webley, 1979.
Wheeler, Nicholas J. *Saving Strangers*. New York: Oxford University Press, 2000.
Wheeler, Nicholas J. and Tim Dunne. "East Timor and the New Humanitarian Interventionism". *International Affairs* 77, no. 4 (2001): 805–27.

6 The UN and regional organisations

Introduction

This chapter explores a range of attitudes towards the UN which influence perspectives on the UNEPS proposal. It is divided into four sections. The first section offers reasons behind respondents' cautious approach to the UN. These are: (1) a rejection of the norms of multilateralism; (2) the view that key bodies within the UN are controlled by irresponsible countries or blocs that represent rival interests; (3) a perceived gap between the UN's mandate and its actions; and (4) the belief that parts of the organisation are incompetent and ineffective.

The second, and shortest section, argues that a belief in the UN's ideals and moral authority is an important factor in clarifying interest in the UNEPS proposal.

The third section discusses a localised version of the proposal – a regional or sub-regional emergency peace service – which waters down UNEPS' original modus operandi but on to which regional norms are grafted to create a unique and tailor-made regional service to attract greater interest and support. We will look at how perceived disadvantages of regional organisations tempered – though did not eliminate – enthusiasm for a more localised response to conflict and mass atrocities. This section also considers the merits of a UN-regional 'hybrid' arrangement.

The fourth section explores ways in which respondents' concerns about the UN – and therefore the UNEPS proposal – might be turned into opportunities. Establishing a more formal distinction between enforcement for humanitarian purposes and enforcement for the purposes of maintaining international peace and security might be one way to do this. Highlighting how a UNEPS might – in practice – improve the performance of UN peacekeeping as a whole could be another useful strategy. Finally, there is potential to create regional or sub-regional variations on the UNEPS proposal, especially one that integrates favourable aspects of UN peacekeeping, such as training, experience and perhaps resources.

Cautious approach to the UN

At one end of the spectrum, respondents are challenging the notion that the UN would be the most legitimate organisation to house a proposed UNEPS. The term the 'UN' is an amorphous one and will mean different things to different actors.

Naturally, the UNSC, into which the UN Charter invests unprecedented political and legal authority to act on behalf of the entire international community, will feature prominently. However, other organisations are also considered to the extent that they influence respondents' views on UNEPS. Concerns about the UN – primarily the UN Security Council (UNSC), UN General Assembly (UNGA) and UN peace operations – remain stumbling blocks to their acceptance of the proposal.

Uncommitted multilateralist

Two Australian respondents took a cautious approach to the UNEPS proposal partly due to their scepticism about multilateralism. While these respondents did not criticise the UN from a personal perspective, they referred to the political culture in which they worked as evidence of the perceived lack of authority of the organisation. One respondent, a senior official in the Australian Department of Foreign Affairs and Trade (DFAT) during former Prime Minister John Howards' tenure, said at the time that Howard was "hard-headed and not a committed multilateralist", predicting that the then government would not support the idea of creating a UNEPS.[1] While the government had "respect for multilateralism", it was not seen as "the necessary conduit for every situation". As suggested in the previous chapter, John Howard often applied a "blunt nationalism" to his relations with Asia and opposed resorting to outside entities, whether they be the UN, human rights conventions or international law which might limit Australian sovereignty.[2]

Howard's approach echoes the views of realists who see the UN as irrelevant because, as Hans Morganthau puts it, the "actions of states are not determined by moral principles and legal commitments but by considerations of interest and power".[3] An extension of this belief is echoed by another respondent whom I interviewed several years later – an Australian Senator in the Liberal Party, which was led by Howard for over a decade but which was in opposition under different leadership at the time the interview was conducted. The Senator said that "most of the Liberal Party aren't international in their thinking: they think more about domestic issues which have a more direct effect on their electorate.... They are sceptical about the UN and its values".[4]

Dominated by 'the other'

Respondents' weak support for the UN, and by extension UNEPS, has a direct relationship with which country or bloc is seen to wield the most power. These respondents are not only critical of the composition of the UN's key bodies; they seem to believe that the current state of affairs will continue indefinitely. One respondent argued that the Group of 77 or the G77 (a group of developing states established in 1964, to pursue common goals and develop leverage in the UN, currently comprising 131 countries) controls the UNGA. Others suggested that the West was the institutional hegemon and criticised the unrepresentative structure of the UNSC. Theoretically, these respondents embody an interesting mixture of assumptions. The first respondent hints at liberal, Western democratic superiority. The second group of respondents takes the opposite position. They decry the composition of the UNSC, especially the dominance of the US. I address each claim in turn.

A retired Australian military officer whose opinions regularly feature in the Australian media claimed: "The UN won't achieve anything until the democracies are in a majority in the General Assembly".[5] Even though the UNSC would be likely to authorise UNEPS' deployments, he argued that the dominance of the G77 in the UNGA – which, he says, comprises irresponsible and untrustworthy states – strips the UN of its legitimacy. He appeared eager to maintain Western political, economic and cultural dominance in the face of powerful "hoodlum states" in the UNGA. He was more interested in the countries that *ought* to be in control. He seems to be applying the liberal idea first expressed by Immanuel Kant – that all non-liberal states are antagonistic, oppressive and are quick to use force – to the majority of states in the UNGA.[6] This respondent's opinions about people and governments outside liberal democratic states indicate that it is unlikely that he would support an international service like UNEPS that is based at the UN.[7]

The second group of respondents believed the UN lacked legitimacy largely because of the formal structure of the UNSC and the actions of its permanent members, especially the perceived dominance of Western powers. The US indeed leads the number of vetoes in the Council.[8] Yet, in recent years, China and Russia have been criticised for their use (or threat of use) of the veto power, in particular for blocking efforts to deploy an enforcement operation in places where atrocities were taking place, such as Darfur, or to respond to the conflict in Syria.

Also implying that the UNSC is controlled by the US and other Western states, one of Indonesia's most prominent TV journalists argued that Indonesians distrust the UN because it is seen to be dominated by "certain powerful nations".[9] A former Indonesian ambassador also criticised the UN – which had implications for his views on the proposed UNEPS – because of what he perceived to be the "machinations" of its powerful members.[10] He referred to the Security Council's endorsement of the Australian-led intervention force in East Timor in 1999, which followed the East Timorese independence referendum. This, he suggested, was a betrayal of his country and the core reason for his negativity, if not hostility, towards the UN.

On a related note, a recently retired Indonesian UN career professional currently involved in activities relating to ASEAN policy reforms said:

> I am speaking as a South East Asian: generally, we don't have a good perspective on the UNSC, it doesn't act in the interests of the world as a whole, it acts mainly for the P5 ... what is France now? Nothing! Just one country. They are part of an important region but Europe is emerging as an entity. We have to look at the realities of the 21st century.[11]

Indeed, the fact that counties in Africa and Asia do not have a permanent seat on the Council even though states from these regions make up the majority in the General Assembly demonstrates the need for more equitable regional representation.[12]

Clearly articulating the implications of such views for the proposed UNEPS, a UNEPS supporter from India who was a former UN peacekeeping commander said that the proposal "won't sell in Asia unless the UNSC is more representative and transparent and includes [the] developing world in decisions.... ".[13] An Australian Senator also argued that the UNEPS proposal cannot be separated from a UNSC reform agenda.[14] His comments reflect the Australian Labor Party's (ALP) commitment to multilateralism, which was particularly pronounced under the leadership of former Prime Minister Kevin Rudd.[15] While these respondents were critical of the UN, it was unclear whether they expected such a transformed international order could ever be achieved.

Similar concerns about the Western dominance of the UNSC plagued earlier proposals for a standing UN peacekeeping force. In 1951, during the Special Committee that was set up to debate Trygve Lie's proposal for a UN Guard, the Soviets declared that it was "one more step in the progression of Anglo-American perversion of United Nations machinery to imperialist ends".[16] Comparable issues about the lack of perceived legitimacy of the UN hampered the idea of a standing UN Volunteer Military Force championed by Brian Urquhart. Commenting on the proposal, Gareth Evans, Australian Minister for Foreign Affairs at the time, expressed concerns about the difficulties proponents of such an idea would face in persuading developing countries to bestow powers on the UNSC to deploy its own force.[17] The assumption was that the Security Council is viewed as unrepresentative and undemocratic and therefore not to be given authority over additional functions and issues.

Not following the rules: "the UNSC is not what the UN Charter says"

Respondents also challenged the legitimacy of the UN, and therefore the UNEPS proposal, because of the obstacles the organisation has faced in achieving its mandate. More specifically, criticisms related to the perceived disconnect between the *intended* means and ends and the *actual* means and ends of peace operations. Cronin and Hurd have shown that an organisation derives its legitimacy in part through the perception that it is following the correct procedures – or "rule following" – especially the terms by which it is given its authority. This does not mean that the rules have to be *fair*, only that they are followed.[18]

A recently retired UN career professional from Indonesia criticised the UN for failing to honour the aspirations in the UN Charter. He argues that "the UNSC is not what the UN Charter says: to act in the interests of maintaining international peace and security. [The members of the UNSC] act in the interests of their own country".[19] He is capturing one of the inherent contradictions in the organisation – it is comprised of representatives seeking to advance the interests of their own government but at the same time it acts on behalf of the world association of states.[20]

The ambassador's grievance is not a new obstacle to establishing a standing peacekeeping service. Dick Leurdijk, who was involved in the Dutch proposal for a UN Rapid Deployment Brigade, pointed out that because a standing peacekeeping service would be contingent upon the UNSC to authorise it, the concept "just takes us full circle, back to the question of national interests".[21] This raises some questions – and potential solutions – explored earlier, such as: how can we ensure that that a proposed UNEPS has a degree of autonomy and is not co-opted by the agenda of the P5? In Chapter 5, I suggested an alternative funding structure could potentially allay concerns that member states would use the proposed service for their own purposes; however, other ideas are also explored below.

The perceived failure of UN members to follow their own rules is most pronounced in the area of peace operations. Specifically, respondents challenged the UN's legitimacy because of their discomfort about the evolution of UN peacekeeping since the organisation's inception. As mentioned in the previous chapter, some expressed their disapproval of the shift from classical peacekeeping operations, which are generally charged with maintaining order between states, to wider, post-Westphalian peace operations which take on the more ambitious job of enforcing peace as well as political, social and economic reconstruction within states.[22] In other words, he is lamenting the fact that peacekeeping just isn't what it used to be because it has deviated from the cardinal principles of neutrality, impartiality and the non-use of force except in self-defence.[23] His views are consistent with key advocates of traditional peacekeeping such as China, India, Cuba and the Non-Aligned Movement.[24]

The recently retired UN career professional mentioned earlier argued that "impartiality is essential". "Once the UN is seen to be partial, it's finished. When de Mello was killed, I said the UN is gone. [The crisis the UN faced in] Somalia started when the UN was linked to the USA".[25] He is referring to the case where Iraqi insurgents blew up the UN's headquarters in Baghdad, Iraq, in 2003 and killed Sergio Vieira de Mello who was the Secretary-General's Special Representative in Iraq at the time. He is also referring to the infamous case in Somalia where the US Rangers, serving in a UN-endorsed peace enforcement operation, broke from impartiality and became directly engaged in the conflict. Eighteen US Rangers were killed and 84 were wounded along with over 300 Somalis.[26] This respondent's attitude was expressed in the Côte d'Ivoire when French forces were deployed to strengthen the UN peacekeeping mission in 2011. Accusations by former Ivorian President, Laurent Gbabgo, that his country was a victim of a "global conspiracy led by France and the United Nations" culminated in attacks on UN peacekeepers.[27]

A further illustration of the sources of decline in the UN's legitimacy can be found in Robert A. Rubinstein's ethnographically rich analysis. He maintains that the UN's loss of "symbolic capital" has contributed to its loss of legitimacy and the effectiveness of its peacekeeping operations.[28] He argues that contributing to the organisation's demise is the growing gap between peacekeeping missions and the local culture, specifically cases where the behaviour of individual peacekeepers has been an anathema to the values on which the organisation was built. Reflecting Rubinstein's argument, a former Indonesian ambassador (mentioned earlier) expresses disdain for the UN saying, in reference to UN peacekeepers, "the UN will sometimes rape like Africa".[29] Indeed, the problem of sexual abuse by UN peacekeepers is now widely recognised by the organisation.[30]

The UN as an ineffective institution

Another source of an organisation's legitimacy, according to Cronin and Hurd, comes from its "performance" or positive results and the accomplishment of its goals. They go on to point out that possessing the ability to act is as important as creating a sense of the right to act, both of which enhance legitimacy.[31] Keohane and Nye also claim that defenders of international organisations "tend to justify them in terms of their apparent efficacy: the essential role they play in protecting international cooperation and providing global public goods".[32] The views of respondents and other actors below illustrate the areas in which the UN is seen to be ineffective and the implications this has for the UNEPS proposal.

Challenging the performance – as well as the moral credentials of the organisation – a retired Australian military officer, who is a darling of the Australian media on all matters relating to the Australian Defence Force (ADF), argued that UNEPS' personnel would not be committed to its mandate, asking the question: "What motivates people to lay down their life? Not the UN because it's so corrupt".[33] This respondent, who spent time working in UN peace operations in South Asia and elsewhere, further explained that his view on the UN derived from what he perceived as "questionable" values of citizens from the G77 – a point discussed earlier.

For example he said: "When I worked for the UN, people from Third World countries were defrauding the system". This same respondent went on to claim that UNEPS would only be effective based on the following condition: "You'd have to change UN culture. The UN's a great idea but it just doesn't work well". Similar criticisms about UN corruption, inefficiency and lack of legitimacy are leveraged by some conservative commentators and newspapers to justify their condemnation of the organisation.[34] Such sentiments were further expressed by a respondent who had spent 20 years as a development worker in Asia and Africa.[35] This respondent also criticised the UN for "employing incompetent consultants and paying them large salaries". Moreover, an Australian senator in the Liberal Party implied that the UN's failure to perform effectively was because of its "bureaucracy and the UNSC". Meanwhile, a former Indian career diplomat, who is currently a political analyst based in Singapore, sardonically questioned: "Has there been a single issue where the UN has managed to settle a problem between states?" He is suggesting that the world body lacks legitimacy since it has failed to achieve its mandate to maintain international peace and security.[36] All three respondents displayed a more than cautious response to the UNEPS proposal. Thus the perception that the UN is an ineffective and inefficient organisation is linked to respondents' reduced support for the UNEPS proposal.

Enthusiastic approach to the UN: support for the UN's ideals and moral authority

At the other end of the spectrum, respondents argued that the UN is a legitimate institution and should be used to house and manage a mechanism like UNEPS. Preferring to focus on its achievements, most in this camp acknowledged – but did not dwell on – the obstacles the UN faces. Their responses echoed David Rieff's words: "People ... often turn to the language of religion, saying, when other justifications fail, that they still 'believe' in the world body".[37] Similarly, scholars such as Ramesh Thakur who, while recognising that states are not equal (despite what the UN Charter says), still advocate UN reforms based on the belief that the UN is our "one and best hope for unity in diversity in a world in which global problems require multilateral solutions".[38] In fact, the belief that the structure of the UNSC is unjust and unrepresentative of contemporary global power dynamics is expressed by the UN's most avid supporters, UN scholars and practitioners alike, yet many are still committed to its reform.[39]

Respondents in this category primarily supported the UN's ideals and insisted that it brings moral authority and legitimacy to peace operations. Sandholtz writes that legitimacy is possible when an organisation's functions and goals are consistent with broader values of society, such as human rights or development assistance. This has been termed "purposive legitimacy".[40] It is a helpful concept to explain some respondents' positive attitudes towards the UN, and therefore the UNEPS proposal.

A respondent from the UN Association in Australia, who was formerly a member of the Australian parliament, believed firmly in the humanistic ideals of the UN Charter. During his political life and as a director of one of the departments in the UN Secretariat, he was committed to realising social and economic ideals, which suggests his faith in the capacity of individuals to effect positive change across nations and globally.[41] Another respondent, an Australian academic in security studies who had spent over a decade working for DFAT and was formerly in the ADF, said that the UN would be an excellent vehicle through which to create a UNEPS. He claimed that "the great advantage of the UN is its moral authority. It's always legitimate".[42]

Echoing this view, in an empirical study of five peace enforcement operations on three continents, Coleman showed that states launch peace enforcement missions within the framework of international organisations primarily because they wish to ensure international legitimacy of these operations.[43] The events leading up to the 2003 war in Iraq also demonstrated the authority of the UNSC. The Bush administration (unsuccessfully) sought the UNSC's approval even though they wanted to avoid the restrictions of multilateralism. Many other governments did not believe they could support the war without it.[44]

Former Japanese Senator Tadashi Inuzuka – a strong UNEPS supporter – concedes that the UN has its faults, but supports UN values of maintaining international peace and security, arguing that it is "still the only representative body of 192 nations that can tackle global security issues collectively".[45] An

Acehnese academic and human rights activist also believed in the UN's purposive legitimacy, saying "the Acehnese, they see UN, they just love it". "They have a strong belief [in it]. Not like they see the Thais, the Singaporeans. The UN uniform psychologically sends a safe nature [*sic*] to the people here. Their highest priority is life".[46] It is likely that this respondent would have supported the UN because of its relationship with GAM (*Gerakan Aceh Merdeka* or the Free Aceh Movement) – an independence movement which fought the Indonesian military in Aceh for 30 years in a separatist war. GAM sought to internationalise the conflict and saw the UN as one avenue through which this could be achieved.[47]

Similarly, a former GAM leader, who became the director of a government agency relating to peacebuilding in Aceh after the war ended, was enthusiastic about the UN because of its moral authority and association with human rights. He said:

> We requested many times for a UN peacekeeping force from the international community but they only recognise the member states and not the insurgent groups. If it [a UN peace operation] had happened many things could have been prevented like atrocities committed by the [Indonesia] military. It's not necessarily an armed peacekeeping force [that we were asking for] but the presence of an international body that would have prevented human rights violations because somebody is watching.[48]

He went on to criticise the international monitors set up to oversee the ceasefire agreement in 2002, which was intended to pave the way for negotiations on a political solution. While these monitors were from Thailand and the Philippines, they did not represent their countries but rather served as individuals responsible to the Henry Dunant Centre, the European organisation that mediated negotiations between the conflicting parties in Aceh between 2000 and 2003.[49] The former GAM leader said the monitoring team was

> very weak ... so when they got attacked they withdrew. They got scared and withdrew their staff from all other centres to [the capital of Aceh] Banda Aceh.... Had there been an independent international mission watching, I don't think they would have attacked and denied the attacks.[50]

This suggests that some members of GAM and their supporters see the UN as a body which tries to prevent the use of armed force, uphold human rights and benefits humanity.

Another example of a respondent who was realistic about the UN's failings – but who was still committed to its ideals and expressed faith in its future – was a representative of the Croatian Mission to the UN. He also personally supported the creation of a UNEPS. His experience working with Security Council members during Croatia's tenure on the Council made him aware of the slow and troubled decision-making process for deploying a peace operation. He said:

The UN is never the institution that can solve problems – it plays the stop-gap role. The UN is a place of ideals, but the problem is the member states, they prevent long-term solutions from being devised ... the Security Council is a political beast...

He insisted that change is possible but with small and measured steps. In reference to the failure of the UN to achieve its ideals, the Croatian diplomat said: "We need to change this but we also need to be aware of this".[51] As mentioned in Chapter 2, the desire to see the UN's ideals realised and its moral authority leveraged is also present in earlier proposals for a standing UN force.[52]

Regional emergency peace service

Amidst all the talk about a permanent *United Nations* Emergency Peace Service, a conversation is taking place on the merits of a permanent or standby regional capacity. Such an arrangement is conceived differently by different actors and shows how the UNEPS proposal can be localised to accommodate a range of regional norms. Acharya argues that opportunities to localise an international norm arise when actors begin to view it as having a potential to contribute to the legitimacy and efficacy of existing institutions without undermining them significantly or fundamentally altering their social identity.[53] Reflecting this process, respondents supported strengthening certain regional or sub-regional organisations to play a similar role as that of the proposed UNEPS, i.e. responding rapidly and effectively to conflict and atrocities. They suggested that a regional peacekeeping service might carry greater legitimacy than one housed at the UN. In normative terms, many of their views reflect the idea that each region of the world *should* be responsible for its own peacekeeping and rapid response to conflict even though most regional organisations lack the capacity to deploy timely and effective peace operations. The African Union Standby Force, for example, with multidisciplinary brigades (police, military and civilians) from five sub-regions, is supposed to be in a position to deploy in 30 days for peacekeeping operations and in 14 days for military interventions. Due to funding shortages, however, this aspiration has never translated into action.[54] There are other regional arrangements, including the European Union Battlegroup and NATO; however, these groups still depend on national political will and the provision of national standby personnel which frequently stymie rapid responses to crises.[55]

This section is sub-divided into three parts: the first and the second parts explore the advantages and disadvantages of regional peacekeeping respectively, including some proposals for a regional capacity. The third part considers the idea of a UN-regional hybrid arrangement.

The advantages of a regional peace service

There are several advantages that respondents associated with regional peacekeeping which led them to advocate a more localised proposal instead of supporting the UNEPS as it was presented to them. The first concerns the perceived commitment of regional peacekeepers. A retired general who commanded a UN peacekeeping force in the former Yugoslavia said that "a concept like UNEPS may possibly strike greater resonance regionally.... In fact, I am increasingly inclined to believe that even peacekeeping operations may possibly be better undertaken under regional auspices. There will be greater commitment".[56]

This relates to a second argument: it is in the interest of regional actors to take an active role in maintaining peace and security in their neighbourhood. Specifically, the regional proximity to a crisis can mean that neighbours will have to live with the instability that conflict causes and therefore have a vested interest in, and commitment to, restoring peace.[57] Such a position has been described as "enlightened self-interest". At least three Australian respondents, two at the Departments of Defence and Foreign Affairs and Trade[58] and one senior official at the Department of Defence,[59] suggested that Australia might take the lead in establishing a regional peacekeeping service that would respond to security threats, including mass human rights violations, in the Asia-Pacific region for this very reason. Australia has already taken an active role in the Pacific region, notably with the Regional Assistance Mission to Solomon Islands, which was allegedly deployed to maintain regional peace and security and address humanitarian concerns.

The third perceived advantage of establishing a regional arrangement is the idea that peacekeepers from the region might have a natural affinity with people and governments in the country of conflict so long as they share a common culture and perhaps ethnic background. This viewpoint reflects a broader call for 'African', 'Arab' and 'Asian' solutions to regional problems. An Indonesian policy analyst who had worked as a director in the ASEAN Secretariat said in reference to the Australian-led international force in East Timor that:

> a white force will always bring up the idea about 'here are the colonisers'.... So actually the Australians would have done better [in East Timor] if they could have taken the forces from the Pacific Island countries ... even with their [Australia's] backing and strategies.[60]

Also touting the merits of regional interventions, based on the view that neighbours are received better by the host state, was a DFAT official who was closely involved with the missions in the Solomon Islands and East Timor. He said that if the UN had been involved in the Solomon Islands "it would have gone over the people's heads". "It's so distant. New York. It's an abstract concept. Whereas their neighbours, they are very tangible".[61] A respondent, who worked for Indonesia's leading political science think tank, also suggested that countries in crisis prefer regional interventions.[62] She referred to the example where former Indonesian President B.J. Habibie attempted to generate support for a South East Asian intervention force in East Timor: neighbouring states were eager to assist but lacked the capacity to do so. This resulted in the deployment of Australian-led multinational forces in East Timor and a subsequent nationalistic backlash in Indonesia. This respondent's regional preferences reflect efforts by the Indonesian government to strengthen regional responses to conflict.[63] There are indeed several examples of ASEAN countries inviting other states in South East Asia to assist in managing internal unrest, which demonstrates growing interest in, and comfort around, regional responses to conflict and mass atrocity crimes.[64]

Another Australian respondent, who formerly held leadership roles in a number of peacekeeping operations and was a prominent international speaker and analyst on global peace operations at the time of the interview, liked the idea of developing an Australian-led standby regional peacekeeping arrangement. Attempting to circumvent accusations of Australia's paternalistic approach to states in the region, he said:

> Let's get Thailand or a country like that to be the champion and for us to provide secondary roles. We must be modest about it even though we know we might be providing 70 per cent of the resources, we must accept 30 per cent of the kudos. That's sometimes hard to get politicians and others to do. We must recognise that we have a great capacity in their country – skilled men and women with great capacity.[65]

The approach promoted by this respondent was to avoid the image problem Australia developed in the Pacific during the era of the former Australian Prime Minister John Howard.[66]

While the suggestion of a sub-regional standby arrangement is far less ambitious than a standing one, this respondent's ideas indicate a growing interest in regional responses to conflict and mass atrocity crimes. They further indicate an interest in optimising the capacity of 'sub-regions' or dealing with regional security issues with selected states or coalitions rather than through all-inclusive regional capacity. This view was echoed by the representative from the Ugandan Permanent Mission to UN.[67]

William Pace, the Executive Director of the WFM, who was involved in the earlier meetings on UNEPS and subsequently became an enthusiastic supporter of the proposal, now advocates a regional incarnation of the service. Pace said:

> My own view has evolved in the last decade: the way we'll get to this service is through regional and sub-regional organisations.... They wouldn't be as they are now – troops are currently supplied nationally. But I see it being supra-national, along the lines of a foreign legion. I don't think you can get it at an AU level, for example, where there are 50 countries, so sub-regional would be more likely.[68]

The idea of sub-regional arrangements responds to concerns cited by an Australian Senator in the Liberal Party who said that, while he was personally interested in some kind of regional iteration of the proposed UNEPS, it would be a challenge to "find an institutional home" for such a service if it were to be based in the Asia-Pacific region.[69] Along these same lines, an architect of the ICISS report and an expert on the UN suggested any initiative to establish a permanent regional service "should be a low key and informal contact to establish the merits of UNEPS", thus reinforcing ideas of "looser" capacity, perhaps along the lines of those discussed above.[70]

Shortcomings of regional peacekeeping

Respondents also had misgivings about regional peacekeeping. The first concern was expressed by a representative from the Bangladeshi Permanent Mission to the UN and related to the lack of unity within certain regions. He said: "Regional initiatives are good but it's important to note that some regions don't work together and that the UN is useful for such situations".[71] While he did not elaborate, it is implied that the geographical proximity to a country does not guarantee regional consensus on how to respond. Furthermore, regional affiliations can lack experience in conducting peace operations. One need look no further than the fledgling AU mission in Darfur to witness the training, skills and capacity shortages of regional operations.[72] With the exception of NATO and the EU, such deficiencies have long been a stumbling block to regional peacekeeping initiatives, especially in the context of sustaining large military operations.[73] Indeed, the capacity and size of the EU Battlegroups need to be increased (maybe to include greater lift capacity and logistics) so that the EU can successfully intervene to tackle large-scale humanitarian crises outside its region.[74] Second, arguing that the questionable human rights records of some states in the Asia Pacific region might hinder the creation of a regional peace service, an Acehnese academic and human rights activist maintained that countries "have their own problems ... the Singaporeans don't know what human rights are sometimes, they are only thinking about money and their economics. We cannot expect too much".[75]

Respondents raised a third concern about a regional hegemon dominating a regional peacekeeping arrangement. A representative of the Permanent Mission of Croatia to the UN argued that "in every region there will always be a 'powerhouse' and this will create problems".[76] This could be, for example, Nigeria in the Economic Community of West African States and Australia in the Pacific Island Forum. Another respondent who worked for a New York-based NGO committed to UN reform said "regional is not always the answer, invested players are not always honest brokers".[77] This problem arose in 2003 with Indonesia's proposal of a South East Asian peacekeeping force.[78] According to a senior academic and political analyst at a prominent Indonesian political science think tank, a central reason why the proposal failed to gain support was because smaller states in the region feared that it would be controlled by Indonesia.[79] Indeed, when asked about a scenario in which Australia – a country with the resources and experience – might take the lead in establishing a regional peacekeeping service, those whom I spoke to in Indonesia were less than enthusiastic.[80]

The best of both worlds? A regional–UN hybrid arrangement

Respondents in this category expressed support for a regional peacekeeping initiative, while equally recognising the importance of UN-endorsed peace operations from moral, practical and legal perspectives (see Table 6.1). The implication was that some of the unfavourable qualities of regional peacekeeping could be offset by the favourable qualities of the UN system. Acharya argues that an important condition for localisation to take place is that some existing aspects of an existing normative order must already be discredited from within. We see this taking place when respondents recognise certain shortcomings of both the regional and UN peacekeeping architecture and therefore try to imagine hybrid alternatives.

Those who supported this idea suggested that the UN's strengths, such as its legitimacy, and international standards in peacekeeping, might be helpful to offset some of the shortcomings of regional interventions. The Indonesian political analyst and former government official cited above said:

> Regional peacekeeping is under Chapter VIII [of the UN Charter].... The UN is actively encouraging existing regional organisations to have their own regional peacekeeping forces ... [this could be] with training provided by UN expertise, [and] some sort of international standard. The regional dynamics could be neutralised by the presence of a UN body. If the UN is actively involved in ensuring norms and standards before it is deployed, such a force has to coordinate with the UN. It's not just Jakarta or Kuala Lumpur making decisions.[81]

Chapter VIII was designed to limit Security Council deliberations to the most severe and intractable disputes, with the Charter encouraging states to use regional organisations as a first step to resolving their conflicts peacefully.[82]

Table 6.1 The perspectives of those who support a regional–UN hybrid arrangement

Organisation	Advantages	Disadvantages
Regional peacekeeping (current or future arrangements)	• Legal authority • Greater commitment from interveners • In the interest of neighbours to respond • "Local faces" addressing "local problems"	• Regional hegemon • Lack of unity • Lack of human rights standards • Lack of capacity/funds
United Nations peacekeeping	• Moral and legal authority • Superior standards in training, skills, norms and doctrine	• There were no specific criticisms of the UN. But respondents' regional preferences suggest that they were not entirely satisfied with UN peace operations

It would therefore be legal for a permanent regional service to deploy without UNSC authorisation if it is not using force or if the consent of the host state is present.[83] Under Chapter VIII, the UNSC may also call on regional organisations, such as NATO, to execute enforcement measures.[84] This respondent's reference to the UN's norms and standards may have been a reference to the UN's Department of Peacekeeping Operations (UNDPKO) principles and guidelines on UN peacekeeping operations (referred to as the Capstone doctrine) and other policies and human rights statements relating to the protection of civilians, and women, peace and security released by the UNSC.[85]

The respondent mentioned above also advocated the creation of a South East Asian peacekeeping service whose operations would possess the legitimacy of the UN, and perhaps receive training from the Organisation, but have personnel from the region in which it is deployed. As a representative from the UNDPKO also remarked, "often regional partners look more to the UN for skills and resources".[86] Thakur and Van Langenhove further point out that the task should be to build effective partnerships between regional and global agencies because regional governance cannot substitute for the UN, while Ban Ki-Moon argued that increasing global–regional collaboration is the key to operationalising the responsibility to protect.[87]

Supporting this view, a prominent international speaker and analyst on global peace operations said that "regional organisations should be in partnership with the UN ...".[88] which is consistent with increasing calls over the last two decades to decentralise some of the UN's activities away from the UNSC and into regional organisations.[89] States have even suggested that regional organisations should take the lead in preventing and responding to mass atrocity crimes.[90] Regional bodies have crucial roles to play in ensuring that civilian protection operations are timely and legitimate. Often, they have better information regarding imminent crises and a more realistic assessment of the need for action to prevent atrocities and protect civilians.

Giving further credence to a localised UNEPS proposal that combines both regional and UN attributes was a former Secretary-General of ASEAN who reiterated support for the UN, while also expressing a preference for regional arrangements. He said:

> Southeast Asia looks at the UN as a venerable body – a platform for all countries of the world to converge and deal with challenges like war and disaster. As part of the international community you need such bodies.... The UN can be a place that formalises the quid pro quo or the settlement [sic] or to get endorsement for a solution that *we find for ourselves*.... Overall, the attitude of people in Southeast Asia [is] that the problems in the region have to be sorted out by the people in the region.... At the end of the day, whatever the solution, it has to be legitimised by the UN.[91]

He is therefore prioritising regional ownership of conflict management but also sees a role for the UN's endorsement of such a process.

Increasing support for UNEPS

What do these perspectives on the UN tell us about generating support for the UNEPS proposal? First, it suggests that an interest in multilateralism and a belief in and commitment to the UN's aspirational values are important prerequisites for an interest in the proposed UNEPS. The remarks of a Senator in the ALP further illustrate this conclusion. The Senator was committed to the UN because he believed that it facilitated interstate cooperation. He said "the UN is the future of the planet", elaborating that "in the past when I was younger and dumber I was a great critic of the UN and older and wiser folk in the ALP took time out to explain to me that multilateralism is the only way forward".[92]

Second, it is important that the proposed body that would authorise a UNEPS – be it the UNSC or the UNGA or some other entity – is seen to represent the values and interests of a broad range of stakeholders. Perceptions are very important here. What actors believe about the UNSC and other UN bodies' legitimated power might be something quite different to the actual text of the treaty that governs them.[93] Furthermore, the unrepresentative composition of the P5 (which has been widely criticised, even by supporters of the UN) is a stumbling block to establishing new UN-based capacities such as a UNEPS. This raises additional questions: is such an undemocratic institution ultimately a 'deal-breaker' for the UNEPS proposal? Do we need to join calls for UNSC reform in order to legitimise and effectively promote UNEPS?

Answers to such questions are hypothetical but are nevertheless worth unpacking, in part because they capture the paradox of advocating a UNEPS. The proposal exists to strengthen UN legitimacy yet the UN's lack of legitimacy – in part due to outdated and undemocratic structures – may in fact be a central factor that weakens support for the idea. Johansen has noted that interest in a UNEPS would grow among under-represented countries of the world if they anticipated fairer forms of representation in the Security Council.[94] Yet, some have concluded that reform is unlikely because the P5 have no incentive to relinquish the veto privilege.[95] The interviews on which a recent report was based indicated that removing or restricting veto power was almost impossible and some even felt restructuring the veto power would not serve to promote international peace and security, but only to complicate matters further.[96] Indeed, amendments to the Charter must be approved by the P5 so paradoxically reforming the UNSC requires approval from the states which enjoy the privilege of dominating it.[97] They would be asking themselves to give up their own power base. The idea of a permanent UN Legion might reveal, in the words of Kinloch, "the limits of the capacity of the organisation to reform itself".[98] Given scepticism about going outside the Security Council for the authorisation of a UNEPS (as discussed in Chapter 5), other cosmopolitan democratic institutions, such as those proposed by Pattison and Hehir,[99] would probably be equally unacceptable and will therefore not be explored here.

We can infer a third conclusion from this analysis about how to increase support for the UNEPS proposal. Even though, for decades now, UN peacekeeping operations have assumed a more robust and pro-active role in complex conflicts where there is no peace to keep, there is the perception that the UN is not mandated to perform such a role. This is naturally because, as discussed earlier, UN peacekeeping doctrine has evolved over time as have the types of conflicts to which they are responding. There is thus an obvious dilemma when some insist that peace operations ought to be impartial; yet the UNEPS proposal touts a robust enforcement capacity that would prevent and respond to atrocities.

This suggests that, for UNEPS to be widely accepted, UN peacekeeping doctrine requires legal clarification. The 2008 Capstone doctrine, other 'policy' documents[100] as well as numerous debates within the Special Committee on Peacekeeping Operations have addressed the shift in theory and practice away from the so-called holy trinity of peacekeeping.[101] Such documents and high-level discussions carry limited weight in some circles, which implies that a legal distinction might be warranted.

It further suggests that a formal division between enforcement for 'new threats' to international peace and security, such as humanitarian crises, and enforcement in response to 'traditional' threats, such as inter-state wars, could be established as a precursor to establishing a UNEPS.[102] As argued by Lauri Mälksoo, broadening the types of threats that require a collective security response means an extension of the UNSC's legal authority and duty to act.[103] The more the Council is required to do, the more important it is that the situations for which it is responsible are clear, understood and widely accepted. For example, Ingvar Carlsson, the Prime Minister of Sweden, recommended along with other members of the Commission on Global Governance that the UN Charter ought to be amended, specifying the circumstances and parameters for any intervention in domestic affairs of states.[104]

Fourth, framing the UNEPS proposal as one way of addressing some of the inefficiencies in the UN might address grievances surrounding the UN's performance. Indeed, efforts made on behalf of UNEPS' advocates to identify the problem-solving attributes of the proposal, as discussed in Chapter 3 and unpacked further in Chapter 7, are one way of doing this. For example, Johansen notes that the selection and terms of service of UNEPS personnel should be based on the "highest professional criteria, not subject to political manipulation, and able to root out dead wood or internal corruption if it occurs".[105] Thus, explicitly identifying the contribution the proposed UNEPS would make to the UN peacekeeping system – or indeed, how it could circumvent some bottleneck – might allay concerns about the organisation's performance that have stymied support for the proposal.

Finally, it is clear that grafting regional peacekeeping norms on to the UNEPS proposal might be a fruitful opportunity to localise it. While questions remain about the constitution and leadership of such a service as well as its regional parameters, interviews reveal that ideas to strengthen regional and especially sub-regional capacities to respond to conflict may garner greater support than those seeking to improve the UN's institutional capability in this area.

Furthermore, while the regional security architecture in Asia and Africa is fairly undeveloped and many of the suggestions for reform are vague, respondents imply that a regional peacekeeping service with the UN's authorisation and support might be more acceptable to the intervened and others in the region. Greater efforts should be devoted to strengthening regional and sub-regional peacekeeping capacities, and the relationship between UN and non-UN components of peace operations should be formalised. These ideas are explored further in the conclusion to this book.

Conclusion

What can we deduce from this analysis about the relationship between the UN and the proposed UNEPS? A very general conclusion is that UNEPS' advocates cannot separate the perceived legitimacy of the organisation, the norms which constitute it, and the way it functions from the credibility of the proposal.

The preceding discussion also highlights four themes that contribute to explaining respondents' views on the UN. First, an interest in multilateralism and a belief in and commitment to the UN's aspirational values are important prerequisites for generating interest in the proposal. Second, the perception that central UN bodies are controlled by states or blocs that represent respondents' cultural and political values and interests is an important factor in attracting supporters. Third, the belief that the UN is not following the rules set out in the Charter was a significant impediment to the acceptance of the UNEPS proposal. Fourth, the perceived ineffectiveness of entities such as the UNSC, the UNGA and the UNDPKO was also a liability for the proposal.

I identify several opportunities to respond to these dilemmas, including establishing a more formal distinction between enforcement for humanitarian purposes and enforcement for the maintenance of international peace. As well as this I stress the importance of highlighting the practical contribution the proposed UNEPS might make to strengthening the performance of the UN as a whole in the areas of peacekeeping, rapid-reaction and preventing atrocities.

This chapter further argues that in light of the growing enthusiasm for regional and sub-regional peacekeeping capacities, a regional version of the UNEPS proposal might attract more interest. Respondents maintained that neighbours have greater commitment to solving problems in the region, an interest in having regional stability and are often more accepted by the intervened. At the same time, negative implications of regional peacekeeping, for example concerns about a regional hegemon dominating such an initiative, are a sobering reminder that regional peacekeeping has its challenges and could benefit from UN support.

There was a tension, however, between respondents' interest in regional responses to conflict and the capacity of various regions to do this effectively or even at all. Suggestions for a regional-UN hybrid arrangement might go some way towards circumventing these obstacles, as discussed further in the conclusion. This suggestion highlights two dynamics in the localisation process whereby respondents prune aspects of the UNEPS proposal that are 'international', such as its composition, and graft attractive aspects of regional peacekeeping arrangements and institutions on to the proposal.

In the following chapter I address the principal problem-solving properties of the UNEPS proposal and consider the extent to which they influence respondents' interest in and support for the idea.

Notes

1 Interview by author, 11 July 2007, Canberra, Australia.
2 Kelly, "Howard's Decade".
3 Morgenthau, *Truth and Power*, 382.
4 Interview by author and Stuart Rees, 8 October 2009, Canberra, Australia.
5 Interview by author and Stuart Rees, 3 July 2007, Sydney, Australia.
6 Cited in Russett, "Liberalism", 102.
7 Interview by author and Stuart Rees, 3 July 2007, Sydney, Australia.
8 Chomsky, "Statement by Professor Noam Chomsky on the Responsibility to Protect", 7.
9 Interview by author, 30 April 2008, Jakarta, Indonesia.
10 Interview by author, 7 May 2008, Jakarta, Indonesia.
11 Interview by author, 9 May 2008, Jakarta, Indonesia.
12 Kinloch, *A UN 'Legion'*, 237.
13 Interview by Kavitha Suthanthiraraj, 2008, location unknown.
14 Interview by author and Stuart Rees, 8 October 2009, Canberra, Australia.
15 "Rudd Pushes for UN Security Council Seat", *ABC News*, 30 March 2008; Flitton, "Rudd Intensifies Security Council Seat Bid", *The Age*.
16 Schwebel, *Justice in International Law*, 311.
17 Hamilton *et al.*, "A UN Volunteer Military Force".
18 Cronin and Hurd, "Introduction", 7.
19 Interview by author, 9 May 2008, Jakarta, Indonesia.
20 Cronin and Hurd, "Introduction", 5.
21 Cited in Kinloch, "Utopian or Pragmatic?", 182.
22 Bellamy, Williams, and Griffin, *Understanding Peacekeeping*, 4.
23 Interview by author, 7 May 2008, Jakarta, Indonesia.
24 Bellamy, Williams, and Griffin, *Understanding Peacekeeping*, 36.
25 Interview by author, 9 May 2008, Jakarta, Indonesia.
26 Wheeler, *Saving Strangers*, 198; Lyons and Samatar, *Somalia*, 59.
27 Reuters, "Propaganda War Rages as Violence Escalates in Abidjan",; United Nations Security Council, *Cross-cutting Report: Protection of Civilians in Armed Conflict*, para. 17.
28 Rubinstein, *Peacekeeping under Fire*, 12–15.
29 Interview by author, 7 May 2008, Jakarta, Indonesia.
30 United Nations, "Problem of Sexual Abuse by Peacekeepers Now Openly Recognized".
31 Cronin and Hurd, "Introduction", 7–11.
32 Keohane and Nye, "Redefining Accountability for Global Governance", 386.
33 Interview by author and Stuart Rees, 3 July 2007, Sydney Australia.
34 "A UN Debacle,| Scandal Makes the Case for Urgent Reform", *The San Diego Union-Tribune*, 2 November, 2005; "'Have You No Shame?' Bibi's Challenge to the UN", *New York Post*, 25 September, 2009; Tony Ryan, "Take Burma or Watch a Million Die", *Newmatilda*, 1 May 2008; Brad Hamilton, "War Criminal Gets UN Job", *New York Post*, 21 November, 2010.

35 Interview by author, 31 March 2008, Sydney, Australia.
36 Interview by author, 16 June 2009, Singapore.
37 Rieff, *A Bed for the Night*, 277.
38 Thakur, *The United Nations, Peace and Security*, 358, 368.
39 Knight, "The Future of the UN Security Council", 19–35; Nambiar, "Afterword", 76.
40 Sandholtz, "Creating Authority by the Council".
41 Interview by author, 28 August 2007, Melbourne, Australia.
42 Interview by Herro and Rees, 18 July 2008, Sydney, Australia.
43 Coleman, *International Organizations and Peace Enforcement*, 278.
44 Cronin and Hurd, "Introduction", 13.
45 Inuzuka, "Terror Elimination Bill",14.
46 Interview by author, 26 November 2009, Aceh, Indonesia.
47 Aspinall, *Islam and Nation*, 41, 44, 228, 233.
48 Interview by author, 23 November 2009, Aceh, Indonesia.
49 Aspinall and Crouch, "The Aceh Peace Process", 10, 32–3.
50 Interview by author, 23 November 2009, Aceh, Indonesia.
51 Interview by Kavitha Suthanthiraraj, 25 June 2010, New York, USA.
52 For example, Lie, *In the Cause of the Peace*, 98–9.
53 Acharya, "How Ideas Spread", 248, 251.
54 Weiss, *What's Wrong with the United Nations and How to Fix It*, 136; Kinloch, *A UN 'Legion'*, 232.
55 Langille, "Preventing Genocide", 299–300.
56 Interview by Kavitha Suthanthiraraj, 18 August 2008, unknown location.
57 Weiss et al., *The United Nations and Changing World Politics*, 20.
58 Interviews by author and Stuart Rees, 11 July 2007, Canberra, Australia.
59 Interview by author, 13 December 2007, Canberra, Australia.
60 Interview by author, 7 May 2008, Jakarta, Indonesia.
61 Phone interview by author, 15 November 2007.
62 Interview by author, 8 May 2008, Jakarta, Indonesia.
63 Asia-Pacific Centre for the Responsibility to Protect, *The Responsibility to Protect in Southeast Asia*, 24.
64 Global Action to Prevent War, Centre for Peace and Conflict Studies, and Centre for Strategic and International Studies, "Peacekeeping and Civilian Protection: Asia-Pacific Perspectives", 12.
65 Interview by author, 14 November 2007, Sydney, Australia.
66 Allen, "Dissenting Voices"; Herro and Rees, *Problems in the Pacific*.
67 Interview by Kavitha Suthanthiraraj, 21 December 2010, New York, USA.
68 Phone interview by author with William Pace, 27 August 2013.
69 Interview by author and Stuart Rees, 8 October 2009, Canberra, Australia.
70 Phone interview by author and Stuart Rees, 2 December 2007.
71 Interview by Kavitha Suthanthiraraj, 18 June 2010, New York, USA.
72 Herro, Lambourne, and Penklis, "Peacekeeping and Peace Enforcement in Africa".
73 Weiss et al., *The United Nations and Changing World Politics*, 21–4; Prantl and Krasno, "Informal Groups of Member States", 317; Langille, *Bridging the Commitment–Capacity Gap*, 212.
74 Pattison, *Humanitarian Intervention and the Responsibility to Protect*, 237.
75 Interview by author, 26 November 2009, Aceh, Indonesia.
76 Interview by Kavitha Suthanthiraraj, 25 June 2010, New York, USA.
77 Suthanthiraraj and Quinn, *Standing for Change*, 36.
78 Association of Southeast Asian Nations, "Indonesia Proposes Southeast Asian Peacekeeping Force".
79 Interview by author, 8 May 2008, Jakarta, Indonesia.
80 Interview by author, 7 and 9 May 2008, Jakarta, Indonesia.
81 Interview by author, 8 May 2008, Jakarta, Indonesia.

82 United Nations, *Charter of the United Nations*, Article 52.
83 Ibid., Article 51.
84 Ibid., Article 53.
85 United Nations Department of Peacekeeping Operations and Department of Field Support, *United Nations Peacekeeping Operations Principles and Guidelines*; UN DPKO/DFS, *DPKO/DFS Lessons Learned*; UN Security Council, *Protection of Civilians in Armed Conflict*; *Resolution 1325*.
86 Interview by Kavitha Suthanthiraraj, 16 November, New York, USA.
87 Thakur and van Langenhove, "Enhancing Global Governance through Regional Integration", 235; UN General Assembly, *Implementing the Responsibility to Protect*, para. 65.
88 Interview by author, 14 November 2007, Sydney, Australia.
89 Boutros-Ghali, *An Agenda for Peace*; Thakur and van Langenhove, "Enhancing Global Governance through Regional Integration".
90 International Coalition for the Responsibility to Protect, "Report on the General Assembly Plenary Debate on the Responsibility to Protect".
91 Interview by author, 16 June 2009, Singapore.
92 Interview by author and Stuart Rees, 8 October 2009, Canberra, Australia.
93 Cronin and Hurd, "Introduction", 12.
94 Johansen, "Cuenca Report", 51.
95 Suthanthiraraj and Quinn, *Standing for Change*.
96 Ibid., 31.
97 United Nations, *Charter of the United Nations*, Article 108.
98 Kinloch, *A UN 'Legion'*, 238.
99 Pattison, "Humanitarian Intervention and a Cosmopolitan UN Force"; Hehir, *The Responsibility to Protect*, 232.
100 UN DPKO/DFS, *DPKO/DFS Lessons Learned*.
101 Curran, "Goodbye Sierra Leone".
102 Kinloch, *A UN 'Legion'*, 226; UN General Assembly, *A More Secure World*, para. 255; Haynes and Stanley, "The UN Needs a 'Fire Brigade' to Douse Regional Conflicts".
103 Malksoo, "Great Powers Then and Now", 110.
104 Carlsson, "Roles for the UN in International Security after the Cold War", 10.
105 Johansen, "Cuenca Report", 60–1.

References

Acharya, Amitav. "How Ideas Spread: Whose Norms Matter? Norm Localization and Institutional Change in Asian Regionalism". *International Organization* 58, Spring (2004): 239–75.

Allen, Matthew. "Dissenting Voices: Local Perspectives on the Regional Assistance Mission to Solomon Islands". *Pacific Economic Bulletin* 21, no. 2 (2006): 194–201.

Asia-Pacific Centre for the Responsibility to Protect. *The Responsibility to Protect in Southeast Asia*. Brisbane: The Asia-Pacific Centre for the Responsibility to Protect, 2009.

Aspinall, Edward. *Islam and Nation: Separatist Rebellion in Aceh, Indonesia*. Stanford, Calif: Stanford University Press, 2009.

Aspinall, Edward and Harold Crouch. "The Aceh Peace Process: Why It Failed". Policy Studies 1. East–West Center, 2003.

Association of Southeast Asian Nations. "Indonesia Proposes Southeast Asian Peacekeeping Force". 21 February 2004. www.aseansec.org/afp/20.htm.

Bellamy, Alex J., Paul Williams and Stuart Griffin. *Understanding Peacekeeping*. Second ed. Cambridge: Polity, 2010.

Boutros-Ghali, Boutros. *An Agenda for Peace: Preventive Diplomacy, Peacemaking and Peace-Keeping. Report of the Secretary-General Pursuant to the Statement Adopted by the Summit Meeting of the Security Council on 31 January 1992*. A/47/277 – S/24111 of 17 June 1992.

Carlsson, Ingvar. "Roles for the UN in International Security after the Cold War". *Security Dialogue* 26, no. 1 (1995): 7–18.

Chomsky, Noam. "Statement by Professor Noam Chomsky to the United Nations General Assembly Thematic Dialogue on the Responsibility to Protect". United Nations, 2009. www.un.org/ga/president/63/interactive/protect/noam.pdf.

Coleman, Katharina P. *International Organizations and Peace Enforcement: The Politics of International Legitimacy*. New York: Cambridge University Press, 2007.

Cronin, Bruce and Ian Hurd. "Introduction". In *The UN Security Council and the Politics of International Authority*, edited by Bruce Cronin and Ian Hurd, 3–22. Abingdon, UK: Routledge, 2008.

Curran, David. "Goodbye Sierra Leone, Hello CAR: On 'New' Peacekeeping Not Being So 'New'". Global Action to Prevent War Blog, 12 March 2014. http://gapwblog.wordpress.com/.

Flitton, Daniel. "Rudd Intensifies Security Council Seat Bid". *The Age*, 22 January 2011. www.theage.com.au/national/rudd-intensifies-security-council-seat-bid-20110121-1a02q.html.

Global Action to Prevent War, Centre for Peace and Conflict Studies, and Centre for Strategic and International Studies. "Peacekeeping and Civilian Protection: Asia-Pacific Perspectives". Convened by Global Action to Prevent War, Centre for Peace and Conflict Studies, Centre for Strategic and International Studies, 11 June 2009. www.globalactionpw.org/wp/wp-content/uploads/jakarta-full-reportv6.pdf.

Hamilton, Brad. "War Criminal Gets UN Job". *New York Post*, 21 November 2010.

Hamilton, Lee, Gareth Evans, Stanley Hoffmann and Brian Urquhart. "A UN Volunteer Military Force: Four Views". *New York Review of Books*, 24 June 1993.

Haynes, Lukas and Timothy W. Stanley. "The UN Needs a 'Fire Brigade' to Douse Regional Conflicts". *The Christian Science Monitor*, 5 July 1994.

Hehir, Aidan. *The Responsibility to Protect: Rhetoric, Reality and the Future of Humanitarian Intervention*. Basingstoke, UK: Palgrave Macmillan, 2012.

Herro, Annie, and Stuart Rees. *Problems in the Pacific: Who You Gonna Call*. Sydney: Centre for Policy Development, 2006.

Herro, Annie, Wendy Lambourne and David Penklis. "Peacekeeping and Peace Enforcement in Africa: The Potential Contribution of a UN Emergency Peace Service". *African Security Review* 18, no. 1 (2009): 49–62.

International Coalition for the Responsibility to Protect. "Report on the General Assembly Plenary Debate on the Responsibility to Protect". International Coalition for the Responsibility to Protect, 15 September 2009. www.responsibilitytoprotect.org/ICRtoP%20Report-General_Assembly_Debate_on_the_Responsibility_to_Protect%20FINAL%209_22_09.pdf.

Inuzuka, Tadashi. "From Article 9 to Chapter 6½: Perspectives from the Discussion on the Terror Elimination Bill". Paper submitted at the Workshop on the Eradication of Armed Conflict co-sponsored by the Australian Centre for Peace and Conflict Studies, the World Federation of United Nations Associations, and the project for a United Nations Emergency Peace Service, 8–10 February 2008, Brisbane, Australia.

Johansen, Robert C. "Expert Discussion of the United Nations Emergency Peace Service: Cuenca Report". In *A United Nations Emergency Peace Service: To Prevent Genocide and Crimes against Humanity*, edited by Robert C. Johansen, 43–74. New York: World Federalist Movement – Institute for Global Policy, 2006.

Kelly, Paul. "Howard's Decade: An Australian Foreign Policy Reappraisal". Lowy Institute Paper 15. Lowy Institute for International Policy, 2006. www.lowyinstitute.org/Publication.asp?pid=522.

Keohane, Robert O. and Joseph S. Nye. "Redefining Accountability for Global Governance". In *Governance in a Global Economy: Political Authority in Transition*, edited by Miles Kahler and David A. Lake, 386–411. Princeton, NJ: Princeton University Press, 2003.

Kinloch, Stephen P. "Utopian or Pragmatic? A UN Permanent Military Volunteer Force". *International Peacekeeping* 3, no. 4 (1996): 166–90.

Kinloch, Stephen. *A UN 'Legion': Between Utopia and Reality*. Abingdon, UK: Routledge, 2012.

Knight, Andrew. "The Future of the UN Security Council: Questions of Legitimacy and Representation in Multilateral Governance". In *Enhancing Global Governance: Towards a New Diplomacy, United Nations University*, edited by Andrew F. Cooper, John English and Ramesh Thakur, 19–37. Tokyo: United Nations University Press, 2002.

Langille, H. Peter. *Bridging the Commitment–Capacity Gap: A Review of Existing Arrangements and Options for Enhancing UN Rapid Deployment*. New York: Center for UN Reform Education, 2002.

Langille, H. Peter. "Preventing Genocide". In *The World and Darfur: International Response to Crimes against Humanity in Western Sudan*, edited by Amanda Grzyb, 281–327. Montreal: McGill Queens University Press, 2009.

Lie, Trygve. *In the Cause of the Peace: Seven Years with the United Nations*. New York: The Macmilliam Company, 1954.

Lyons, Terrence, and Ahmed I. Samatar. *Somalia: State Collapse, Multilateral Intervention, and Strategies for Political Reconstruction*. Washington DC: Brookings Institution Press, 1995.

Malksoo, Lauri. "Great Powers Then and Now: Security Council Reform and Response to Threats to Peace and Security". In *United Nations Reform and the New Collective Security*, edited by Peter G Danchin and Horst Fischer, 94–114. Cambridge: Cambridge University Press, 2010.

Morgenthau, Hans J. *Truth and Power: Essays of a Decade, 1960–70*. New York: Praeger, 1970.

Nambiar, Satish. "Afterword". In *A United Nations Emergency Peace Service: To Prevent Genocide and Crimes against Humanity*, edited by Robert C. Johansen. New York: World Federalist Movement – Institute for Global Policy, 2006.

Pattison, James. "Humanitarian Intervention and a Cosmopolitan UN Force". *Journal of International Political Theory* 4, no. 1 (2008): 126–45.

Pattison, James. *Humanitarian Intervention and the Responsibility to Protect: Who Should Intervene?* New York: Oxford University Press, 2010.

Prantl, Jochen and Jean E. Krasno. "Informal Groups of Member States". In *The United Nations: Confronting the Challenges of a Global Society*, edited by Jean E. Krasno, 311–57. Boulder, Colo: Lynne Rienner Publishers, 2004.

Reuters. "Propaganda War Rages as Violence Escalates in Abidjan". 13 March 2011. www.france24.com/en/20110313-propaganda-war-rages-violence-escalates-abidjan-civil-war-press-newspapers.

Rieff, David. *A Bed for the Night: Humanitarianism in Crisis*. New York: Simon & Schuster, 2002.

Rubinstein, R. A. *Peacekeeping under Fire: Culture and Intervention.* Boulder, Colo: Paradigm Publishers, 2008.

"Rudd Pushes for UN Security Council Seat". *ABC News*, 30 March 2008.

Russett, Bruce. "Liberalism". In *International Relations Theories: Discipline and Diversity*, edited by Tim Dunne, Milja Kurki and Steve Smith. New York: Oxford University Press, 2010.

Ryan, Tony. "Take Burma or Watch a Million Die". *Newmatilda*, 1 May 2008. http://newmatilda.com/2008/05/01/take-burma-or-watch-million-die.

Sandholtz, Wayne. "Creating Authority by the Council: The International Criminal Tribunals". In *The UN Security Council and the Politics of International Authority*, edited by Bruce Cronin and Ian Hurd, 131–53. Abingdon, UK: Routledge, 2008.

Schwebel, Stephen M. *Justice in International Law*. Cambridge: Cambridge University Press, 1994.

Suthanthiraraj, Kavitha and Mariah Quinn. *Standing for Change in Peacekeeping Operations: Project for a United Nations Emergency Peace Service (UNEPS)*. New York: Global Action to Prevent War, 2009.

Thakur, Ramesh. *The United Nations, Peace and Security: From Collective Security to the Responsibility to Protect*. Cambridge: Cambridge University Press, 2006.

Thakur, Ramesh, and Luk van Langenhove. "Enhancing Global Governance through Regional Integration". *Global Governance* 12 (2006): 233.

United Nations. *Charter of the United Nations*. New York: United Nations, 1945.

United Nations. "Problem of Sexual Abuse by Peacekeepers Now Openly Recognized, Broad Strategy in Place to Address It, Security Council Told: Head of Peacekeeping, Adviser to Secretary-General Brief". SC/8649, Department of Public Information, 23 February 2006.

United Nations Department of Peacekeeping Operations and Department of Field Support. *United Nations Peacekeeping Operations Principles and Guidelines*. New York: United Nations, 2008.

UN Department of Peacekeeping Operations/Department of Field Support. *DPKO/DFS Lessons Learned Note on the Protection of Civilians in UN Peacekeeping Operations: Dilemmas, Emerging Practices and Lessons*. New York: United Nations, 2010.

UN General Assembly. *A More Secure World: Our Shared Responsibility. Report of the Secretary-General's High-Level Panel on Threats, Challenges and Change*. A/59/565 of 2 December 2004.

UN General Assembly. *Implementing the Responsibility to Protect: Report of the Secretary-General*. A/63/677 of 12 January 2009.

UN Security Council. *Resolution 1325*. S/RES/1325 of 31 October 2000.

UN Security Council. *Protection of Civilians in Armed Conflict*. S/PV.5703 of 22 June 2007.

UN Security Council. *Cross-Cutting Report: Protection of Civilians in Armed Conflict*. No. 3. Security Council Report, 29 October 2010. www.securitycouncilreport.org/site/c.glKWLeMTIsG/b.6354943/k.C7D2/CrossCutting_Report_No_3brProtection_of_Civilans_in_Armed_Conflictbr29_October_2010.htm.

Weiss, T.G. *What's Wrong with the United Nations and How to Fix It*. Malden, Mass: Polity, 2009.

Weiss, Thomas G., David P. Forsythe, Roger A. Coate and Kelly-Kate Pease. *The United Nations and Changing World Politics*. Sixth edn. Boulder, Colo: Westview Press, 2010.

Wheeler, Nicholas J. *Saving Strangers*. New York: Oxford University Press, 2000.

7 Towards a pragmatic policy proposal

Introduction

A central feature that makes a policy proposal attractive is the extent to which it is seen as a viable solution to perceived problems. UNEPS' supporters sometimes frame UNEPS in this way by identifying shortcomings in the UN peacekeeping system and presenting UNEPS as a solution.[1]

This chapter explores attitudes towards the main problem-solving ideas on which the proposed UNEPS is based. It firstly shows there was a tension between those who favoured strengthening the peacekeeping status quo, based on states' ad-hoc troop contributions, and advocates of a permanent UN standing capacity. The belief that UNEPS would replicate what the UN is already doing in certain areas or that precious resources would be wasted to maintain such a service at high readiness can explain the position of the former. In response to these criticisms, I suggest that framing UNEPS as complementary to a range of UN programmes and activities as well as emphasising the insurmountable limitations of the current standby arrangement system might strengthen the pragmatic credentials of the proposal. I also argue that a proposed UNEPS would probably be expected to be used in multiple sites at the same time, and perform a range of essential activities when not deployed, which might respond to the concerns that UNEPS would become a "white elephant".

The second part of this chapter explores the views of the so-called cosmopolitans on the composition of UNEPS. They supported the proposal partly based on the belief that it would eliminate the time-gap between the adoption of a UN Security Council resolution and the deployment of peacekeepers. There is another tension: this time between those who supported a multidimensional and multifunctional service comprising troops, police and civilians, and those supporting the establishment of a UN security force. Such divergent views raise questions about UNEPS' composition as well as how the proposal is framed: is it a force or a service?

The final section considers the projected size and cost of a UNEPS. While some respondents argue that it would be too small, I maintain that such claims are unpersuasive for a range of reasons. Objections to its proposed size highlight the importance of clarifying UNEPS' limited mandate and deployment time as well as the need to devote more attention to assumptions made by UNEPS' advocates that national armed forces will be available to replace the service after it withdraws. Contention surrounding the proposed cost of the service – namely that it is too high – points to the need to consider alternative funding schemes that do not rely on governments, as well as the possibility of pruning UNEPS' numbers. This might be a politically astute move to generate the initial support with an eye to increasing its size down the track.

Acknowledging the need to improve UN peace operations

Acceptance of the inadequacies of the UN peacekeeping system was fairly uncontroversial among respondents. Indeed, the need to improve the international community's rapid-response capability is almost universally recognised.[2] A plenitude of books, articles and reports have been written about the shortcomings of the UN peacekeeping system, rapid reaction and the resourcing of peace operations.[3] Specifically, though, respondents highlighted two shortcomings: (1) the failure of peacekeepers to respond rapidly and effectively to crises; and (2) the lack of preventative deployments. The belief that it is the responsibility of the international community – through the United Nations – to prevent armed conflict seems to underpin their views.

Among those who cited the first shortcoming was a representative from the Australian Agency for International Development who remarked, "I don't accept that what we are doing at the moment is good enough".[4] He is pointing to the slow deployment of peacekeepers who are often poorly prepared to deal with the conflict. Respondents also expressed concern about the challenges peace operations face once on the ground. A representative from the Malaysian Ministry of Foreign Affairs who spent several years at the Malaysian Permanent Mission to the UN also recognised the limitations of the organisation saying, "Operations can be bogged down because of lack of resources".[5] As mentioned in Chapter 5, others still cited as cause for concern the difficulties peacekeepers acting under a Chapter VII mandate face in protecting civilians. They complained about the absence of uniform training among peacekeepers, and their lack of understanding about how to protect civilians on the ground as well the minimal resources available to them.

Those who lamented the lack of preventative deployments included a representative from the UN Office of the Special Adviser on Genocide Prevention who said,

> peacekeeping missions come after the crisis – we don't have preventative peacekeeping, it often happens after the deaths have occurred and often on [a] mass scale. How do prevention and intervention interact – we need to bring this into the mindset of the policy makers [and] the Department of Peacekeeping Operations ... [it is] much easier to enter early prior to the crisis than after.[6]

This respondent is almost correct in claiming that preventative peacekeeping does not exist. The only preventative deployments that have taken place – such as in Macedonia (1992), the Democratic Republic of the Congo (2003, 2006) and Libya (2011) – were made possible primarily because of troops and resources from Europe and the US. A representative from OHCHR sounded alarm bells about the absence of preventative mechanisms available to the international community saying,

> I was in Burundi recently for the elections and violence could have easily broken out – in such situations there are minimal contingency plans as there are no deterrence options – we were very lucky that it went smoothly but that was luck not planning![7]

Despite the apparent consensus on the shortcomings confronting the current peacekeeping system, there were mixed views on how to respond.

Advocates of modest reforms

Perceived practical disadvantages of creating an independent standing capacity like UNEPS were an obstacle to the support that the proposal received. Respondents' central arguments were that: (1) there are already UN agencies devoted to preventing and responding rapidly to crises; and (2) to maintain such a capacity in high readiness at considerable cost to the UN is a waste of resources. Several respondents claimed that strengthening the current standby 'rapid deployment' arrangements would be a more effective use of resources.

The arguments presented in this section are underpinned by a normative dimension which Pugh helpfully articulates.[8] He claims that the dominant view of peacekeeping "serves the purpose of an existing order within which problem-solving adjustments can occur".[9] The "concentration on 'working with what we've got' may yield important practical lessons", he writes, but it reinforces the underlying values and structures of the prevailing international order.[10] Normatively speaking, it appears that respondents below are uncomfortable with – or concerned about others' discomfort with – the transformative global order that a standing UN peacekeeping service would both reflect and put into effect. US Senator Jesse Helms, for example, in reference to an earlier proposal for a small UN rapidly deployable mission headquarters, cautioned that it would undermine the system of sovereign states.[11]

Fixing what we've got

Those who argued in favour of strengthening the existing peacekeeping system included a representative from the Australian Agency for International Development who said, "first, we need to get the UN system more coherent and flexible. The challenge is to use the existing tools to get the international community to respond better and coordinate".[12] Mounting a similar argument, a senior representative from the Australian Department of Foreign Affairs and Trade (DFAT) said that, "there are already agencies within the UN who do

118 *Towards a pragmatic policy proposal*

this kind of thing".[13] "This kind of thing" is a reference to the deployment of multidimensional peace operations. She went on to argue that:

> they don't do them as well as we'd like them to. They need to work in a coordinated way. Why not concentrate on trying to make this better rather than setting up a whole new system? This [UNEPS] could potentially be one more actor in a whole range of actors trying to work out how to work together.[14]

An Indonesian journalist likewise said that while the UNEPS idea was "very ambitious, very noble", the first step should be to ensure the existing standby mechanisms are made more effective.[15] This respondent was presumably alluding to the UNSAS which, as discussed in the introduction and in Chapter 2, is plagued with similar deployment delays and shortages of personnel and equipment to those faced by the UNDPKO and the UN Department of Field Support (UNDFS).

Calls to improve the current UN standby arrangements are not new. Based on official government positions, renewed focus on standby systems enjoys greater political support than creating a new standing capacity like UNEPS. This has been the trend since the cold war years, as mentioned in Chapter 2. UN member states, including South Korea, Rwanda and the United States, have highlighted the need to strengthen international standby and rapid reaction capacities to ensure that the UN has the ability to intervene, should peaceful measures fail to protect populations from mass atrocities.[16]

The director of GAPW, Bob Zuber, captures the challenge of convincing people of the value of the UNEPS proposal, while avoiding the trap of presenting it as a panacea to all the woes of the UN peacekeeping system. He pointedly remarked: "How to talk about UNEPS in a way that doesn't oversell but keeps it relevant?"[17] One response to the view that the UN already does what the UNEPS proposal seeks to do is to frame it as a complementary service, thereby emphasising how it would support or supplement existing national, regional and UN responses to conflict. For example, the proposed UNEPS would be a first-in, first-out capacity and could buttress failing missions in specific areas.[18] Such a frame explicitly highlights the gaps a UNEPS could fill in the UN's peace and security architecture. In this way, it avoids claims that it would be a silver bullet and accusations that it would be a white elephant.

In addition, it is important to underscore the inherent and insurmountable limitations of the UN Standby Arrangement System – that is, it will always be held hostage to governments' whim when it comes to the provision of national armed forces, equipment and other resources. Peace operations will therefore suffer chronic deployment delays because there is no guarantee that troops will be provided to meet the requirements of a mission. Indeed, not one of the participating states agreed to contribute additional troops to UNAMIR, the peacekeeping operation deployed at the time of the Rwandan genocide, to help avert the atrocities that ensued.[19] In sum, the above concerns remind us that we cannot divorce discussions on a UNEPS from the broader challenges facing the

UN's efforts to achieve peace and security. This is significant because there is a risk of talking about UN reform proposals such as UNEPS in a vacuum without due consideration of the structures and processes that already exist.

A waste of resources – "people sitting around waiting for a crisis"

Part of the aversion to standing forces are oft-cited practical obstacles, specifically that UNEPS would be an inefficient use of UN resources. An Indonesian political analyst said: "armies get bored. If they don't have crises to respond to they create trouble".[20] She is alluding to the issue of how to justify and manage the up-keep of a standing capacity when it is not deployed. This point is echoed by a senior official in DFAT, Michael Potts, who was the First Assistant Secretary of the International Organisations and Legal Division at the time this comment was made. As part of his critique of the UNEPS proposal at the Senate Standing Committee on Foreign Affairs, Defence and Trade inquiry into Australia's involvement in peacekeeping operations, Potts said, "you would have your forces perhaps sitting idle".[21] Raising similar concerns that a UNEPS would be costly and potentially redundant, a former UN career diplomat from Austria said, "the idea of a standing arrangement means that people are sitting around waiting for a crisis. Yet there is a battle for a UN post for $150,000 per year".[22] He is highlighting the existing financial strain the UN is under and arguing that the organisation's scarce resources would be wasted on a standing service that might not always be utilised.

A former principal military advisor in UNDPKO also cited the issue of cost and wasted resources, which contributed to his lack of support for the proposal. Challenging the feasibility of sustaining a UNEPS in high readiness, he asked:

> who's going to pay them while they are sitting? Nobody will want to pay to maintain a force at that readiness. You can do a certain amount of training but what happens when that finishes? People are prepared to go into a training cycle for two to three months but if they don't get deployed what are you going to do? They are like an insurance policy.[23]

The same practical concerns about the 'standing' nature of the service also plagued the first UNSG's idea of a UN Guard in the middle of last century, with South Africa arguing that it would be difficult to keep the force constantly occupied which could pose morale problems. China, India and the UK also shared some of these concerns.[24] Similar obstacles re-emerged to haunt Brian Urquhart's proposal of a standing UN Volunteer Military Force. Gareth Evans, then Foreign Minister of Australia, agreed with Urquhart's idea on moral grounds but raised concerns that "given rotational needs, up to half the core force would be non-operational a good deal of the time".[25]

Almost anticipating a retort to these criticisms, Peter Langille writes that UNEPS personnel would be co-located at a new UN base under a static operational headquarters and "among the primary tasks of this HQ would be to: organise, plan, prepare, train, coordinate and support UNEPS. It must ensure the unity of effort and purpose necessary for prompt, well-integrated, sophisticated responses".[26] Moreover, the former UN High Commissioner for Refugees, Sadako Ogata, has said about former French politician and co-founder of Médecins Sans Frontières Bernard Kouchner's idea for a permanent international force to prevent atrocities that "there are too many places in the world where it could intervene! Once deployed, who would take over if needed elsewhere?"[27] While her observation raises other issues about the duration a proposed UNEPS ought to deploy and the feasibility of contingency plans to sustain an operation that UNEPS started, it further responds to concerns that the proposed service would be "sitting around" and wasting precious UN resources.

Advocates of a standing service – the cosmopolitans

This section is devoted to exploring perspectives of the so-called cosmopolitans – those who support the UNEPS proposal, albeit with some qualifications. Many of them believe that their interest in empowering the UN and preventing R2P crimes might be achieved through extending or transforming the existing international order by creating a standing international service that is not held hostage to states' contributions.

Respondents explained that their support for the proposed UNEPS stemmed from the belief that it would eliminate the time-gap between a Security Council mandate and the deployment of peacekeepers because there would be fewer immediate demands on governments to provide personnel for the challenging and often dangerous initial stages of an operation. As a representative from the Malaysian Ministry of Foreign Affairs said about the proposal – "It makes sense ... if the Council decides to intervene, it is incumbent upon member states to translate that decision and move quickly on the ground. Why delay?" Buttressing his support was the belief that UNEPS would have a positive impact on peacekeeping, in particular rapid deployment, as well as the legitimacy of the UN because it would help the Council carry out its mandate.[28] Similar beliefs also influenced politicians from the US and Japan to draft bills for their respective parliaments calling for the creation of a permanent UNEF.[29]

The causal idea that a permanent UN service could have solved a problem or 'plugged a hole' in the current UN peacekeeping system in the area of prevention and rapid reaction is, of course, a central proposition made by UNEPS' architects as well as others who have advocated the creation of a UN standing peacekeeping capacity in the past. William Frye, for example, was motivated to propose a small permanent UN force because of the sluggish, ad-hoc method of assembling UN peacekeeping missions.[30] Likewise, Brian Urquhart suggested a standing UN Volunteer Military Force to respond in the early stages of violence because of the perennial problem of deployment delays or missions with inadequate numbers of troops.[31]

There were some tensions, however, surrounding respondents' perspectives on the composition of the proposed UNEPS and its projected cost and size. These debates are explored below.

UNEPS as a service

A key problem-solving credential of the proposed UNEPS is that a multidimensional and multifunctional service, comprising not just troops but also police and civilians, would respond to governments' inability or unwillingness to contribute such personnel.[32] It would also, claim UNEPS' advocates, overcome the challenges such diverse professionals face in working together cohesively in peace operations. Given this proposed cadre of international civil servants with a range of expertise, UNEPS' personnel would undertake a wide variety of activities, for example, "deterring belligerents and defending the mission, as well as civilians at risk"[33]; civilian policing; disaster relief and humanitarian assistance; human rights monitoring and education; de-mining, de-mobilisation and disarmament (DDR); and reconstruction, reintegration and reconciliation.[34]

Some of these activities resemble those undertaken by peacekeepers in multidimensional operations, and yet the term 'multidimensional' is used only sporadically to refer to the UNEPS proposal in advocacy and educational material.[35] As mentioned earlier, although the military remain the backbone of most multidimensional peace operations, such missions also include police and civilian personnel (for example, electoral observers and human rights monitors). While these operations generally lack the programme funding and technical expertise required to implement effective peacebuilding programmes comprehensively, they can be mandated by the Security Council to play a catalytic role in critical peacebuilding activities, such as DDR, mine action and security sector reform and other rule of law-related activities.[36]

So even though multidimensional peace operations undertake more tasks than the proposed UNEPS would, a considerable number of the existing activities of the former overlap with those of the latter. Unlike most multidimensional peace operations, UNEPS would deploy different personnel, equipment and supplies in 'modular formation' to allow for "prompt 'tailoring' or selection of elements appropriate to mission-specific requirements".[37] In other words, only a few aspects of the service might deploy at any one point in time.

Respondents in this category supported a proposed UNEPS that would deploy its personnel in stages based on the peace and conflict life-cycle. Those interested in a standing multidimensional capacity believed that this would be the most effective mechanism to prevent a crisis and stop another from recurring. A representative from the OHCHR argued that the most effective means of dealing with conflict and atrocities is for the UN to have different capacities at its disposal. He said:

> [UNEPS] could have been applied at the elections in Côte d'Ivoire. UNEPS could be composed of small specialised modules that could be deployed according to the circumstance and I think especially to prevent the mass crimes. Would the President of Côte d'Ivoire have acted as confidently if a competent international military was available nearby for rapid deployment? I think the Security Council needs a range of options

available to it to respond within a small window. This should range from rapidly deployable civilian capacity to limited and targeted military intervention. Small focused military options are critical – member states need to be educated on the cost savings and effectiveness over ineffective multidimensional operations.[38]

The OHCHR official is raising the issue of the lack of skilled military and civilian experts available at short notice to prevent atrocities. He illustrates his concern by referring to the violence that occurred in Côte d'Ivoire in the lead-up to, and after, the second round of presidential elections on 28 November 2010. In particular, defeated leader Laurent Gbagbo's forces systematically targeted actual and perceived supporters of President-elect Alassane Ouattara. Human Rights Watch documented killings, enforced disappearances and rape by pro-Gbagbo forces along political and ethnic lines, amounting to crimes against humanity.[39]

Other respondents also argued that UNEPS should comprise a range of personnel ready to conduct different tasks in 'staggered' or modulated interventions. While these respondents should not technically be classified as cosmopolitans because of their scepticism about UNEPS' political feasibility, their comments highlighted their support of the multidimensional composition of the proposed service as well as the need to understand at what stage in a conflict certain features of the service would be used.

A former senior official in UNDPKO and member of the ADF said that, while it is acceptable to use force to protect civilians, UNEPS must be part of a larger package. He argued that members of a standing peacekeeping capacity should have the skills a country in crisis needs to stave off a catastrophe: "It must apply them [these skills] as quickly as possible. It will go through phases: humanitarian response and conflict phase, the peace-building phase…".[40] Similarly, an Indonesian defence analyst said, "the military should be in the frontline at the start – we need security and safety. Our analysis is that three months should be enough. Then we move to other stages of the operation". Another Indonesian defence analyst, who had spent time in the Indonesian military and working in a senior position in the ASEAN Secretariat, also highlighted the importance of knowing when to deploy certain elements of an intervention service. He said: "When do you send in the police force? The military? The civilians?… The various possibilities will have to be built in to the [UNEPS] concept".[41] Answers to such questions would illustrate the potential function and utility of a UNEPS at a particular time and place, and would be useful for UNEPS proponents to consider more deeply.

Respondents' support for a multidimensional and multifunctional UNEPS echoes observations made by Michael Doyle and Nicholas Sambanis, two well-known international relations scholars who have written significant works on peacekeeping. They argue that, while consent-based multidimensional peacekeeping operations can end violence and pave the way for institutional and political reforms that help to secure sustainable peace, protracted conflicts, such as those in Bosnia and East Timor, require both enforcement and reconstruction programmes implemented "in the right order".[42]

Influencing those who supported a multidimensional UNEPS seemed to be the idea that peace operations ought to contribute to the construction of a liberal international order made up of democratic states. Richmond points out that this type of thinking arises from a liberal desire to "resolve" conflict – to reproduce a positive peace or aid national recovery and expedite the eventual removal of the underlying causes of internal war through multidimensional peace operations.[43] This is in contrast to the negative peace or the cessation of violence that a permanent UN force (made up solely of police and the military) would be responsible for achieving. Consequently, Richmond writes that "peace" now legitimates, and rests upon, long-standing and deep interventions in conflict zones via a "peacebuilding consensus".[44]

Mary Kaldor, Co-Director of the Centre for the Study of Global Governance and a Professor of Global Governance at the London School of Economics, critiques the NATO-led airstrikes in Libya using this lens. Kaldor argues that NATO's sole reliance on military attacks from the air was a mistake. She maintains that international peacekeepers, comprising military, police and civilians, should have been deployed to help protect civilians in the liberated areas, provide humanitarian and reconstruction assistance, support a democratic political process, and arrest those indicted by the International Criminal Court.[45] These expectations echo respondents' support for a multidimensional UNEPS that would undertake both enforcement action and certain peacebuilding measures as a means of planting seeds for sustainable peace.

UNEPS as a force

The political sensitivity surrounding a standing force has already been established in previous chapters. But what about its practical utility? David Penklis, a former senior executive in UN Peacekeeping Field Operations and Headquarters Department of Management Chief (and currently with the UNDPKO and UNDFS) is the principal respondent supporting the creation of a standing military force, without civilian personnel. Penklis' idea is reminiscent of the proposal for a UN Rapid Deployment Police and Security Force comprising at least 6,000 volunteers recruited globally and directly employed by the UN. It was championed by Congressmen James McGovern (Democrat – Michigan) and Amo Houghton (Republican – New York) in 2001.[46]

One reason why Penklis supports separating military and civilian peacekeeping capacities is to avoid the potential 'clash' of professional cultures (even though the logic behind designing an integrated service is to overcome such clashes). Penklis argues that there are:

> very different deep-seated beliefs and professional cultures in the military, police and civilian elements. In particular, there is a strong contrast between human rights and military views. Individuals, or more definitely large

groups such as battalions, bring their own culture and experiences to a peacekeeping operation that can influence the organisation.[47]

Penklis, Lambourne and I have argued elsewhere that a standing military *force* with adequate equipment and supplies – including helicopters, ground support and intelligence apparatus – could have overcome some of the practical obstacles faced by the UNAMIR (1993–4) and the AU Mission in Sudan and UN support packages in Darfur (2006–8). Filling these gaps might have helped to alleviate the short-term suffering of the civilian populations.[48]

The crux of Penklis' opposition to multidimensional peace operations in general and the multidimensional nature of the UNEPS proposal in particular is the belief that they would result in overlapping personnel and activities, and poorly executed services. Rather than introducing civilian peacekeepers who would be less familiar with the situation on the ground than those already in the field, he maintains that the existing in-country international civilian presence must be strengthened.[49] Penklis, whose PhD thesis explored the coordination deficits within, and significant overlaps between, UN field operations, laments that:

> there is little or no consideration, when a [multidimensional] peacekeeping operation mandate is interpreted by UNDPKO and UNDFS, of allocating the activity to the often already existing UN Agencies in that country.... This is due to perceived difficulties in coordinating the allocation of activities with UN Agencies at the headquarters and field levels, lack of resources in the agencies, and the self-sufficiency perception that the whole UNSC mandate should be implemented by the peacekeeping operation.... This is further compounded as multidimensional peacekeeping operations provide for a comprehensive range of activities and functions to implement the main portion of the mandate from the UNSC from within the peacekeeping operation without proper consideration of the UN Agencies, creating functional and programmatic overlaps in the area of field operations.[50]

Penklis argues that, ideally, UN peacekeeping operations should "not have a humanitarian or development component or undertake peacebuilding activities" which would make them "less complex and primarily deployed with sufficient capacity to undertake security and stability activities".[51] Institutionally, this would mean that both UNDPKO and UNDFS should be "streamlined and downsized, with their efforts focused on UN military, police and security issues".[52] While, Penklis' thesis stops short of recommending the creation of a UNEPS, when interviewed about his views on the proposal, he suggested that a standing UN force could go some way towards reducing the need to deploy complex, expensive multidimensional peacekeeping operations. He also suggested that UN agencies, such as the UN Development Programme, should be strengthened in the lead-up to and after military intervention in lieu of providing the proposed UNEPS with a civilian component.[53]

Like Penklis, Lieutenant General (retired) Satish Nambiar, a Force Commander and Head of Mission of the United Nations Protection Force and UNEPS supporter, warned against creating a UNEPS that would overlap with the activities of existing UN mechanisms. He writes: "given the fact that action has been initiated for setting up a United Nations Peacebuilding Commission and support infrastructure, it would be best that the UNEPS does not assume this responsibility".[54]

Expressing a similar message about maximising the effectiveness of existing national and international civilian capacities – but in the context of peacebuilding in the immediate aftermath of conflict – the UNSG writes:

> the need for rapid deployment should not outweigh careful consideration as to how to draw on capacities that are already on the ground, both national and international. There is almost always international capacity on the ground as conflict ends and, in some cases, humanitarian actors and assets are the only international actors present beyond a national capital. These operational capacities can be critical to support the quick delivery of basic services, particularly as people begin to return. Mechanisms to rapidly reinforce these existing capacities, including through [UN] agencies' own surge capacities and rosters, are an essential element of a postconflict response. In particular, where humanitarian actors are engaged in activities that coincide with immediate peacebuilding priorities, the fastest way to scale up those activities is to augment the capacities and resources of these humanitarian actors.[55]

A representative from UNDPKO further highlights the challenges of integrating new rapid response capacities into conflict or pre-conflict zones. She said that:

> it is important to evaluate the role of the team of experts [who are preparing to deploy], there might be a negative output to the 'immediate' response. It is important to analyse and reformulate the [UNEPS] proposal, if necessary – everyone is concerned with rapid response, which I agree is critical, but we must also do this properly and not cause more problems.[56]

While she does not specifically mention the coordination issues cited by Penklis, her remarks implicitly caution against hasty deployments of rapid reaction teams that might introduce superfluous or poorly executed services.

In sum, there is a tension between those supporting the creation of a permanent multidimensional service versus those supporting a permanent force, raising questions about the goal and composition of a proposed UNEPS. This discussion further highlights whether UNEPS' advocates should heed the advice of those endorsing a UN standing force for pragmatic reasons at the risk of isolating those for whom such a force triggers alarm bells because of its militaristic connotations. Answers to such questions will be considered in the conclusion to this book, given they also relate to the issue of an un-armed UNEPS, discussed in

The size and cost of UNEPS

The projected size and cost of a UNEPS is another problem-solving idea underpinning the proposal. I deal with each subject in turn. First in terms of size, UNEPS would comprise around 18,000 personnel of which about 10,000 would be troops that provide sufficient disincentives to dissuade, deter or repel (further) violence.[57] "A strong police presence to restore law and order" and "an array of useful civilian services to address human needs" would presumably make up the remaining 8,000. The 10,000 troops would be divided between two mobile mission headquarters which means that a UNEPS operation might only comprise 5,000 of them.[58] Some argued that a service of around 18,000 personnel is far too ambitious politically, while others, ignoring political intransigencies and focusing on practical considerations, insisted that such a force would have little chance of preventing or responding to crises effectively.

Those arguing that a service comprising 5,000–10,000 troops would simply be an inadequate response to many crises included a prominent UNEPS' advocate and Chief Executive Officer of a US-based NGO focused on conflict prevention, human rights and strengthening the United Nations.[59] He points out that the US politicians he has spoken to about the proposal believe that UNEPS, in its current format, needs to be much larger – that is, around 54,000 personnel. Richard N. Haass, an American diplomat who is known for his hawkish position on foreign relations, has also said, in reference to a proposal for a UN permanent military force of approximately the same size as UNEPS, that "it is easy to see how such a small force would be overwhelmed".[60] Likewise, Clark and Sohn argued, in relation to the size and expense of a proposed standing peacekeeping force, that in order to stay within the costs that states would be willing to fund, such a force would need to be so small that it could only be used against the smallest states. Thus, pending complete disarmament, they concluded that a permanent force that would undertake enforcement measures is impractical.[61]

Jonathan Gilmore has also challenged the projected size of a UNEPS. He writes that it is "significantly smaller than some existing UN peacekeeping missions" and:

> [g]iven the wide range of military, civilian and policing roles with which UNEPS is concerned, alongside its short, mandate deployment periods, the overall size of the proposed force appears insufficient to carry out these tasks in a consistent enough manner.[62]

Adam Roberts makes a similar point about previous proposals for a standing UN military force.[63] He argues that the practical tasks envisaged for UN standing forces are so varied (such as responding to wars, civil war and mass killings;

expediting the deployment of peacekeeping forces to support ceasefires and peace agreements, etc.) that, if these tasks remained on one standing force's agenda, it would likely be required for more operations than it could manage. This criticism could equally be applied to UNEPS. Roberts also points out that the various types of military expertise, equipment and force structure required for each activity would exceed the capability of one UN standing force.[64] While these are fair points, there are some counter-arguments.

First, the Rwanda experience demonstrates what might be accomplished at short notice with a small military force. Major-General Romeo Dallaire, who commanded the UNAMIR, argued that a force of only 5,000 troops with a Chapter VII mandate could have stopped the genocide even if deployed 24 hours after it began on 7 April 1994.[65] The Independent Inquiry into the actions of the UN during the 1994 genocide in Rwanda also concluded that even the reduced force of 2,500 (if fully deployed) should still have been able to stop or at least minimise the massacres.[66] So while a UNEPS might not be able to address all situations, it could still help in some of them. Furthermore, as Robin Collins of the World Federalist Movement-Canada points out, a much larger force – politically speaking – "will be intimidating to some smaller states, and too much of a good thing for those who perceive themselves already as the de facto world police".[67]

Second, as Peter Langille notes, UNEPS would have a modular structure where small deployable elements could be used at the earliest stages of a mission. This would allow for simultaneous deployments of military, police or civilian packages to different operations, should the need arise. This does not mean that it would necessarily 'do the job' of a multidimensional operation but rather that it could kick-start several tasks soon after the Security Council gave the green light. It could also support ad-hoc coalitions where member states have not contributed enough troops, or other personnel or resources.

Criticisms raised above on the size of a UNEPS also contain two lessons for advocates to consider. First, it is important to be clear about the situations to which UNEPS would respond. Specifically, UNEPS, like many previous iterations of a permanent UN force, is not designed for large-scale or sustained war fighting and is not a UN army. It would fill the gap between a UNSC resolution and the deployment of peacekeepers, until a larger operation is deployed (if that is deemed necessary) and conduct a range of other activities outlined and explored throughout this book.

Second, objections to the proposed size of the service further highlight the need to consider the role that national militaries would play when taking over at the point when UNEPS withdraws. Indeed, Gilmore critiques the UNEPS literature for insufficiently addressing the challenges facing national militaries. Specifically, he argues that the success of the proposed UNEPS would depend largely on the willingness and capacity of national armed forces to continue effectively the work that a UNEPS intervention started.

Related to the size of the proposed service is its cost. UNEPS would cost US$2.5 billion to create and around US$1 billion per year to sustain which, according to its promoters, would save the international community billions of dollars in post-conflict reconstruction.[68] Paying for the UN's peace operations has always been a source of political debate and, at times, controversy. While financing UN peacekeeping is based on the scale of assessments for the UN's regular budget, the P-5 pay an extra 25 per cent for peacekeeping in addition to their regular UN assessment.[69] The UNDPKO's estimated cost of UN peace operations between 2008 and 2009 was around US$7.1 billion. But because many rich states had not paid their peacekeeping dues on time, by the end of 2008, the level of outstanding contributions to peace operations was just under US$3 billion. Financial crisis is only avoided because states agree to lend money and equipment to the UN.[70]

In light of the financial challenges confronting UN peacekeeping, it is understandable that the estimated cost of UNEPS might appear to be (too) politically bold. Yet Urquhart makes three points to justify the argument that a standing UN service would save the international community significant funds in the long-term: (1) as violence spreads, larger forces are required; (2) these forces are usually needed for longer periods of time; and (3) in both international and civil wars, the fighting destroys much of the infrastructure which necessitates peacebuilding and expensive post-conflict reconstruction.[71] For example, the experience of the preventative deployment of a relatively small multinational force (UN Preventive Deployment Force) to Macedonia in 1994 showed that prevention tends to be easier, less demanding and less costly.[72] And, of course, prevention has the important benefit of saving lives.

Despite such arguments on the cost-effectiveness of prevention, a respondent, who was formerly an ALP member in the Australian House of Representatives and director in the UN Secretariat, argued that the current UNEPS proposal is politically intractable. He said that the estimated cost to set up UNEPS "is the budget of the whole of the UN for a year". He went on to comment that the "UN has had no significant increase in its budget for 15 years. You are talking about [for] one initiative doubling the budget".[73] While his second point is incorrect – in 2011 the budget for the entire UN system (excluding the international financial institutions) was around US$13 billion[74] – he is pointing out that a proposal which requires a large chunk of the total UN budget would not garner the support needed for implementation. He said, "it might make more sense to start with 100 or 500 [personnel] next year rather than 18,000. These things have to be built up slowly". An Australian Senator in the Liberal Party raised similar concerns saying "the problem is where are we going to get the money and who will contribute?"[75] The perception that the UNEPS proposal is so radical that it would not attract broad political support seemed to reduce the Senator's interest. Adam Roberts has also cast a pall upon the financial feasibility of a UN standing force, writing:

> I find it hard to imagine that states, which in any case have proven to be notoriously mean in paying their UN dues, are suddenly going to pop up with money for a force they were reluctant to provide from their own troops anyway.[76]

The issue of cost plagued earlier proposals for UN rapid reaction tools too. In response to Lie's idea of a UN Guard, South Africa expressed concern about the cost in light of what the UN could afford, while the Soviets argued that the cost might exceed the annual budget of the UN.[77] Another proposal for a standing UN force that was strangled at birth in the late 1950s by countries' unwillingness to shoulder the necessary financial costs was William Frye's idea for a small permanent UN force.[78] The force would have comprised about 7,000 troops either recruited as individual volunteers or borrowed from member states or a mixture of both (which was his preference) for six months to two years. Frye suggested that if the contributing states could cover the start-up costs of equipping the troops with light arms, uniforms, vehicles and other standard equipment, the annual budget for 7,000 men might be as low as US$25 million.[79] Though Frye's proposal was rather modest in both size and cost, with the financial difficulties the UN was experiencing even a small additional cost seemed inconceivable.[80]

More recently, a representative from the Australian Permanent Mission to the UN pointed out that the Special Committee on Peacekeeping Operations (known as the C34) looked at a number of standing capacity or enhanced rapid deployment capacity (ERDC) options for Lebanon, Darfur and the Democratic Republic of the Congo. He explained that "standing capacity options were discussed and they [the C34] asked who would contribute troops – no one (except France in Lebanon) said yes. There was no appetite for these options".[81] Indeed, the C34 concluded in their report by the working group on enhanced rapidly deployable capacities that the concept of ERDC "is currently not viable, given the lack of appropriate financial arrangements and support from Member States for this purpose".[82]

To avoid UNEPS becoming hostage to the ebbs and flows of national politics, a permanent UN service might need to be financed outside the regular UN budget, as prefaced in Chapter 4. This idea has led historically to suggestions about taxes on certain items of trade such as arms, air travel or taking a portion of national defence budgets. Others have suggested the UN could control the right to exploit resources from the oceans.[83] Similar initiatives have been proposed to overcome traditional impasses in UN budgets and to increase its limited resources. One such initiative is a proposed tax on international currency transactions – the so-called Tobin tax – which would provide the UN with independent revenues to alleviate the Organisation's reliance on member states' contributions.[84] But, as Kinloch points out, while such solutions could provide a standing force with a degree of autonomy, it could not make it independent as it would still need capabilities such as transport and "projection capability" (the ability to intimidate and implement policy by threatening or using force in a distant area).[85]

It is worth considering the wisdom of reducing the size, and therefore the cost, of the service, as one respondent suggested. If history is anything to go by, former UNSG Trygve Lie's first proposal of a small Guard Force was almost immediately truncated to 800 men (although it still did not attract the requisite political support).[86] The existing UN Standing Police Capacity provides a promising example, suggesting that ambitious initiatives might generate the necessary political support if they have modest beginnings. The Police Capacity has been operational since 2007 and the then Under-Secretary-General for Peacekeeping Operations, Alain Le Roy, noted that it "has proven to be an effective rapidly deployable tool to help start up new operations and reinforce existing ones".[87] Its numbers, however, are still below the recommendations from the 2004 High Level Panel on Threats, Challenges and Change because they still rely on member states to contribute officers.[88]

Conclusion

Examining UNEPS from a problem-solving perspective suggests that if the proposal is seen to respond to systemic shortcomings in UN peacekeeping it is more likely to receive support. Those who believed that UNEPS was an unhelpful answer to the UN's peacekeeping woes generally showed little interest in it. At the same time, even when some respondents understood that a UNEPS would, in theory, plug holes in the peacekeeping system, if they did not believe that it had political and practical saliency this reduced support for the proposal. In such cases, respondents tended to make concrete suggestions to localise the proposal to increase their or others' support. An aversion to, or comfort surrounding, cosmopolitan norms also influenced respondents' opposition to, or support for, the technical aspects of the proposal, respectively. This indicates that while the UNEPS proposal must be viewed as a 'roadmap' to address the shortcomings in the current peacekeeping system, its technical aspects alone will not necessarily generate interest in the proposal.

The analysis in this chapter sheds light on at least four dimensions that help us understand how the UNEPS proposal might be implemented. First, framing UNEPS as a service that would strengthen the UN's capacity to prevent, and respond rapidly and effectively to, crises through the provision of well-trained, equipped and coordinated peacekeepers is an effective strategy to attract interest in the proposal. The relevance of such a frame in the context of POC operations is discussed in the following chapter. Emphasising that UNEPS would be a tool that would complement – rather than replicate – the structures and processes of the existing UN peacekeeping system would further highlight the specific gaps a UNEPS could fill. Finally, giving more attention to the activities UNEPS would perform when not deployed would go some way toward countering arguments that the proposed service would waste money.

Second, it is necessary to clarify UNEPS' composition given the tension between those advocating a multidimensional service and those in favour of a UN force – a task I take on in the following chapter. The third aspect that emerged from this analysis was whether the projected size of the service is appropriate. In response to those who argued that it might be too small, I listed several reasons why this was an invalid argument: a small elite force could have made a significant difference in preventing the Rwandan genocide; UNEPS is designed to respond to certain situations that suit its capabilities, not to all crises; and UNEPS would not function as a large multidimensional peace operation but rather would kick-start preventative or responsive operations that would be eventually taken over by another mission composed of national militaries. Greater attention could also be paid to the role of national militaries in UNEPS' interventions.

I have suggested significantly reducing the size of the proposed service in an effort to increase the proposal's political salience and with a view to increasing the numbers in the future. As for those who challenged the proposed cost of a UNEPS, arguing that it was too much for an organisation already struggling to collect its dues, I argue that establishing an alternative and independent funding structure to raise, at least in part, the funds for the service might allay such concern.

I now proceed to the conclusion of the book and explore the implications of this research for how the UNEPS proposal might be designed, advocated and implemented.

Notes

1. Ogata, *The Turbulent Decade*.
2. Roberts, "Proposals for UN Standing Forces", 100.
3. Durch *et al.*, *The Brahimi Report*; Jett, *Why Peacekeeping Fails*; Ladley, "Peacekeeper Abuse, Immunity and Impunity"; Weiss, *What's Wrong with the United Nations and How to Fix It*; UN General Assembly, *Report of the Panel on United Nations Peace Operations*.
4. Interview by author, 11 July 2007, Canberra, Australia.
5. Interview by author, 2 December 2009, Kuala Lumpur, Malaysia.
6. Interview by Kavitha Suthanthiraraj, 10 June 2010, New York.
7. Interview by Kavitha Suthanthiraraj, 2 December 2010, New York.
8. Pugh, "Peacekeeping and Critical Theory".
9. Ibid., 41.
10. Ibid.
11. Scully, "Armed Troops Sought for UN".
12. Interview by author and Stuart Rees, 11 July 2007, Canberra, Australia.
13. Interview by author and Stuart Rees, 11 July 2007, Canberra, Australia.
14. Interview by author and Stuart Rees, 11 July 2007, Canberra, Australia.
15. Interview by author, 30 April 2008, Jakarta, Indonesia.
16. International Coalition for the Responsibility to Protect, "Report on the General Assembly Plenary Debate on the Responsibility to Protect".
17. Interview with Bob Zuber, 23 August 2013, New York.
18. I am grateful to Bob Zuber for highlighting the importance of "complementarity" in discussion about a UNEPS.
19. UN General Assembly, *Supplement to an Agenda for Peace*, para. 43.
20. Interview by author, 8 May 2008, Jakarta, Indonesia.
21. Senate Foreign Affairs, Defence And Trade Committee, "Australia's Involvement in Peacekeeping Operations".
22. Interview by author, 24 October 2007, Sydney, Australia.
23. Interview by author, 14 November 2007, Sydney, Australia.
24. Schwebel, *Justice in International Law*, 312.
25. Hamilton *et al.*, "A UN Volunteer Military Force".
26. Langille, "Preventing Genocide", 301–2.
27. Cited in Kinloch, *A UN 'Legion'*, 229.

28 Interview by author, 2 December 2009, Kuala Lumpur, Malaysia.
29 Global Action to Prevent War, "To Prevent Genocide and Crimes against Humanity"; Katsumi, "The Upper House Adopts a Dpj Bill Proposing to Facilitate the Establishment of a New UN Service".
30 Frye, *A United Nations Peace Force*, ix–xi, 32.
31 Urquhart, "For a UN Volunteer Military Force", 3.
32 UN General Assembly, *Report of the Panel on United Nations Peace Operations*, para. 108; Durch, "United Nations Police Evolution", 15; Chandran et al., "Rapid Deployment of Civilians for Peace Operations", para. 9a.
33 Langille, "Preventing Genocide", 303.
34 Ibid., 302; Langille, *Bridging the Commitment–Capacity Gap*.
35 World Federalist Movement, "United Nations Emergency Peace Service"; Costa Vaz, "Forging the Basis of Legitimacy for UNEPS", 84.
36 United Nations Department of Peacekeeping Operations and Department of Field Support, *Principles and Guidelines*, 21–26. See also former UNSG Boutros-Ghali's definition of multidimensional UN approach to peacekeeping – UN General Assembly, *Supplement to an Agenda for Peace*, para. 21.
37 Langille, "Preventing Genocide", 303.
38 Interview by Kavitha Suthanthiraraj, 2 December 2010, New York.
39 Human Rights Watch, "Oral Statement to the Human Rights Council on Côte d'Ivoire".
40 Interview by author, 14 November 2007, Canberra, Australia.
41 Interviews by author, 7 May 2008, Jakarta, Indonesia.
42 Doyle and Sambanis, "Peacekeeping Operations", 344.
43 Richmond, "UN Peace Operations and the Dilemmas of the Peacebuilding Consensus", 83.
44 Ibid., 84. Richmond is actually mounting a critique of the liberal peacebuilding consensus.
45 Kaldor, "Libya: War or Peacekeeping".
46 Langille notes, however, that the technical details of such a force, like its design, composition and preparation, require further investigation. Langille, *Bridging the Commitment–Capacity Gap*, 14.
47 Penklis, "Implications of the 1993 to 2008 Burundi Peace Process", 123.
48 Herro, Lambourne, and Penklis, "Peacekeeping and Peace Enforcement in Africa".
49 Interview by author with David Penklis, 12 November 2009, Sydney, Australia.
50 Penklis, "Implications of the 1993 to 2008 Burundi Peace Process", 114–15.
51 Ibid., 272.
52 Ibid.
53 Interview by author with David Penklis, 12 November 2009, Sydney, Australia.
54 Nambiar, "Afterword", 76.
55 UN Secretary-General, *Report of the Secretary-General on Peacebuilding in the Immediate Aftermath of Conflict*, para. 61.
56 Interview by Kavitha Suthanthiraraj, 16 November 2010, New York.
57 Langille, "Preventing Genocide", 303; Johansen, "Cuenca Report", 46.
58 Langille, "UNEPS Composition (Draft)".
59 Interview by Kavitha Suthanthiraraj, 2008, unknown location.
60 Cited in Kinloch, "Utopian or Pragmatic?", 175.
61 Cited in Bowett, *United Nations Forces*, 317.
62 Zuber and Curran, "Peacekeeping and Rapid Reaction", 16–17.
63 Roberts, "Proposals for UN Standing Forces", 99, 125.
64 Ibid., 125.
65 Feil, "Preventing Genocide", 8.
66 UN Security Council, *Report of the Independent Inquiry into the Actions of the United Nations During the 1994 Genocide in Rwanda*.

67 Collins, "Gp Responses: Shouldn't UNEPS Advocacy Be Front and Centre?".
68 Langille, *Preparing for a UN Emergency Peace Service*, 5.
69 Bellamy, Williams and Griffin, *Understanding Peacekeeping*, 61.
70 Ibid., 64.
71 Urquhart, "Prospects for a UN Rapid Response Capability", 31.
72 Langille, *Bridging the Commitment–Capacity Gap*, 73.
73 Interview by author, 28 August 2007, Melbourne, Australia.
74 Weiss, *What's Wrong with the United Nations and How to Fix It*, 197.
75 Interview by author and Stuart Rees, 8 October 2009, Canberra, Australia.
76 Cited in Kinloch, "Utopian or Pragmatic?", 176.
77 Schwebel, *Justice in International Law*, 312.
78 Frye, *A United Nations Peace Force*, 78.
79 Ibid.
80 Cox, *Prospects for Peacekeeping*, 75.
81 Interview by Kavitha Suthanthiraraj, 30 June 2010, New York.
82 United Nations General Assembly, *Report of the Special Committee on Peacekeeping Operations and Its Working Group*, para. 77.
83 Kinloch, *A UN 'Legion'*, 209–10.
84 Weiss, *What's Wrong with the United Nations and How to Fix It*, 196–7.
85 Kinloch, "Utopian or Pragmatic?", 177.
86 Schwebel, *Justice in International Law*, 309; Roberts, "Proposals for UN Standing Forces", 102.
87 Le Roy, "Remarks of the under Secretary-General for Peacekeeping Operations".
88 UN General Assembly, *A More Secure World*, 25; Suthanthiraraj and Quinn, *Standing for Change*.

References

Bellamy, Alex J., Paul Williams and Stuart Griffin. *Understanding Peacekeeping*. Second ed. Cambridge: Polity, 2010.
Bowett, D.W. *United Nations Forces: A Legal Study*. New York: Praeger, 1964.
Chandran, Rahul, Jake Sherman, Bruce Jones with Shepard Forman, Anne le More, Yoshino Funaki and Andrew Hart. "Rapid Deployment of Civilians for Peace Operations: Status, Gaps, and Options". NYU Center on International Cooperation, April 2009. www.cic.nyu.edu/peacebuilding/docs/Deployment_annex_links.pdf.
Collins, Robin. "Gp Responses: Shouldn't UNEPS Advocacy Be Front and Centre?" Global Policy, 13 November. 2013. www.globalpolicyjournal.com/blog/13/11/2013/gp-responses-shouldn%E2%80%99t-uneps-advocacy-be-front-and-centre.
Costa Vaz, Alcides. "Forging the Basis of Legitimacy for UNEPS: South American Perspectives". In *A United Nations Emergency Peace Service: To Prevent Genocide and Crimes against Humanity*, edited by Robert C. Johansen, 83–6. New York: World Federalist Movement – Institute for Global Policy, 2006.
Cox, Arthur M. *Prospects for Peacekeeping*. Washington DC: Brookings Institution, 1967.
Doyle, Michael W. and Nicholas Sambanis. "Peacekeeping Operations". In *The Oxford Handbook on the United Nations*, edited by Thomas G. Weiss and Sam Daws, 323–48. Oxford: Oxford University Press, 2007.
Durch, William J. "United Nations Police Evolution, Present Capacity and Future Tasks". Prepared for the GRIPS State-Building workshop: 'Organizing police forces in post-conflict peace-support operations.' National Graduate Institute for Policy Studies, 27–28 January 2010. www.3.grips.ac.jp/~pinc/data/10–03.pdf.

Durch, William J., Victoria K. Holt, Caroline R. Earle and Moira K. Shanahan. *The Brahimi Report and the Future of UN Peace Operations*. Washington DC: Henry L. Stimson Center, 2003.

Feil, Scott R. "Preventing Genocide: How the Early Use of Force Might Have Succeeded in Rwanda: A Report to the Carnegie Commission on Preventing Deadly Conflict". New York: Carnegie Commission on Preventing Deadly Conflict, 1998.

Frye, William R. *A United Nations Peace Force*. London: The Carnegie Endowment for International Peace, 1957.

Global Action to Prevent War. "To Prevent Genocide and Crimes against Humanity: Diverse Perspectives on a Standing, Rapid-Reaction UN Emergency Peace Service". Symposium Report on the United Nations Emergency Peace Service Initiative. Convened at Rutgers Law School, Rutgers University, New Jersey, 29 March 2007. www.globalactionpw.org/wp/wp-content/uploads/rutgers_uneps_conference_report_2007.pdf.

Hamilton, Lee, Gareth Evans, Stanley Hoffmann and Brian Urquhart. "A UN Volunteer Military Force: Four Views". *New York Review of Books*, 24 June 1993.

Herro, Annie, Wendy Lambourne and David Penklis. "Peacekeeping and Peace Enforcement in Africa: The Potential Contribution of a UN Emergency Peace Service". *African Security Review* 18, no. 1 (2009): 49–62.

Human Rights Watch. *Oral Statement to the Human Rights Council on Côte d'Ivoire*. Human Rights Watch, 15 June 2011. www.hrw.org/en/news/2011/06/15/oral-statement-human-rights-council-c-te-d-ivoire.

International Coalition for the Responsibility to Protect. "Report on the General Assembly Plenary Debate on the Responsibility to Protect". International Coalition for the Responsibility to Protect, 15 September 2009. www.responsibilitytoprotect.org/ICRtoP%20Report-General_Assembly_Debate_on_the_Responsibility_to_Protect%20FINAL%209_22_09.pdf.

Jett, Dennis C. *Why Peacekeeping Fails*. New York: Palgrave, 2001.

Johansen, Robert C. "Expert Discussion of the United Nations Emergency Peace Service: Cuenca Report". In *A United Nations Emergency Peace Service: To Prevent Genocide and Crimes against Humanity*, edited by Robert C. Johansen, 43–74. New York: World Federalist Movement – Institute for Global Policy, 2006.

Kaldor, Mary. "Libya: War or Peacekeeping". Open Democracy, 5 April 2011. http://fair-andunbalancedblog.blogspot.com/2011/04/libya-war-or-peacekeeping.html.

Katsumi, Takahiro. "The Upper House Adopts a Dpj Bill Proposing to Facilitate the Establishment of a New UN Service". 2008. http://uneps-japan.blogspot.com/search?updated-min=2008–01–01T00%3A00%3A00%2B09%3A00&updated-max=2009–01–01T00%3A00%3A00%2B09%3A00&max-results=6.

Kinloch, Stephen P. "Utopian or Pragmatic? A UN Permanent Military Volunteer Force". *International Peacekeeping* 3, no. 4 (1996): 166–90.

Kinloch, Stephen. *A UN 'Legion': Between Utopia and Reality*. Abingdon, UK: Routledge, 2012.

Ladley, Andrew. "Peacekeeper Abuse, Immunity and Impunity: The Need for Effective Criminal and Civil Accountability on International Peace Operations". *Politics and Ethics Review* 1, no. 1 (2005).

Langille, H. Peter. *Bridging the Commitment–Capacity Gap: A Review of Existing Arrangements and Options for Enhancing UN Rapid Deployment*. New York: Center for UN Reform Education, 2002.

Langille, H. Peter. "UNEPS Composition (Draft)". Paper presented at the Workshop on the Eradication of Armed Conflict, Brisbane, 8–10 February 2007.

Langille, H. Peter. "Preventing Genocide". In *The World and Darfur: International Response to Crimes against Humanity in Western Sudan*, edited by Amanda Grzyb, 281–327. Montreal: McGill Queens University Press, 2009.

Langille, H. Peter. *Preparing for a UN Emergency Peace Service*. Friedrich Ebert Stiftung, August 2012. http://library.fes.de/pdf-files/iez/09282.pdf.

Le Roy, Alain. "Remarks of the under Secretary-General for Peacekeeping Operations, Mr Alain Le Roy, to the Special Committee on Peacekeeping Operations". United Nations, 23 February 2009. www.un.org/en/peacekeeping/articles/article230209.htm.

Nambiar, Satish. "Afterword". In *A United Nations Emergency Peace Service: To Prevent Genocide and Crimes against Humanity*, edited by Robert C. Johansen. New York: World Federalist Movement – Institute for Global Policy, 2006.

Ogata, Sadako N. *The Turbulent Decade: Confronting the Refugee Crises of the 1990s*. New York: WW Norton & Company, 2005.

Penklis, David. "Implications of the 1993 to 2008 Burundi Peace Process for United Nations Peacekeeping Operations". Thesis submitted for the degree of Doctor of Philosophy, The University of Sydney, 2011.

Pugh, Michael. "Peacekeeping and Critical Theory". *International Peacekeeping* 11, no. 1 (2004): 39–58.

Richmond, Oliver. "UN Peace Operations and the Dilemmas of the Peacebuilding Consensus". *International Peacekeeping* 11, no. 1 (2004): 83–101.

Roberts, Adam. "Proposals for UN Standing Forces: A Critical History". In *The United Nations Security Council and War: The Evolution of Thought and Practice since 1945*, edited by Vaughan Lowe, Adam Roberts, Jennifer Welsh and Dominik Zaum, 99–130. New York: Oxford University Press, 2008.

Schwebel, Stephen M. *Justice in International Law*. Cambridge: Cambridge University Press, 1994.

Scully, Sean. "Armed Troops Sought for UN". *Washington Times*, 1 June, 2000. www.globalpolicy.org/component/content/article/199/40970.html.

Senate Foreign Affairs, Defence And Trade Committee. Australia's Involvement in Peacekeeping Operations. Australian Senate, 21 August 2007. http://parlinfo.aph.gov.au/parlInfo/download/committees/commsen/10470/toc_pdf/5635–3.pdf;fileType=application%2Fpdf#search=%22committees/commsen/10470/0003%22.

Suthanthiraraj, Kavitha and Mariah Quinn. *Standing for Change in Peacekeeping Operations: Project for a United Nations Emergency Peace Service (UNEPS)*. New York: Global Action to Prevent War, 2009.

United Nations Department of Peacekeeping Operations and Department of Field Support. *United Nations Peacekeeping Operations Principles and Guidelines*. New York: United Nations, 2008.

UN General Assembly. *Supplement to an Agenda for Peace: Position Paper of the Secretary-General on the Occasion of the Fiftieth Anniversary of the United Nations*. A/50/60 of 25 January 1995.

UN General Assembly. *Report of the Panel on United Nations Peace Operations*. A/55/305 of 21 August 2000.

UN General Assembly. *A More Secure World: Our Shared Responsibility. Report of the Secretary-General's High-Level Panel on Threats, Challenges and Change*. A/59/565 of 2 December 2004.

UN General Assembly. *Report of the Special Committee on Peacekeeping Operations and Its Working Group*. A/63/19 of 23 February–20 March 2009.

UN Secretary-General. *Report of the Secretary-General on Peacebuilding in the Immediate Aftermath of Conflict*. A/63/881–S/2009/304 United Nations General Assembly/ United Nations Security Council, 11 June 2009.

UN Security Council. *Report of the Independent Inquiry into the Actions of the United Nations During the 1994 Genocide in Rwanda*. S/1999/1257 of 16 December 1999.

Urquhart, Brian. "For a UN Volunteer Military Force". *New York Review of Books*, 10 June 1993, 3–4.

Urquhart, Brian. "Prospects for a UN Rapid Response Capability". In *UN Rapid Reaction Capabilities: Requirements and Prospects*, edited by David Cox and Albert Legault. Cornwallie, Ottawa: Canadian Peacekeeping Press, 1995.

Weiss, T.G. *What's Wrong with the United Nations and How to Fix It*. Second ed. Malden, Mass: Polity, 2012.

World Federalist Movement. "United Nations Emergency Peace Service". n.d. www.wfm-igp.org/site/wfm/united%2Bnations%2Bemergency%2Bpeace%2Bservice.

Zuber, Robert and David Curran. "Peacekeeping and Rapid Reaction: Towards the Establishment of Cosmopolitan Capacities for Rapid Deployment". Division of Peace Studies at the University of Bradford, Global Action to Prevent War and Armed Conflict, the World Federalist Movement Canada, 8 July 2013. www.bradford.ac.uk/ssis/media/ssis/peacestudies/Bradford-Write-Up-Sept.pdf

8 Conclusion
Moving beyond the UNEPS proposal?

Introduction

Edward Luck, former Special Advisor to the UN on the Responsibility to Protect, once said that "the course of [UN] reform tends to be decidedly unpredictable. Rarely does a reform wave end up where its initiators expected".[1] The story this book has told suggests that the UNEPS proposal could follow a similarly unpredictable path. I have shown that in the face of various challenges confronting the proposal, increasing the support it receives might mean reworking some of its core attributes – grafting different norms and other ideas on to the proposal, pruning those that are particularly controversial, and framing it to incite the interest, if not enthusiasm, of a broad range of stakeholders. Such modifications have operational and procedural implications for the proposed body, which would affect the mandate, composition, funding structure, authorisation body, size and cost.

Deviating from a single-minded 'campaign' based on the principal features of a UNEPS is not always a popular approach, as indicated in Chapter 2. Some members of the UNEPS' network insist that exploring alternative visions of the original prototype might detract from the coherence and potential policy relevance of the proposal and so they favour retaining "a compelling, cost-effective idea" for when it is needed.[2] Such an approach, however, is not the one this book has taken and it makes no apologies for this.

Where does this leave us? What should UNEPS 'look like' and how should it be promoted now we have considered the views of a diverse range of actors from far-flung regions of the world? This chapter summarises the key findings of the book and evaluates perspectives that have not yet been considered on localising the proposal. It first argues that establishing an un-armed standing service, explored in Chapter 4, would not be a pragmatic solution to the shortcomings facing the civilian dimensions of peace operations and the UN's responsibility to prevent atrocities. It recommends instead strengthening the mandate and capacity of the UNPBC, as well as those of UN field agencies at points where there is a risk of violence or atrocities breaking out. Next, I argue that establishing a standing capacity that would be limited to security forces should be favoured over a multidimensional and multifunctional service comprising police, troops and civilians. This recalibrated proposal should be: (1) framed as a 'service' rather than a 'force' that would protect civilians from armed conflict; and (2) significantly pruned in terms of its size in order to create a much smaller (and less intrusive) capacity. There could also be a version of this proposal that would solely address natural disasters. Each type of service would fill a gap in the UN's peace and security architecture as well as its system of disaster response. I highlight the importance of distinguishing UNEPS from other external actors in a conflict zone to ensure that it has its own identity and does not increase the vulnerabilities of existing peace operations and UN field activities. Finally, I reinforce and elaborate upon the advantages of a permanent regional or sub-regional capacity, using the Asia-Pacific and African regions as examples. I argue that support from the UN might help to advance efforts to establish a regional standing capacity, especially in Africa. In short, this chapter proposes various iterations of the UNEPS that might be supplements or viable alternatives to the UNEPS proposal as we know it today.

A standing civilian service – not the way to go

One dilemma confronting the UNEPS proposal that influences the support it receives relates to whether it would be made up of civilians or whether it would include troops that could use force to uphold its mandate. Those advocating a civilian service did so for several reasons. The first was normative – it is the 'right' response to conflict. The second was practical – it is the most effective approach to averting conflict and it is the only type of UN standing capacity that would receive political support. Broadly speaking, those espousing a civilian service showed an interest in strengthening the international community's capacity to help states to prevent violent conflict and atrocity crimes within their own territory. I called these a 'peacebuilding service' and a non-violent R2P prevention service, respectively.

Would such localised iterations of UNEPS be a viable alternative – a means to circumvent the obstacles facing the proposal? I have concluded, probably not. But let us consider arguments on both sides. On one hand, there is a lack of deployable civilian capacities in UN peace operations, including project managers, financial personnel and post-conflict officers. Civilians now represent approximately 20 per cent of all UN peacekeepers[3] and Ban Ki-moon has reinforced the importance of an "effective emergency civilian surge" in the context of peacekeeping and the protection of civilians.[4] The problems with civilians in UN peace operations relate to the time it takes to identify, recruit and deploy appropriate staff to the field, as well as the ability to retain staff.[5] Chandran and colleagues cite the example of the United Nations Mission in the Central African Republic and Chad which was mandated on September 25, 2007.[6] A year later, 91 per cent of civilian peacekeeping positions had not been filled. Furthermore, de Coning argues that none of the organisations that undertakes peace operations, including the AU, the European Union, the Organization for Security and Co-operation in Europe and the UN, has managed to develop the capability to deploy suitably qualified and experienced civilian peacekeepers in a reasonable time and in the numbers required.[7] In other words, it is not only a matter of getting adequate numbers of personnel on the ground in good time but also getting the right personnel.

But, as a representative from the OHCHR noted, we cannot expect too much because "the development of rapid civilian capacity deployment teams within peacekeeping missions is very much in its infancy".[8] Ban confirms this observation, saying in relation to R2P that:

> it is often difficult to identify and mobilize sufficient numbers of police and civilian cadres with the skills and training required to deal with crimes relating to the responsibility to protect, just as it can be hard to find their military counterparts.[9]

At first sight, this deficit appears promising for both the non-violent preventative and rebuilding dimensions of the UNEPS proposal. As such, a standing civilian capacity could conceivably address the personnel gaps identified in UN peace operations by providing well-trained civilian specialists at short notice and for a short period of time at different points in a mission's life-cycle.

But there are more persuasive arguments, I believe, countering this proposition. First, de Coning maintains that the UN already receives a large number of well-qualified applicants for advertised civilian positions (approximately 1,500 per position of which about half are suitable).[10] There are also multiple civilian rosters where individuals are pre-trained, pre-identified and placed on standby so that they are ready to deploy when the need arises.[11] From this perspective, the problem is not the *availability* of qualified, well-trained personnel but rather the "structural bottlenecks" and the informal nature of the UN's recruitment system – specifically, the central role played by personal contacts or "knowing someone on the inside".[12] Consequently, Solli and colleagues make the case for a significant overhaul of the UNDFS and UNDPKO recruitment architecture.[13] De Coning suggests that the best way to ensure the UN has enough well-trained civilian peacekeepers available at short notice is for the UN Secretariat to focus on "improving the UN recruitment system, with the aim of reducing the time it takes to hire new staff and to improve internal standing capacities and rosters. It also needs to improve the quality of the personnel in the field".[14] He argues that "the focus should thus be on addressing these shortcomings, rather than on developing new rosters and rapid deployment systems that will require considerable time and resources, and that have a poor track record of success". This argument indicates that the lack of promptly deployable civilian personnel might not be most effectively addressed through the creation of a standing civilian capacity, as some respondents have suggested, but by ensuring that the existing system that recruits and deploys civilian peacekeepers is operating effectively.

Second, some argue that there is a risk that multidimensional peace operations could duplicate or displace civilian roles that would be better performed by local authorities or other civilian actors (both local and international) with more appropriate mandates.[15] As explored in Chapter 7, there are already a number of UN field agencies (not to mention NGOs) that are undertaking peacebuilding activities. As Penklis demonstrated through his analysis of the peace operation in Burundi between 1993 and 2008, the work of UN agencies and others can be compromised by mandate and functional overlaps in various stages of the peace process.[16] An Australian academic who specialises in defence studies and international relations highlights similar concerns about a potential overlap between the proposed UNEPS and the work of UN agencies. He argues:

> the broader issue of coordination within the UN system [needs to be considered]. You need a mechanism by which these tensions can be resolved. This is a challenge because the UN is not a single organisation. It's a family of moderately disconnected organisations.... The UN has always struggled with the issue of coordination.[17]

Penklis maintains that the best way to strengthen the UN's non-violent conflict prevention and rebuilding activities is to buttress existing mechanisms rather than to introduce a new actor (like a civilian or multidimensional UNEPS) into a conflict zone or an environment where there is a risk of conflict breaking out. Improving the current system could reduce the coordination deficits and overlaps between UN field operations, such as UN agencies and peacekeeping missions.[18] The Integrated Assessment Planning Team released a report in December 2013 that supports this general conclusion. The report noted that a UN "agency, fund or programme may be best placed to carry out a mandated task [of a UN peace operation]" and consequently recommended that when planning and designing peace operations the "duplication of structures" should be avoided.[19] As a means of preventing such duplications, Penklis specifically conceives of a more active role for the UNPBC wherein it would manage the UN's engagement in the whole peace process, including the UNSC, UNGA, and the Economic and Social Council (ECOSOC) on mandates and coordinated programme activities.[20] As it currently stands, the UNPBC is restricted to acting only in post-conflict contexts and was tasked specifically with identifying and bridging the gaps in coordination of the international community's efforts to support peacebuilding in countries emerging from violent conflict.

This discussion raises the question: would strengthening existing institutions and mechanisms that are capable (or have the potential) of preventing R2P crimes be a better use of resources than introducing a new entity like a civilian UNEPS? I believe, yes. The responsibility to *prevent* remains the most underdeveloped aspect of the R2P doctrine. Despite the dearth of information, reforming the UNPBC as a means of preventing R2P crimes could be a good way forward. Reminiscent of Penklis' suggestion, Bellamy argues for a more active role for the UNPBC which would place greater importance on prevention in addition to its current focus on post-conflict peacebuilding. This was indeed part of the original vision for the UNPBC and is consistent with the view of a peace and conflict cycle where post-conflict peacebuilding is continuous with conflict prevention.[21]

The 2004 Report of the Secretary-General's High-Level Panel on Threats, Challenges and Change, for example, which recommended the creation of a UNPBC stated that the core function of the UNPBC should be to "identify countries that are under stress and risk sliding towards State collapse" and to provide "proactive assistance in preventing that process from developing further".[22] The Global Partnership for the Prevention of Armed Conflict (GPPAC),[23] a network of civil society organisations involved in peacebuilding and conflict prevention based in The Hague, expressed disappointment that the original proposal to include a prevention mandate was not followed through. In a background paper published in September 2006, GPPAC indicated that the resolutions creating the UNPBC "seem to allow a member state to request advice when it is on the verge of "lapsing into conflict" only in "exceptional cases".[24] According to GPPAC, "given that the impacts of armed violence escalate when fighting breaks out, this was a regrettable sacrifice in the negotiations that established the body".[25] The report of a roundtable discussion on "Peacebuilding and the Roles of Civil Society Organisations: How does it look from Geneva?", hosted by the Quaker UN Office in Geneva (QUNO) in May 2006, also indicated that it was hoped that there would be "more continuity between the work of conflict prevention initiatives and those of peacebuilding with the development of the PBC".[26] QUNO maintained in a briefing published on its website in 2007 that even though the initial mandate of the UNPBC was largely focused on post-conflict situations, there was "potential for the Commission to eventually address the conflict spectrum in a holistic way – including preventive strategies in the early stages of conflict becoming violent".[27]

The expansion of the UNPBC mandate could make it an institutional vehicle for addressing the preconditions of R2P crimes.[28] Commentators have argued that we need a more detailed understanding of the tools that are most effective when mass atrocities are likely. This would include identifying the specific triggers for mass atrocity crimes.[29] Modestly reforming the UNPBC could mean giving it an advisory role whereby it would work with national governments and other stakeholders to develop action plans and provide ideas to the UNSC, UNGA and ECOSOC. With the engagement of national leaders and international assistance, the UNPBC could help develop context-sensitive plans for preventing civil wars and mass atrocities.[30] Bellamy suggests that the UNPBC could also focus on generating policies to help governments promote equitable economic growth and sustainable democratisation, and that a modified UNPBC might coordinate security, including the deployment of robust military and police forces.[31]

The wisdom of a UN force

The above discussion regarding the coordination of civilian and military actors at various stages of a peace process directly relates to whether a permanent multidimensional and multifunctional standing service is in fact the most pragmatic response to the woes of the current peacekeeping system, especially in the context of preventing atrocities. Many respondents who were interested in a UNEPS tended to endorse a proposal that would comprise troops, police and civilians. These personnel would contribute (albeit in the short term) to preventing mass violence through robust peace enforcement as well as paving the way for sustainable peace by kick-starting or supplementing peacemaking and peacebuilding measures. On the one hand, the view that such a service is a logical solution to the absence of rapidly deployable, well-trained, equipped and coordinated multidimensional peacekeepers is popular. On the other hand, Penklis' argument – to strengthen existing in-country UN agencies and programmes that are already conducting peacemaking and peacebuilding activities – suggests that establishing a standing force comprised *solely* of police and troops might be the more appropriate way forward. A similar initiative was proposed by the United States Congress in the form of the United Nations Rapid Deployment Act. The Act called on the US to work with the UNSG and other member states to establish a UN Rapid Deployment Police and Security Force of about 6,000 volunteers from around the world. Peter Langille drafted a possible structure for this unit which provides a valuable starting point for further investigation.[32]

While a Rapid Deployment Police and Security Force (or something like it) would make sense from an organisational perspective, political issues stand in the way. As discussed in Chapters 2, 4 and 5, the sensitivities surrounding the idea of a standing force are widespread. Where does this leave those who wish to create a permanent UN force that would enjoy broad support? There is no easy answer to this question and there is an undeniable tension between the pragmatic and the normative here. Such a tension raises three issues that might soften the blow of a standing security force. The first is the language used to describe this re-imagined proposal or how to frame it. Langille argues that the term "standing force" or "rapid reaction force" has hampered efforts to establish UNEPS-type capacities. He points out that the term "emergency service" was crafted to attract a significant support base, and that "rapid deployment" receives a comparably warm reception.[33] If the UNEPS proposal is to be pruned of its civilian components and associated goals and tasks, it is essential that it is framed in a way that is least likely to incite outright rejection, such as that suggested by Langille. At a minimum, this would mean replacing the word 'force' with 'service'. The second point relates to the size of the proposed service. As discussed in the previous chapter, significantly pruning its size in order to create a much smaller (and less intrusive) capacity might be an effective strategy to garner support. Third, altering UNEPS' mandate could further contribute to the acceptability of a relatively small UN force. As discussed in Chapters 4 and 5, respectively, there was an interest in localising UNEPS so that it would respond to natural disasters, or be responsible for POC peacekeeping missions. I have already argued that the former would be a valuable contribution to the international community's toolbox but what about the latter? Would a standing force that is framed as supporting or commencing POC Missions be needed from a problem-solving perspective?

POC missions

The short answer is, yes. But before I elaborate, let us recap some of the finer points of this localised version of the UNEPS proposal. It would require advocates to focus on practical factors hindering peacekeepers' ability to protect civilians such as the timing of deployment and the minimal resources that are available to them in such missions. Highlighting these features seemed to increase interest in the proposal among those who were committed to both the POC Mission norm and strengthening the effectiveness of the UN in this area, but who were at the same time cautious about the invasive character of military interventions against the wishes of the host-state. POC Missions, we recall, require the consent of the state in question and are committed to being perceived as neutral by both sides. This observation suggests that these features would need to be introduced into the proposal and highlighted by its promoters.

The introduction to this book explained how peacekeepers face a number of obstacles in their efforts to protect civilians. Given the interest respondents showed in understanding and addressing such challenges, I now explore this theme in slightly more detail in the context of a possible role for a UNEPS. While the UNDPKO has highlighted the increasing relevance of POC to peacekeeping operations in practice, peacekeepers can lack the requisite skills and training, as well as the operational guidance and conceptual clarity, to allow them to protect civilians effectively.[34] Moreover, there is a dearth of information on the extent to which POC actually influences daily operational matters.[35] And only recently has UNDPKO (with the UNDFS) provided strategic direction to troop and police contributing states on what the "protection of civilians under imminent threat of physical violence" actually means – but it has not yet conducted scenario-based or detailed task-driven training.[36]

UNDPKO has also developed a *Framework for Drafting Comprehensive POC Strategies in UN Peacekeeping Operations* which provides basic parameters and principles for drafting POC strategies. While the Framework marks an important milestone in the development of a common understanding of POC in the UN system, it only provides general guidance.[37] Another challenge facing POC Missions is that even though the UNSC has regularly referenced the protection of civilians "under imminent threat of physical violence" in mandates for UN-led peacekeeping operations authorised under Chapter VII of the UN Charter,[38] peacekeepers are still under the authority of their respective governments, which sometimes may prevent them from taking the necessary risks required to protect civilians.[39] And, of course, there is the general problem that all missions face of slow-deploying peacekeepers who often arrive too late to protect civilians.

Could a UNEPS address these shortcomings faced by POC Missions? My answer is not all, but some of them, even with a truncated size and composition. Its personnel could be trained as 'protection specialists' with the service possessing operational expertise in protecting civilians from violence in conflict, and potentially including atrocity crimes (as the line between POC missions and R2P missions are blurred in practice). UNEPS' personnel could undertake a range of protection measures, ensuring security and supporting actions that reduce or eliminate the ability of (likely) perpetrators to threaten the population. Preparing for such activities would take time and could be undertaken when the service is not deployed. Emphasising what is involved in training personnel for the missions they would be conducting would go some way toward countering arguments, explored in Chapter 7, that the proposed service would be a white elephant.

We see a glimpse of the UN's willingness to deploy peacekeepers who are mandated and have the capacity to protect civilians proactively with the inception of the United Nations Force Intervention Brigade in the North Kivu region of the Democratic Republic of the Congo (DRC). The Brigade, comprising around 3,000 troops from Tanzania, South Africa and Malawi, was deployed in mid-2013 and charged specifically with carrying out offensive operations to neutralise armed groups that threatened the state's authority and civilian security.[40] This is the most ambitious mandate (in military terms) that a UN peace operation has ever been given. The Brigade was deployed in part to buttress the existing UN mission in the DRC (MONUSCO) which, despite having a protection mandate, failed to protect civilians adequately[41] because peacekeepers lacked clarity on whether POC functions should be 'reactive' or 'defensive', as well as lacking adequate training.[42] While some commentators raised questions about the Brigade's potential to jeopardise an eventual political agreement,[43] others lauded it for rebuilding the credibility of the UN and providing a refreshing departure from the often passive approach that has given peacekeepers a bad reputation.[44]

The proposed UNEPS might be able to perform a similar role to the Brigade, which would mean deploying with the consent of the host state as well as with the UNSC's authorisation. While this is merely a suggestion on how UNEPS could plug holes in POC missions, it is an invitation for UNEPS' proponents to investigate and propose ways in which the service might explicitly function in a POC peacekeeping context – both strategically and tactically. Importantly, this analysis highlights the value of *framing* UNEPS as a tool that would conduct and support POC missions.

A standing force that is designed to prevent or respond rapidly to R2P crimes would also – from a practical perspective – be a valuable tool for the UN and enhance its ability to prevent and respond effectively to mass killings. As with the challenges confronting POC missions, the UN faces multiple problems in its efforts to prevent and respond rapidly to R2P crimes: deployment delays, poorly equipped peacekeepers, peacekeepers having a limited or unclear authority to act and states' unwillingness to provide peacekeepers for peace enforcement operations. Furthermore, because peacekeepers are not generally trained in how to respond to genocide, UNDPKO avoids situations where its missions are called to respond to such acts.[45]

If UNEPS is framed as a tool to operationalise R2P – as discussed in Chapter 5, a proposition I would not recommend – it would make sense to include a caveat in the proposal stating that it would deploy only with UNSC authorisation and not against the wishes of the state in question. This is most similar to an R2P Pillar Two Mission which, as stated in Chapter 3, is deployed when there is a risk of atrocity crimes being committed. I argued in Chapter 5 that incorporating a higher litmus test for those wishing to intervene with more detailed precautionary principles could allay fears that such interventions would cause more harm than good.

Distinguishing UNEPS from the rest

A localised UNEPS – smaller, with a slightly different mandate, and composed solely of security forces – would be working in volatile situations alongside a range of government, non-government, regional and UN actors. This raises the question: how would UNEPS be distinguishable by the host population as well as the warring parties from existing in-country programmes, services and other intervention forces? As one prominent Australian academic puts it:

> How would you make a force distinctively recognisable without running the risk that they would be identified with other separate recognisable forces that might be floating around in a particular conflict area? Maybe dress them up as 'Clowns Sans Frontières'.

In other words, he is suggesting that making the service appear visually different from other actors in the conflict zone might provide it with a unique identity. This was the original rationale behind the blue helmets worn by UN peacekeepers. It differentiated them from other actors in a conflict zone. Perhaps another colour ought to be introduced to further distinguish a POC UNEPS from the rest.

Similar issues surrounding the need for a clear division between offensive operations and non-offensive ones have been raised with the Brigade in the DRC. Robert Zuber asked whether it would increase the vulnerabilities of the peace operation, MONUSCO, which is not conducting such an aggressive operation or other UN field activities. He suggests that the Brigades could benefit from some institutional distance from other UN activities on the ground.[46] NGOs working in the Kivi region have also expressed concern that they will be linked to military action. For its part, the M23 rebel group has suggested that the Brigade will need to work in different areas to the other peacekeepers. M23 spokesman Rene Abandi said:

> It's a very complicated situation for us.... Blue helmets come with an offensive mandate while others are deployed in the same areas with a peacekeepers' mandate. They have really to separate areas so that we can make the distinction.[47]

Such issues will clearly need to be thought through in both the conceptual and implementation stages of the proposed UNEPS. My general point, however, is that UNEPS will, in some way, need to 'look different' to the other actors in conflict.

Managing and authorising a UNEPS

If the proposed UNEPS were solely to comprise security forces, under what authority would it deploy? UNEPS' proponents suggested that the UNSC should be the first point of call but, if the Council is blocked due to a veto of a P-5 member, UNEPS could obtain the green light from either the UNGA, under the Uniting for Peace Resolution, or perhaps at the discretion of the Secretary-General. While, at first sight, this seems like a sensible range of options, this selection will probably ignite suspicion among those who are already cautious about a standing UN peacekeeping capacity being overused or misused.

Only the UNSC is seen as providing adequate assurance that such a service would not be open to abuse and would not deploy in situations where a P-5 member had vital national interests at stake. Even so, there were also misgivings about the potential manipulation of the proposed service by its principal funders. I responded to such concerns in part by suggesting the introduction of an independent funding structure that could placate fears that UNEPS would be co-opted by powerful states.

The composition of the UNSC, especially the P-5, also affected the support the UNEPS proposal received. Even those who placed sufficient trust in the Council to consider supporting a UNEPS that would be deployed with UNSC authorisation might require additional safeguards – specifically, consent from the state into whose territory UNEPS would intervene – to assure them that such a service would not be used for purposes other than those for which it was intended. Of course, such a safeguard would prevent it from deploying in situations where the state itself was the perpetrator of atrocities or conflict; however, perhaps it is a concession that UNEPS' advocates will need to make in order to generate widespread support for the idea.

A standing force predicated on the conditions above would mean it would not be able to respond to a situation such as the war in Syria where a political solution and pressure from regional and international power-brokers appear to be the missing ingredients for peace. It might, however, provide the institutional mechanism to implement Security Council resolutions passed on 22 February 2014 ordering both sides to permit the delivery of humanitarian aid.[48] It could do so by creating a humanitarian corridor though which essential provisions might pass.

The United Nations

Perspectives on the UN varied in this study, which directly affected the perceived legitimacy and viability of the proposed UNEPS. Reform of the Security Council is undoubtedly needed and called for by some of the Organisation's most ardent supporters.[49] Indeed, explaining the conundrum of the UNSC, Kennedy writes that "everyone agrees that the present structure is flawed; but a consensus on how to fix it remains out of reach".[50] Bellamy rightly notes that the more the UNSC is asked to do and adjudicate on, the more important the

Council's own legitimacy becomes, in particular the extent to which it is seen to be representative, accountable and transparent.[51] The success of the UNEPS proposal and wider UN reforms is closely linked to reforming the UNSC. Different reform proposals (size, veto, regional representation, categories of membership, and working methods) that have been developed over the years have so far not been implemented. A more representative body that reflects the needs and concerns of UNEPS' stakeholders – those who are likely to be recipients of an intervention or affected in other ways by one – would no doubt increase the desirability of a proposed UNEPS.

Despite its shortcomings, a commitment to the UN and its ideals is also crucial in generating the opportunity to create a UN standing capacity that saves lives. As discussed in Chapters 6 and 7, people must believe, at least to a degree, in the norms underpinning multilateralism and cosmopolitanism in order to look past the failings of the Organisation and strive for change. They must believe in the potential of the UN to reform itself and rise above its politicking. It is hard to see how a UNEPS will ever be established unless belief in the UN is kept alive. Short of radical reforms to the Council, other less drastic but still ambitious steps might be taken to restore legitimacy to the world body responsible for international peace and security and, in turn, strengthen interests in the UNEPS proposal. These include establishing a formal shift in UN peacekeeping doctrine away from the so-called holy trinity of peacekeeping (neutrality, impartiality and the non-use of force except in self-defence), as well as a clearer distinction between enforcement for humanitarian purposes and enforcement for the maintenance of international peace and security.

A regional EPS and UN regional-hybrid

Opportunities to localise the proposal at a regional or sub-regional level, at times with some involvement from the UN, also influenced levels of support for a UNEPS. Interests in regional responses to conflict and atrocities are growing and have been proposed as an answer to the violence against civilians in Syria.[52] Soner Cagaptay, a senior fellow at the Washington Institute for Near East Policy, argued that Turkey should support an air-based intervention to protect UN-designated safe havens where civilians could seek refuge. The mission, according to Cagaptay, would be an "all-Muslim military force" composed of both Turkish and Arab militaries.[53] He suggested that Qatar and Saudi Arabia, who are funding the opposition, could work with Turkey to protect the safe havens. While these ideas never materialised, they symbolise a growing interest in 'regional responses to regional problems'. Mary Kaldor, moreover, has argued in the case of Libya that the deployment of international peacekeepers, especially if they were drawn from Arab and Africans countries, would have been a constructive alternative to the NATO airstrikes.[54]

As discussed in Chapter 6, there was greater comfort surrounding the idea of regional responses to conflict, partly because of perceived cultural and political familiarity of neighbours or potential interveners. Some, especially from Australia, also showed an interest in responding to conflict in their region based on the view that it is in Australia's interest to have a peaceful neighbourhood. While the security architecture in the Asia-Pacific is still relatively undeveloped, what is important here is that some suggested that a regional intervention with UN authorisation and support might be more acceptable to both the intervened and others in the region.

The idea of establishing a regional peacekeeping capacity is supported by the Council for Security Cooperation in the Asia Pacific (CSCAP) – a track-two organisation that aims to facilitate dialogue on regional security issues – which convened a *Study Group on the Responsibility to Protect*. In its 2011 report, CSCAP recommended that national governments, regional arrangements and the region's global partners should work towards establishing "a regional standing capacity for preventing and responding to genocide, war crimes, ethnic cleansing and crimes against humanity".[55] Such a capacity would be used "at the request of the host-state and the UN, in order to prevent the four R2P crimes or respond to their commission in a timely and decisive manner".[56] While the funding, composition and institutional home of such a service requires further consideration, it shows both the need to and interest in pursing such avenues, conceptually and in practice.

The idea of a regional-UN 'hybrid' was also popular. Such a proposal would see the UN authorise, train and possibly fund a regional force but it would comprise, and be led by, personnel from the region. There are many steps that must be taken to pursue this avenue and these will vary according to the region and sub-region. But let us take Africa as an example because it has the advantage of the AU's constitution which, under Article 4(h), allows the organisation to intervene forcefully in "grave circumstances" – those of war crimes, genocide and crimes against humanity – in countries that have signed up to the treaty. Although not without its problems (both political and procedural),[57] the AU constitution shows the commitment made by African leaders to provide the legal and normative foundations for an institutional capacity to implement R2P. Plus, there is already the skeleton of such a capacity on its way to being fully operational – the African Standby Force (ASF).

The ASF, we recall, refers to multidisciplinary brigades of police, military and civilians from five sub regions, which are supposed to be in a position to deploy in 30 days for peacekeeping operations and in 14 days for military interventions. The ASF has been called a 'moving target' because of the inability of the Africans to settle on a clear concept.[58] There was an internal debate about whether the ASF's rapid deployment capability would be standing or standby, that is, under the control of each of the five regions in peacetime. Specifically, key AU officials argued in 2007 for a standing high-readiness capability that would deploy under the mandate of the Peace and Security Council; however, African Ministers of Defence and Security agreed in 2008 that states in each of the five regions would retain control of their rapid deployment capability.[59]

Work on the ASF has been underway since 2004 but has been hampered by many obstacles which have resulted in its inability to intervene rapidly, stop atrocities, and defeat spoilers. This is because the readiness of the five regional brigades varies. The most advanced is in East Africa but the other four are either works in progress or exist only in a rudimentary way. Promising signs, however, include the establishment of a brigade headquarters, centres of excellence have been identified and units have been pledged by member states.[60] Overall, however, there has been a general unwillingness and inability of many African states to assume political, materiel and financial responsibility for peace operations, which means they rely on outside support.[61] This has led some to predict that the ASF concept "will not be fully implemented in the foreseeable future".[62] Furthermore, while bilateral and multilateral assistance has been forthcoming in some areas, for example in training, such assistance is motivated by each partner's own interests and priorities rather than the needs and preferences of the stakeholders of the ASF – the Africans themselves.[63]

One solution to obstacles facing the ASF could be to get the UN more involved. So far, Jakkie Cilliers argues that the "degree of support and succour that the UN has provided to the ASF has been a disappointment. Instead of leading, the UN has followed".[64] Kofi Annan's report, *In Larger Freedom*, recommended introducing memoranda of understanding between the United Nations and individual regional organisations that would govern the sharing of information, expertise and resources. The UN would, in particular circumstances, use assessed contributions (those conditional on membership to the UN) to finance regional operations authorised by the Security Council.[65] Jakkie Cilliers proposes a single point of entry for international funders wanting to assist the AU to replace the current 'donor scramble' and duplication of efforts.[66] Arthur Boutellis and Paul D. Williams also make some broad recommendations to strengthen the AU-UN partnership in the area of peace operations: (1) harmonising the decision-making processes of the two councils (the UNSC and the AU's Peace and Security Council); (2) filling some of the key capacity gaps in the AU's representation in New York; and (3) developing more effective modes of communication between the elected African members of the UNSC and the AU's Peace and Security Council in Ethiopia.[67] While such suggestions are not explicitly aimed at rendering the ASF more fully operational, if they were implemented they might go some way towards advancing the ASF beyond its current form.

The potential and pitfalls of the ASF is the topic of an entire book and I make no claims to resolve it here. I wish to point out that the discussion of a standing force has already been tabled as part of the conceptual evolution of the ASF, and that some capacity shortages, largely due to the unwillingness or inability of African leaders to honour their commitments, could be addressed by ensuring the UN is more fully engaged.[68] In sum, there is an array of possibilities for regional and sub-regional peacekeeping arrangements. Such proposals could also be seen, in the short-term, as a means of strengthening the international community's capacity to prevent and respond rapidly to atrocities before an international capacity such as a UNEPS is finally established.

A final word

The idea of a UN Legion, as discussed in Chapter 2, is older than the UN itself. For decades cosmopolitan thinkers and politicians have tried to establish a supranational entity that would not be reliant on the political whims of sovereign states. The UN got close to creating this kind of arrangement with the dawn of peacekeeping operations, which have become considerably more ambitious and far-reaching over the years. The organisation has widened its definition of a "threat" to collective security to which peace operations and other collectives may respond with coercive force to include intra-state conflict and genocide and other atrocities.[69] While the UN has taken notable steps to implement the international community's responsibility to protect civilians from atrocities and armed conflict, there are still gaps to be filled, especially in the areas of peace operations. It seems remarkable that many of the complaints Lakhdar Brahimi expressed about UN peacekeeping in 2000 – late arriving ill-trained, equipped and coordinated peacekeepers – are still applicable today. Until these problems are adequately addressed, calls for a UN 'Legion' will continue to arise.

This final chapter has argued in favour of a recalibrated set of proposals based on the concerns and preferences of a wide selection of stakeholders. It has evaluated ideas that were identified in previous chapters and offered a number of conclusions. First, the best way to support the UN's ability to prevent conflict and atrocity crimes from occurring and through non-violent means is not with a standing UN civilian capacity but rather through buttressing the UNPBC and the existing in-country international civilian presence. It further argues that the creation of a standing UN security force – rather than a complex multidimensional capacity – would make the best sense given existing coordination deficits and overlaps between UN field agencies and peace operations. I maintain that sensitivities surrounding such a capacity might be partly overcome through reducing the size of the proposed force, ensuring that it is framed in a way that is least likely to incite outright rejection, and presenting it as a tool to conduct or contribute to POC Peacekeeping Operations or a first-responder to natural disasters. It is important that such a force is visually distinguishable from other actors in a conflict zone to avoid confusion with politically neutral actors or those without an offensive mandate. I argued that ideas for regional and sub-regional standing arrangements are also promising. While certain details of these proposed regional arrangements require further exploration, this chapter reinforces the potential of such a capacity in the Asia-Pacific and Africa and argues that support from the UN might help to facilitate their implementation.

Some proponents of a permanent UN capacity saw such an idea as a precursor to the eventual abolition of national militaries.[70] So, despite the ambitious nature of establishing – even a fairly small – UN standing service, they viewed it as the first step towards the more revolutionary move of global disarmament. In this book, I have taken a different position, asking: what would it take for a UNEPS to be created in the first place? The localised versions of the proposal that have been condensed in this chapter and explored in greater detail previously might be treated as 'trail-blazers' towards the eventual establishment of a UNEPS. In the same way that traditional peacekeeping operations, which were initially charged with monitoring a peace that had already been reached by belligerents, gradually evolved into missions with the mandate and capacity to use force to create peace where there was none to be found, some of the ideas explored in this book – if implemented – could one day herald a UNEPS, as we understand it today. The different variations could also be pursued *alongside* the proposed UNEPS to maximise the chance that much-needed reforms that would strengthen the institutional capacities to protect civilians might in the short to medium term be realised. It is my hope that the findings in this book might contribute to how the UNEPS idea is approached by its proponents and provide some insights for those interested in strengthening the rapid-deployment tools available to the international community to prevent war and protect civilians.

Notes

1 Luck, "Reforming the United Nations", 390.
2 Anonymous book reviewer, 2013.
3 Coning, "Civilian Peacekeeping Capacity".
4 UN Secretary-General, "Human Protection and the 21st Century United Nations".
5 Coning, "Civilian Peacekeeping Capacity", 581.
6 Chandran *et al.*, "Rapid Deployment of Civilians for Peace Operations", 2.
7 Coning, "Civilian Peacekeeping Capacity", 577.
8 Interview by Kavitha Suthanthiraraj, 2 December 2010, New York, USA.
9 UN General Assembly, *Implementing the Responsibility to Protect*, para. 39.
10 Coning, *Civilian Capacity in United Nations Peacekeeping and Peacebuilding Missions*, 3.
11 Ibid.
12 Solli *et al.*, "Training in Vain?" 425.
13 Ibid., 425–6.
14 Coning, *Civilian Capacity in United Nations Peacekeeping and Peacebuilding Missions*, 4.
15 Ghani and Lockhart, *Fixing Failed States*; Deschamp, "Victims of Violence", 20.
16 Penklis, "Implications of the 1993 to 2008 Burundi Peace Process", 161.
17 Interview by author, 13 December 2007, Canberra, Australia.
18 Penklis, "Implications of the 1993 to 2008 Burundi Peace Process", 161, 162, 168.
19 Integrated Assessment and Planning Working Group, *Integrated Assessment and Planning Handbook*.
20 Penklis, "Implications of the 1993 to 2008 Burundi Peace Process", 270.
21 Evans, *Cooperating for Peace*.
22 UN General Assembly, *A More Secure World*, para. 83.
23 GPPAC was formed in 2002 in response to a recommendation in UN Secretary-General Kofi Annan's 2001 report on the *Prevention of Armed Conflict*. Annan, *Prevention of Armed Conflict*.
24 Heemskerk, "Getting the Peacebuilding Commission Off the Ground", 6.
25 Ibid.
26 Quaker UN Office, "Peacebuilding and the Roles of Civil Society Organisations".
27 Quaker UN Office, "The United Nations and the Prevention of Violent Conflict".
28 Bellamy, *Global Politics and the Responsibility to Protect*, 111.
29 Welsh, Quinton-Brown, and MacDiarmid, "Brazil's 'Responsibility While Protecting' Proposal".

30 Bellamy, *Global Politics and the Responsibility to Protect*, 113.
31 Ibid., 113, 119–20.
32 Langille, *Bridging the Commitment–Capacity Gap*, 84–8.
33 Global Action to Prevent War, "UNEPS Research, Policy and Outreach Meeting".
34 Holt and Berkman, *The Impossible Mandate?* 8; Holt, Taylor and Kelly, "Protecting Civilians in the Context of UN Peacekeeping Operations", 99–100, 121.
35 Francis and Popovski, "Responsibility to Protect and the Protection of Civilians", 91.
36 The Challenges Partnership, the Asia Pacific Civil–Military Centre of Excellence, "Challenges of Strengthening the Protection of Civilians in Multidimensional Peace Operations: Summary Report", 8.
37 Francis and Popovski, "Responsibility to Protect and the Protection of Civilians", 85–6, 93.
38 Holt and Berkman, *The Impossible Mandate?* 5.
39 Bellamy, Williams and Griffin, *Understanding Peacekeeping*, 57.
40 UN News Centre, "Tanzanian Troops Arrive in Eastern Dr Congo as Part of UN Intervention Brigade".
41 UN Security Council, *Resolution 1856*, para. 2; Reynaert, "Monuc/Monusco and Civilian Protection in the Kivus".
42 Holt, Taylor, and Kelly, "Protecting Civilians in the Context of UN Peacekeeping Operations", 99, 202.
43 Zuber, "The Politics of 'Doing Something'".
44 Kulish and Sengupta, "New UN Brigade's Aggressive Stance in Africa Brings Success, and Risks".
45 Francis and Popovski, "Responsibility to Protect and the Protection of Civilians", 91.
46 Zuber, "The Politics of 'Doing Something'".
47 IRIN, "NGOs Concerned About New Drc Intervention Brigade".
48 UN Security Council, *Resolution 2139*.
49 Thakur, *The United Nations, Peace and Security*; Knight, "The Future of the UN Security Council".
50 Kennedy, *The Parliament of Man*, 76.
51 Bellamy, *Responsibility to Protect*, 23.
52 Zuber, "Restraining Order: Dampening Enthusiasm for the Use of the Veto on Atrocity Crimes".
53 Cagaptay, "The Case for Organizing a Military Force from Muslim Countries to Intervene in Syria".
54 Kaldor, "Libya: War or Peacekeeping".
55 Council for Security Cooperation in the Asia Pacific, "Study Group on the Responsibility to Protect", 3.
56 Ibid., para. 52.
57 Bellamy, "Whither the Responsibility to Protect?", 158–60.
58 Bachmann, "The African Standby Force".
59 Robinson, "The Eastern Africa Standby Force", 7.
60 Engel and Porto, "The African Union's New Peace and Security Architecture", 20.
61 Okek, "An Evolving Model of African-Led Peace Support Operations?"; Boutellis and Williams, "Peace Operations, the African Union, and the United Nations", 13.
62 Burgess, "The African Standby Force", 129.
63 Bachmann, "The African Standby Force"; Ramsbotham *et al.*, *The Implementation of the Joint Africa/G8 Plan*.
64 Cilliers, *The African Standby Force*, 18.
65 UN General Assembly, *In Larger Freedom*, paras 213 and 215.
66 Cilliers, *The African Standby Force*, 13.
67 Boutellis and Williams, "Peace Operations, the African Union, and the United Nations".

68 The UN involvement is by no means a panacea to the ASF. Some commentators insist that for the ASF to be fully operational and to reflect the needs and aspirations of its main stakeholders – the Africans – AU member states must make a conscious effort to increase their political, conceptual and, especially, financial commitment. Bachmann, "The African Standby Force?"
69 UN General Assembly, *A More Secure World*; UN General Assembly, *2005 World Summit Outcome*.
70 Johansen and Mendlovitz, "The Role of Enforcement of Law in the Establishment of a New International Order"; Langille, *Preparing for a UN Emergency Peace Service*; Clark and Sohn, *Introduction to World Peace through World Law*.

References

Annan, Kofi A. *Prevention of Armed Conflict*. New York: United Nations, 2001.
Bachmann, Olaf. "The African Standby Force: External Support to an 'African Solution to African Problems'?". *IDS Research Reports* 2011, no. 67 (2011): 1–73.
Bellamy, Alex J. "Whither the Responsibility to Protect? Humanitarian Intervention and the 2005 World Summit". *Ethics & International Affairs* 20, no. 2 (2006): 143–69.
Bellamy, Alex. *Responsibility to Protect: The Global Effort to End Mass Atrocities*. Cambridge: Polity, 2009.
Bellamy, Alex. *Global Politics and the Responsibility to Protect: From Words to Deeds*. London: Routledge, 2011.
Bellamy, Alex J., Paul Williams and Stuart Griffin. *Understanding Peacekeeping*. Cambridge: Polity Press, 2004.
Boutellis, Arthur and Paul D. Williams. "Peace Operations, the African Union, and the United Nations: Toward More Effective Partnerships". International Peace Institute, April 2013 . www.ipinst.org/~ipinst/media/pdf/publications/ipi_rpt_peace_operations_revised.pdf.
Burgess, Stephen. "The African Standby Force, Genocide, and International Relations Theory". *Genocide Studies and Prevention* 6, no. 2 (2011): 121–33.
Cagaptay, Soner. "The Case for Organizing a Military Force from Muslim Countries to Intervene in Syria". *The New Republic*, 9 February 2012. www.tnr.com/article/world/100514/syria-bosnia-soft-intervention-velveteen.
Challenges Partnership, the Challenges Secretariat, the Asia Pacific Civil–Military Centre of Excellence. "Challenges of Strengthening the Protection of Civilians in Multidimensional Peace Operations: Summary Report". 3rd International Forum for the Challenges of Peace Operations. Challenges Partnership, the Challenges Secretariat, the Asia Pacific Civil–Military Centre of Excellence, 27–29 April 2010. www.challengesforum.org/cms/images/pdf/Challenges_Forum_2010_SummaryReport.pdf.
Chandran, Rahul, Jake Sherman, Bruce Jones, with Shepard Forman, Anne le More, Yoshino Funaki, and Andrew Hart. "Rapid Deployment of Civilians for Peace Operations: Status, Gaps, and Options". April NYU Center on International Cooperation, 2009. www.cic.nyu.edu/peacebuilding/docs/Deployment_annex_links.pdf.
Cilliers, Jakkie. *The African Standby Force: An Update on Progress*. Pretoria: Institute for Security Studies, 2008.
Clark, Grenville, and Louis Sohn. *Introduction to World Peace through World Law*. Cambridge, Mass: Harvard University Press, 1958.
Coning, Cedric de. *Civilian Capacity in United Nations Peacekeeping and Peacebuilding Missions*. Policy Brief 4. Norwegian Institute of International Affairs (NUPI), 2011.

Coning, Cedric de. "Civilian Peacekeeping Capacity: Mobilizing Partners to Match Supply and Demand". *International Peacekeeping* 18, no. 5 (2011): 577–92.

Council for Security Cooperation in the Asia Pacific. "Study Group on the Responsibility to Protect: Final Report". Council for Security Cooperation in the Asia Pacific, June 2011. www.r2pasiapacific.org/documents/CSCAP%20Study%20Group%20on%20RtoP%20 Report%20FINAL.pdf.

Deschamp, Brian. "Victims of Violence: A Review of the Protection of Civilians Concept and Its Relevance to Unhcr's Mandate". PDES/2010/11. UNHCR Policy Development and Evaluation Service, September 2010. www.unhcr.org/cgi-bin/texis/vtx/search?page=search&docid=4c99d0ba9&query=bryan%20protection%20of%20civilians.

Engel, Ulf and Joao Gomes Porto. "The African Union's New Peace and Security Architecture: Towards an Evolving Security Regime". In *Regional Organizations in African Security*, edited by Fredrik Soderbaum and Rodrigo Tavares, 14–28. Abingdon, UK: Routledge, 2013.

Evans, Gareth. *Cooperating for Peace: The Global Agenda for the 1990s and Beyond*. Sydney: Allen & Unwin, 1993.

Francis, Angus and Vesselin Popovski. "Responsibility to Protect and the Protection of Civilians: A View from United Nations". In *The Laws of Protection: Protection of Civilians and the Responsibility to Protect*, edited by Angus Francis, Vesselin Popovski and Charles Sampford, 82–97. Tokyo: United Nations University Press, 2012.

Ghani, Ashraf and Clare Lockhart. *Fixing Failed States: A Framework for Rebuilding a Fractured World*. Oxford: Oxford University Press, 2009.

Global Action to Prevent War. "UNEPS Research, Policy and Outreach Meeting". Convened at Rutgers Law School, Rutgers University, New Jersey, 30 March 2007.

Heemskerk, Renske. "Background Paper: Getting the Peacebuilding Commission Off the Ground – How to Include Civil Society on the Ground". Organised by Friedrich-Ebert-Stiftung New York Office and the Global Partnership for the Prevention of Armed Conflict, New York, 5 September 2006.

Holt, Victoria K. and Tobias C. Berkman. *The Impossible Mandate? Military Preparedness, the Responsibility to Protect and Modern Peace Operations*. Washington DC: The Henry L. Stimson Center, 2006.

Holt, Victoria, Glyn Taylor and Max Kelly. "Protecting Civilians in the Context of UN Peacekeeping Operations: Successes, Setbacks and Remaining Challenges". Independent study jointly commissioned by the Department of Peacekeeping Operations and the Office for the Coordination of Humanitarian Affairs, 2009. www.peacekeepingbestpractices.unlb.org/pbps/Library/Protecting%20Civilians%20in%20the%20 Context%20of%20UN%20PKO.pdf

Integrated Assessment and Planning Working Group, UN. *Integrated Assessment and Planning Handbook*. UN Policy on Integrated Assessment and Planning, December 2013.

Integrated Regional Information Networks. "NGOs Concerned About New Drc Intervention Brigade". *IRIN*, 31 May, 2013. www.irinnews.org/report/98140/ngos-concerned-about-new-drc-intervention-brigade.

Johansen, Robert C. and Saul H. Mendlovitz. "The Role of Enforcement of Law in the Establishment of a New International Order: A Proposal for a Transnational Police Force". *Alternatives: Global, Local, Political* 6, no. 2 (1980): 307–37.

Kaldor, Mary. "Libya: War or Peacekeeping". Open Democracy, 5 April 2011. http://fair-andunbalancedblog.blogspot.com/2011/04/libya-war-or-peacekeeping.html.

Kennedy, Paul. *The Parliament of Man: The Past, Present, and Future of the United Nations*. New York: Random House, 2007.

Knight, Andrew. "The Future of the UN Security Council: Questions of Legitimacy and Representation in Multilateral Governance". In *Enhancing Global Governance: Towards a New Diplomacy*, edited by Andrew F. Cooper, John English and Ramesh Thakur, 19–37. Tokyo: United Nations University Press, 2002.

Kulish, Nicholas and Somini Sengupta. "New UN Brigade's Aggressive Stance in Africa Brings Success and Risks". *New York Times*, 12 November, 2013. www.nytimes.com/2013/11/13/world/africa/new-un-brigades-aggressive-stance-in-africa-brings-success-and-risks.html?pagewanted=2&_r=0.

Langille, H. Peter. *Bridging the Commitment–Capacity Gap: A Review of Existing Arrangements and Options for Enhancing UN Rapid Deployment*. New York: Center for UN Reform Education, 2002.

Langille, H. Peter. *Preparing for a UN Emergency Peace Service*. Friedrich Ebert Stiftung, August, 2012. http://library.fes.de/pdf-files/iez/09282.pdf.

Luck, Edward C. "Reforming the United Nations". In *The United Nations: Confronting the Challenges of a Global Society*, edited by Jean E. Krasno, 359–97. Boulder. Colo: Lynne Rienner Publishing, 2004.

Okek, Jide Martyns. "An Evolving Model of African-Led Peace Support Operations? Lessons from Burundi, Sudan (Darfur) and Somalia". In *Peacekeeping in Africa: The Evolving Security Architecture*, edited by Marco Wyss and Thierry Tardy, 37–53. Abingdon, UK: Routledge, 2014.

Penklis, David. "Implications of the 1993 to 2008 Burundi Peace Process for United Nations Peacekeeping Operations". Thesis submitted for the degree of Doctor of Philosophy, The University of Sydney, 2011.

Quaker UN Office. "Peacebuilding and the Roles of Civil Society Organisations: How Does It Look from Geneva?" Quaker House, 4 May 2006. ftp://budgie3.ethz.ch/gcsp-migration09/e/publications/GPP-2010/Background/project_milestones/4%20MAY%2006.pdf.

Quaker UN Office. "The United Nations and the Prevention of Violent Conflict". n.d. www.quno.org/preventionUN.htm.

Ramsbotham, Alex, Alhaji M.S. Bah, Fanny Calder and Chatham House. *The Implementation of the Joint Africa/G8 Plan to Enhance African Capabilities to Undertake Peace Support Operations*. London: Chatham House (2005).

Reynaert, Julie. "Monuc/Monusco and Civilian Protection in the Kivus". International Peace Information Service, 2011. http://reliefweb.int/sites/reliefweb.int/files/reliefweb_pdf/node-390401.pdf.

Robinson, Colin. "The Eastern Africa Standby Force: History and Prospects". *International Peacekeeping* 21, no. 1 (2014): 20–36.

Solli, Audun, Benjamin de Carvalho, Cedric de Coning and Mikkel F. Pedersen. "Training in Vain? Bottlenecks in Deploying Civilians for UN Peacekeeping". *International Peacekeeping* 18, no. 4 (2011): 425–38.

Thakur, Ramesh. *The United Nations, Peace and Security: From Collective Security to the Responsibility to Protect*. Cambridge: Cambridge University Press, 2006.

UN General Assembly. *A More Secure World: Our Shared Responsibility. Report of the Secretary-General's High-Level Panel on Threats, Challenges and Change*. A/59/565 of 2 December 2004.

UN General Assembly. *In Larger Freedom: Towards Development, Security and Human Rights for All. Report of the Secretary-General*. A/59/2005 of 21 March 2005.

UN General Assembly. *Resolution Adopted by the General Assembly: 60/1. 2005 World Summit Outcome*. A/RES/60/1 of 24 October 2005.

UN General Assembly. *Implementing the Responsibility to Protect: Report of the Secretary-General*. A/63/677 of 12 January 2009.

UN News Centre. "Tanzanian Troops Arrive in Eastern Dr Congo as Part of UN Intervention Brigade". *UN News Centre*, 10 May, 2013. www.un.org/apps/news/story.asp?NewsID=44876#.Uv1TivmSyZN.

UN Secretary-General. Cyril Foster Lecture 2011 on "Human Protection and the 21st Century United Nations". UN News Centre, 2 February 2011. www.un.org/apps/news/infocus/sgspeeches/statments_full.asp?statID=1064.

UN Security Council. *Resolution 1856*. S/RES/1856 of 22 December 2008.

UN Security Council. *Resolution 2139*, 22 February 2014.

Welsh, Jennifer, Patrick Quinton-Brown and Victor MacDiarmid. "Brazil's 'Responsibility While Protecting' Proposal: A Canadian Perspective". Canadian Centre for the Responsibility to Protect, 12 July 2013. http://ccr2p.org/?p=616.

Zuber, Robert. "The Politics of 'Doing Something'". 2013. http://gapwblog.wordpress.com/2013/08/.

Zuber, Robert. "Restraining Order: Dampening Enthusiasm for the Use of the Veto on Atrocity Crimes". 30 October 2013, Global Action to Prevent War Blog. http://gapwblog.wordpress.com/tag/responsibility-to-protect/.

Selected bibliography

Acharya, Amitav. "How Ideas Spread: Whose Norms Matter? Norm Localization and Institutional Change in Asian Regionalism". *International Organization* 58, Spring 2004: 239–75.

Asia-Pacific Centre for the Responsibility to Protect. "Implementing the Responsibility to Protect: Asia-Pacific in the 2009 General Assembly Dialogue". Asia-Pacific Centre for the Responsibility to Protect, October 2009. www.r2pasiapacific.org/documents/final_un_ga_debate_july_2009.pdf.

Bellamy, Alex. *Responsibility to Protect: The Global Effort to End Mass Atrocities*. Cambridge: Polity, 2009.

Bellamy, Alex. *Global Politics and the Responsibility to Protect: From Words to Deeds*. London: Routledge, 2011.

Bellamy, Alex J., Paul Williams and Stuart Griffin. *Understanding Peacekeeping*. Second ed. Cambridge: Polity, 2010.

Bowett, D.W. *United Nations Forces: A Legal Study*. New York: Praeger, 1964.

Boutros-Ghali, Boutros. *An Agenda for Peace: Preventive Diplomacy, Peacemaking and Peace-Keeping. Report of the Secretary-General Pursuant to the Statement Adopted by the Summit Meeting of the Security Council on 31 January 1992*. New York: United Nations A/47/277 – S/24111 of 17 June 1992.

Brahimi, Lakhdar. *Report of the Panel on United Nations Peace Operations [Brahimi Report]*. New York: United Nations, 2000.

Breakey, Hugh. "The Protection of Civilians in Armed Conflict: Four Concepts". In *Norms of Protection: Responsibility to Protect, Protection of Civilians and Their Interaction*, edited by Angus Francis, Vesselin Popovski and Charles Sampford, 40–61. Tokyo: United Nations University Press, 2012.

Breakey, Hugh. "The Responsibility to Protect and the Protection of Civilians in Armed Conflict: Overlap and Contrast". In *Norms of Protection: Responsibility to Protect, Protection of Civilians and Their Interaction*, edited by Angus Francis, Vesselin Popovski and Charles Sampford, 62–81. Tokyo: United Nations University Press, 2012.

Caballero-Anthony, Mely and Belinda Chng. "Cyclones and Humanitarian Crises: Pushing the Limits of R2P in Southeast Asia". *Global Responsibility to Protect* 1, no. 2 (2009): 135–55.

Campbell, John L. "Institutional Analysis and the Role of Ideas in Political Economy". *Theory and Society* 27, no. 3 (1998): 377–409.

Caritas Australia, Global Action to Prevent War, Centre for Peace and Conflict Studies. "Right to Protection: Whose Responsibility and How? Summary Report". Caritas Australia, Global Action to Prevent War, Centre for Peace and Conflict Studies,

4 September 2008. http://sydney.edu.au/arts/peace_conflict/research/AH_Conference%20report%202.pdf.

Chandran, Rahul, Jake Sherman, Bruce Jones with Shepard Forman, Anne le More, Yoshino Funaki and Andrew Hart. "Rapid Deployment of Civilians for Peace Operations: Status, Gaps, and Options". NYU Center on International Cooperation, April 2009. www.cic.nyu.edu/peacebuilding/docs/Deployment_annex_links.pdf.

Clark, Grenville and Louis Sohn. *Introduction to World Peace through World Law*. Cambridge, Mass: Harvard University Press, 1958.

Coning, Cedric de. *Civilian Capacity in United Nations Peacekeeping and Peacebuilding Missions*. Policy Brief 4. Norwegian Institute of International Affairs (NUPI), 2011.

Coning, Cedric de. "Civilian Peacekeeping Capacity: Mobilizing Partners to Match Supply and Demand". *International Peacekeeping* 18, no. 5 (2011): 577–92.

Cooper, Andrew F. and John English. "International Commissions and the Mind of Global Governance". In *International Commissions and the Power of Ideas*, edited by Ramesh C. Thakur, Andrew F. Cooper and John English, 1–26. Tokyo: United Nations University Press, 2005.

Council for Security Cooperation in the Asia Pacific. "Study Group on the Responsibility to Protect: Final Report". Council for Security Cooperation in the Asia Pacific, June 2011. www.r2pasiapacific.org/documents/CSCAP%20Study%20Group%20on%20RtoP%20Report%20FINAL.pdf.

Cox, Robert. "Social Forces, States, and World Orders: Beyond International Relations Theory". *Millennium: Journal of International Studies* 10, no. 2 (1981): 126–55.

Cronin, Bruce and Ian Hurd. *The UN Security Council and the Politics of International Authority*. Abingdon, UK: Routledge, 2008.

Durch, William J. *Twenty-First-Century Peace Operations*. Washington DC: United States Institute of Peace Press, 2006.

Durch, William J. "United Nations Police Evolution, Present Capacity and Future Tasks". Prepared for the GRIPS State-Building workshop: 'Organizing police forces in post-conflict peace-support operations.' National Graduate Institute for Policy Studies, 27–28 January 2010. www.3.grips.ac.jp/~pinc/data/10–03.pdf.

Durch, William J. "Cross-Cutting Issues in Protection of Civilians for UN Peace Operations. International Forum for the Challenges of Peace Operations". 27 April 2010. http://challengesforum.org/cms/images/pdf/Forum2010_WilliamDurch.pdf.

Finnemore, Martha and Kathryn Sikkink. "International Norm Dynamics and Political Change". *International Organization* 52, no. 4 (1998): 887–917.

Francis, Angus and Vesselin Popovski. "Responsibility to Protect and the Protection of Civilians: A View from United Nations". In *The Laws of Protection: Protection of Civilians and the Responsibility to Protect*, edited by Angus Francis, Vesselin Popovski and Charles Sampford, 82–97. Tokyo: United Nations University Press, 2012.

Frye, William R. *A United Nations Peace Force*. London: The Carnegie Endowment for International Peace, 1957.

Global Action to Prevent War. "To Prevent Genocide and Crimes against Humanity: Diverse Perspectives on a Standing, Rapid-Reaction UN Emergency Peace Service. Symposium Report on the United Nations Emergency Peace Service Initiative. Convened at Rutgers Law School, Rutgers University, New Jersey, 29 March 2007. www.globalactionpw.org/wp/wp-content/uploads/rutgers_uneps_conference_report_2007.pdf.

Global Action to Prevent War. "Timely Response to the Threat of Mass Atrocities: Implementing the Responsibility to Protect". 2012. www.thesimonsfoundation.ca/highlights/conference-report-timely-response-threat-mass-atrocities-implementing-responsibility-prot.

Global Action to Prevent War and The Project for a UN Emergency Peace Service. *UNEPS in Context: Third Pillar Capacities and First Pillar Responses*. 7 and 8 December 2010. www.globalactionpw.org/wp/wp-content/uploads/uneps-report1.pdf.

Goldstein, Judith and Robert O. Keohane, eds. *Ideas and Foreign Policy: Beliefs, Institutions, and Political Change*. Ithaca, NY: Cornell University Press, 1993.

Government of Canada. *Towards a Rapid Reaction Capability*. Ottawa: Government of Canada. September 1995.

Hamilton, Lee, Gareth Evans, Stanley Hoffmann and Brian Urquhart. "A UN Volunteer Military Force: Four Views". *New York Review of Books*, 24 June, 1993.

Hehir, Aidan. *The Responsibility to Protect: Rhetoric, Reality and the Future of Humanitarian Intervention*. Basingstoke, UK: Palgrave Macmillan, 2012.

Herro, Annie, Wendy Lambourne and David Penklis. "Peacekeeping and Peace Enforcement in Africa: The Potential Contribution of a UN Emergency Peace Service". *African Security Review* 18, no. 1 (2009): 49–62.

Holt, Victoria K. and Tobias C. Berkman. *The Impossible Mandate? Military Preparedness, the Responsibility to Protect and Modern Peace Operations*. Washington DC: The Henry L. Stimson Center, 2006.

Holt, Victoria, Glyn Taylor and Max Kelly. "Protecting Civilians in the Context of UN Peacekeeping Operations: Successes, Setbacks and Remaining Challenges". Independent study jointly commissioned by the UN Department of Peacekeeping Operations and the Office for the Coordination of Humanitarian Affairs, 2009. www.peacekeepingbestpractices.unlb.org/pbps/Library/Protecting%20Civilians%20in%20the%20Context%20of%20UN%20PKO.pdf

Inuzuka, Tadashi. "From Article 9 to Chapter 6½: Perspectives from the Discussion on the Terror Elimination Bill". Paper submitted at the Workshop on the Eradication of Armed Conflict co-sponsored by the Australian Centre for Peace and Conflict Studies, the World Federation of United Nations Associations, and the project for a United Nations Emergency Peace Service, 8–10 February 2008, Brisbane, Australia.

International Coalition for the Responsibility to Protect. "Report on the General Assembly Plenary Debate on the Responsibility to Protect". International Coalition for the Responsibility to Protect, 15 September 2009. www.responsibilitytoprotect.org/ICRtoP%20Report.

International Commission on Intervention and State Sovereignty. *The Responsibility to Protect*. Ottawa: International Development Research Centre, 2001.

Johansen, Robert C. "Expert Discussion of the United Nations Emergency Peace Service: Cuenca Report". In *A United Nations Emergency Peace Service: To Prevent Genocide and Crimes against Humanity*, edited by Robert C. Johansen, 43–74. New York: World Federalist Movement – Institute for Global Policy, 2006.

Johansen, Robert C. "Proposal for a United Nations Emergency Peace Service to Prevent Genocide and Crimes against Humanity". In *A United Nations Emergency Peace Service: To Prevent Genocide and Crimes against Humanity*, edited by Robert C. Johansen, 23–41. New York: World Federalist Movement – Institute for Global Policy, 2006.

Johansen, Robert C., ed. *A United Nations Emergency Peace Service: To Prevent Genocide and Crimes against Humanity*. New York: World Federalist Movement – Institute for Global Policy, 2006.

Johansen, Robert C. and Saul H Mendlovitz. "The Role of Enforcement of Law in the Establishment of a New International Order: A Proposal for a Transnational Police Force". *Alternatives: Global, Local, Political* 6, no. 2 (1980): 307–37.

Krasner, Stephen. *Sovereignty: Organized Hypocrisy*. Princeton, NJ: Princeton University Press, 1999.

Selected bibliography

Kuperman, Alan J. "Humanitarian Hazard: Revisiting Doctrines of Intervention". *Harvard International Review* 26, no. 1 (2004): 64–9.

Kuperman, Alan J. "A Model Humanitarian Intervention? Reassessing Nato's Libya Campaign". *International Security* 38, no. 1 (2013): 105–36.

Keck, Margaret E. and Kathryn Sikkink. *Activists Beyond Borders: Advocacy Networks in International Politics*. Ithaca, NY: Cornell University Press, 1998.

Kinloch, Stephen. *A UN 'Legion': Between Utopia and Reality*. Abingdon, UK: Routledge, 2012.

Langille, H. Peter. *Bridging the Commitment–Capacity Gap: A Review of Existing Arrangements and Options for Enhancing UN Rapid Deployment*. New York: Center for UN Reform Education, 2002.

Langille, H. Peter. "Preventing Genocide". In *The World and Darfur: International Response to Crimes against Humanity in Western Sudan*, edited by Amanda Grzyb, 281–327. Montreal: McGill Queens University Press, 2009.

Langille, H. Peter. *Preparing for a UN Emergency Peace Service*. Friedrich Ebert Stiftung, August 2012. http://library.fes.de/pdf-files/iez/09282.pdf.

Leurdijk, Dick A., ed. *A UN Rapid Deployment Brigade: Strengthening the Capacity for Quick Response*. The Hague: Netherlands Institute of International Relations, 1995.

Lie, Trygve. *In the Cause of the Peace: Seven Years with the United Nations*. New York: The Macmilliam Company, 1954.

Miller, Andrew S. "Universal Soldiers: UN Standing Armies and the Legal Alternatives". *Georgetown Law Journal* 81 (1992): 773–828.

Morgenthau, Hans J. *Politics among Nations: The Struggle for Power and Peace*. Fourth ed. New York: Knopf, 1948.

Morgenthau, Hans J. *The Decline of Domestic Politics*. Chicago: University of Chicago Press, 1958.

Nambiar, Satish. "Afterword". In *A United Nations Emergency Peace Service: To Prevent Genocide and Crimes against Humanity*, edited by Robert C. Johansen. New York: World Federalist Movement – Institute for Global Policy, 2006.

Penklis, David. "Implications of the 1993 to 2008 Burundi Peace Process for United Nations Peacekeeping Operations". Thesis submitted for the degree of Doctor of Philosophy, The University of Sydney 2011.

Pattison, James. "Humanitarian Intervention and a Cosmopolitan UN Force". *Journal of International Political Theory* 4, no. 1 (2008): 126–45.

Pattison, James. *Humanitarian Intervention and the Responsibility to Protect: Who Should Intervene?* Oxford: Oxford University Press, 2010.

Roberts, Adam. "Proposals for UN Standing Forces: A Critical History". In *The United Nations Security Council and War: The Evolution of Thought and Practice since 1945*, edited by Vaughan Lowe, Adam Roberts, Jennifer Welsh and Dominik Zaum, 99–130. New York: Oxford University Press, 2008.

Robinson, Colin. "The Eastern Africa Standby Force: History and Prospects". *International Peacekeeping* 21, no. 1 (2014): 20–36.

Schwebel, Stephen M. *Justice in International Law*. Cambridge: Cambridge University Press, 1994.

Solli, Audun, Benjamin de Carvalho, Cedric de Coning and Mikkel F. Pedersen. "Training in Vain? Bottlenecks in Deploying Civilians for UN Peacekeeping". *International Peacekeeping* 18, no. 4 (2011): 425–38.

Suthanthiraraj, Kavitha and Mariah Quinn. *Standing for Change in Peacekeeping Operations: Project for a United Nations Emergency Peace Service (UNEPS)*. New York: Global Action to Prevent War, 2009.

Thakur, Ramesh. *The Responsibility to Protect: Norms, Laws and the Use of Force in International Politics*. London: Routledge, 2011.
United Nations. *Charter of the United Nations*. New York: United Nations, 1945.
United Nations Department of Peacekeeping Operations and Department of Field Support. "United Nations Peacekeeping Operations Principles and Guidelines". New York: United Nations, 2008.
United Nations Department of Peacekeeping Operations and Department of Field Support. *DPKO/DFS Lessons Learned Note on the Protection of Civilians in UN Peacekeeping Operations: Dilemmas, Emerging Practices and Lessons*. New York: United Nations, 2010.
UN Economic and Social Council. *Resolution 2004/5: Strengthening of the Coordination of Emergency Humanitarian Assistance of the United Nations*. 2005/4 of 15 July 2005.
UN General Assembly. *Supplement to an Agenda for Peace: Position Paper of the Secretary-General on the Occasion of the Fiftieth Anniversary of the United Nations*. A/50/60 of 25 January 1995.
UN General Assembly. *Report of the Panel on United Nations Peace Operations*. A/55/305 of 21 August 2000.
UN General Assembly. *A More Secure World: Our Shared Responsibility. Report of the Secretary-General's High-Level Panel on Threats, Challenges and Change*. A/59/565 of 2 December 2004.
UN General Assembly. *Resolution Adopted by the General Assembly: 60/1. 2005 World Summit Outcome*. A/RES/60/1 of 24 October 2005.
UN General Assembly. *Implementing the Responsibility to Protect: Report of the Secretary-General*. A/63/677 of 12 January 2009.
UN Security Council. *Resolution 1325*. S/RES/1325 of 31 October 2000.
UN Security Council. *Protection of Civilians in Armed Conflict*. S/PV.5703 of 22 June 2007.
Urquhart, Brian. "For a U.N. Volunteer Military Force". *New York Review of Books*, 10 June 1993, 3–4.
Weiss, T. G. *What's Wrong with the United Nations and How to Fix It*. Second ed. Malden, Mass: Polity, 2012.
Wendt, A. "Anarchy Is What States Make of It: The Social Construction of Power Politics". *International Organization* 46, no. 2 (1992): 391–425.
Wendt, Alexander. "Constructing International Politics". *International Security* (1995): 71–81.
Wendt, Alexander. *Social Theory of International Politics*. Cambridge: Cambridge University Press, 1999.
World Federalist Movement. *UNEPS Backgrounder*. n.d. www.worldfederalistscanada.org/uneps%20backgrounder.pdf.
Zuber, Robert and David Curran. "Peacekeeping and Rapid Reaction: Towards the Establishment of Cosmopolitan Capacities for Rapid Deployment". Division of Peace Studies at the University of Bradford, Global Action to Prevent War and Armed Conflict, the World Federalist Movement Canada, 8 July 2013. www.bradford.ac.uk/ssis/media/ssis/peacestudies/Bradford-Write-Up-Sept.pdf

Index

Aceh, Indonesia 66, 99
Acharya, Amitav 38, 47, 48–9, 100, 104
Ackermann, Alice 63
African Standby Force (ASF) 100, 148–9
African Union (AU) 3, 28, 138, 148; Peace and Security Council in Ethiopia 149
Agenda for Peace (Boutros-Ghali) 19
Amnesty International 46, 62
ancient Greece 15
Angola 20
Annan, Kofi 18; *In Larger Freedom* report 149
armed conflict, prevention of *see* conflict prevention
armed forces *see* military; national militaries; troops
Arusha Peace Accords 20
Association of Southeast Asian Nations (ASEAN) 6, 60, 65, 76; Intergovernmental Commission on Human Rights 76
atrocities 27, 41, 42, 44, 46; prevention of 2, 5, 8, 27, 38, 43, 45, 50, 58, 68, 141; (direct prevention 42, 61, 64–5; structural prevention 42, 60–3, 64)
Australia 27; Regional Assistance Mission to Solomon Islands 101; and regional peacekeeping 101
Austria 27
authorisation of UNEPS 43, 44, 50, 84, 85, 86, 106, 144–5, 146
Axworthy, Lloyd 25

Badescu, Cristina G. 39
balance of consequences criterion 23
Ban Ki-moon 41, 42, 60, 105, 138, 139
Barber, Lois 26, 28
Beck, Ulrich 76
Belgium 27

Bellamy, Alex 39, 64, 79, 81, 140, 141, 146–7
bilateral economic relationships 80, 86
Bosnia 1, 21, 23, 123
Boutellis, Arthur 149
Boutros-Ghali, Boutros 150; *An Agenda for Peace* 19
Brahimi Report (*Report of the Panel on UN Peace Operations*) 3, 21
Brazil 27
Breakey, Hugh 43, 44
Britain *see* United Kingdom (UK)
Brunei 62
Burundi 140

C34 (UN Special Committee on Peacekeeping Operations) 129
Cabarello-Anthony, Mely 67
Cagaptay, Soner 147
Cambodia 20, 62, 76
Cameroon 27, 28
Campbell, John 46
Canada, *Towards a Rapid Reaction Capability* report 22–3
Capstone doctrine 105, 107
Carlsson, Ingvar 107
Cassidy, Fikry 62
Central African Republic (CAR) 46, 138
Centre for Peace and Conflict Studies (University of Sydney) 29
Chad 138
Chandran, Rahul 138
Charlesworth, Hilary 82
Chesterman, Simon 44
China 119
Chng, Belinda 67
Chomsky, Noam 78
Cillers, Jakkie 149
Citizens for Global Solutions 25, 29

Index 163

civilian peacekeepers 2, 21, 38, 58, 121, 126, 138–41, 142; deployment problems 3, 25, 139; duplication of efforts 139–40; inadequate numbers of 47, 50; recruitment 139; separation from military 123–4; training 3, 25
civilians, protection of 21, 44–5, 46, 50, 116, *see also* Protection of Civilians (POC), R2P
Clark, Grenville 17, 126
classical realism 77, 78
Cold War period 16–18
Coleman, Katharina P. 98
Collier, Paul 62
Collins, Robin 127
Commission on Global Governance 107
communications systems 3
composition of UNEPS 115, 120, 121–6, 130
conflict prevention 8, 45–6, 50, 59, 116–17, 128, 140, 141
Congo: UN operations in (1960 to 1964) 17; *see also* Democratic Republic of the Congo
Coning, Cedric de 138–9, 139
consent-based intervention 84–5, 86, 143, 146
constructivism 39, 47
Cooper, Andrew F. 41
corruption, UN 97
Corten, Olivier 44
cosmopolitans/cosmopolitanism 77, 78, 80–1, 84, 86, 115, 120–6, 147
cost of UNEPS 8–9, 38, 47, 50, 83, 116, 119, 120, 127–9, 131
Costa Vaz, Alcides 26, 28
Côte d'Ivoire 96, 121–2
Council for Security and Cooperation in the Asia Pacific (CSCAP) 148
Cox, Robert 47
Crawford, Neta 39
Crimea, Russian intervention in 78
crimes against humanity 2, 4, 5, 7, 26, 29, 42, 45, 47, 60, 66, 79, 148
critical theory 47
Cronin, Bruce 95, 97
Cuenca conference (2005) 26, 41, 43, 45, 59, 80

Dallaire, Romeo 20, 127
Darfur 1, 29, 103, 124, 129; African Union/United Nations Hybrid Operation in 3
Davies, Lord David 15
Dean, Jonathan 27
Delian League 15

Democratic Republic of the Congo (DRC) 85, 117, 129, 144, 145
democratisation 62, 141
deployment delays 2–3, 21, 25, 46, 116, 118, 120, 139
diplomacy 18, 20
direct prevention of conflict/atrocities 42, 61, 64–5
Doyle, Michael 122–3
Draft Statute for the Formation and Operation of the United Nations Emergency Peace Service 29
DRC *see* Democratic Republic of the Congo (DRC)
Dumbarton Oaks Conference (Washington DC, 1944) 4

EarthAction 26
East Timor 23, 76, 85, 94, 101–2, 123
economic breakdown 64
economic growth and development 62, 141
economic relationships, bilateral 80, 86
ECOSOC *see* UN Economic and Social Council
English, John 41
Ethiopia 149
ethnic cleansing 1, 2, 23, 81, 148
European Union Battlegroups 3, 100, 103
European Union (EU) 138; Operation Artemis in DRC (2003) 85
Evans, Gareth 39, 95, 119

Falk, Richard 25
Finnemore, Martha 39
Fiott, Daniel 28
force: non-use of 58–70, 96, 147; use of 2, 8, 16, 43, 44, 68, 74–88; (as doing more harm than good 74, 79–80, 83–4, 86; and host country consent 84–5, 86)
Forced Migration 67–8
Forsberg, Randy 27
France 4
Francis, Angus J. 44
Free Aceh Movement (GAM) 99
French Foreign Legion 4
Friedrich-Ebert-Stiftung 28
Friends of Rapid Deployment (FORD) 24
Frye, William R. 18, 120, 129
funding structure of UNEPS 83, 85, 86, 96, 116, 129, 131, 146

GAM (*Gerakan Aceh Merdeka*) 99
GAPW *see* Global Action to Prevent War (GAPW)

Gbabgo, Laurent 96, 122
gender 5, 63
genocide 1, 2, 4, 5, 7, 26, 29, 42, 45, 60, 63, 74, 78, 144, 148, 150; Kosovo 81; preconditions for 64; Rwanda 1, 20, 21, 118, 127, 130
Genocide Convention 42
Genocide and Crimes Against Humanity symposium (2003) 25
Gilmore, Jonathan 8, 126, 127
Glanville, Luke 75
Global Action to Prevent War (GAPW) 6, 25, 27, 28, 29, 30, 42, 44, 46
Global Conference on the Prevention of Genocide (Montreal, 2007) 28
Global Partnership for the Prevention of Armed Conflict (GPPAC) 141
Goldstein, Judith 47
GPPAC *see* Global Partnership for the Prevention of Armed Conflict
Greece 68
Group of 77 (G77) 93, 94

Haass, Richard N. 126
Habibie, B.J. 85, 101
Haiti 66
Hammarskjøld, Dag 25
Hehir, Aidan 106
Helms, Jesse 117
Henry IV of France 15
Henry Dunant Centre 99
High Level Panel on Threats, Challenges and Change (2004) 130, 141
Holzgrefe, J.L. 44
Howard, John 77–8, 93, 102
human rights 5, 23, 38, 39, 61, 74, 76
Human Rights Watch 122
human security 62
humanitarian assistance 5, 24, 25, 45, 59, 66, 67, 68, 121, 123, 125, 146
humanitarian intervention 18, 23, 44, 79, 81, 92, 103, 108
Humanitarian POC 45
Hurd, Ian 95, 97

ICISS *see* International Commission on Intervention and State Sovereignty
identity 39, 40
impartiality 2, 96, 107, 147
imperialism 78
India 119
Indonesia 27, 76, 101–2, 103
Institute for World Order 18
Integrated Assessment Planning Team 140

intelligence 3
interests 39, 40; *see also* national interests
International Coalition for the Responsibility to Protect 29
International Commission on Intervention and State Sovereignty (ICISS) 23, 43, 44, 59, 83, 84, 85
International Committee of the Red Cross 45
international community 7, 9, 23, 42, 43, 50, 58, 60, 67, 74, 116
International Criminal Tribunal for the former Yugoslavia 42
International Criminal Tribunal for Rwanda 41
International Force for East Timor (INTERFET) 85
international human rights law 5, 44, 60
international humanitarian law 5, 38, 44, 60
International Law Association 59
International Peace Research Association 28
international (police) force 14, 15, 18, 19
Inuzuka, Tadashi 4, 28, 98
Ira Wallach Fund for the Eradication of Genocide 27
Iraq 66, 96; US-led invasion of (2003) 82, 98
Italy 15

Johansen, Robert 18, 24, 26, 41–2, 43, 45, 59, 80, 106
just cause criterion 23, 44
just war doctrine 23, 83

Kaldor, Mary 123, 147
Kant, Immanuel 94
Keck, Margaret E. 48
Kennedy, Paul 146
Keohane, Robert O. 47, 97
Khagram, Sangeev 39
Kinloch, Stephen 7, 106, 129
Koops, Joachim 28
Kosovo, NATO intervention in 44, 79, 81
Kouchner, Bernard 120
Krasner, Stephen 75
Kratochwil, Friedrich V. 40, 47
Kraus, Don 25, 26, 29
Krook, Mona L. 48
Kuperman, Alan 79, 83

Lambourne, Wendy 124
Langille, Peter 4, 14, 22, 24–6, 28, 30, 43, 45, 119–20, 127, 142
Laos 62

Index 165

last resort criterion 23
Le Roy, Alain 130
League of Nations 15
Lebanon 129
Lee Kuan Yew 76
legitimacy 98; purposive 98; UN 94, 95–7, 106, 120, 147
Leurdijk, Dick 96
Liberia 45, 63
Libya 3, 79, 82, 117, 123, 147
Lie, Trygve 4, 16–17, 59, 79, 95, 128–9, 129
Lito, Melina 29
localisation, theory of 38, 47, 48–9
logistics 3
Luck, Edward 137

M23 rebel group 145
Macedonia 117, 128
Mahathir bin Mohamad 76
Malaysia 76, 81, 82
McGovern, James 123
Mendez, Juan 4, 44
Mendlovitz, Saul 18, 25, 26, 27, 29, 43
Miler, Andrew 7
military 2, 21, 25, 38, 58, 121; separation from civilian peacekeeping 123–4; *see also* national militaries; troops
Military and Police Advisors Community in the Permanent Mission of Austria to the UN 28
Mindanao 66
MONUSCO 144, 145
moral hazard 79
Morgenthau, Hans 77, 78, 93
Mozambique 19, 20
multidimensional service 2, 24, 38, 47, 50, 115, 118, 121–3, 124, 125, 137–8, 141–2
multifunctional service 24, 47, 50, 115, 121, 122, 137–8, 141–2
multilateralism 93, 98, 106, 108, 147
Multinational Standby High Readiness Brigade 2
Myanmar 66, 79

Nambiar, Satish 26, 28, 125
national interests 77, 84, 95
national militaries 127, 131, 150; availability of 15–16, 19, 118; strengthening of 8
NATO (North Atlantic Treaty Organisation) 22, 24, 100, 103; intervention in Kosovo 44, 79, 81; intervention in Libya 3, 79, 82, 123, 147
natural disasters 5, 45, 50, 58, 65–8, 138, 142, 150
neocolonialism 3
Netherlands 15; report on UN rapid reaction capability 22
neutrality 2, 96, 147
New Zealand 24
Non-Aligned Movement 77, 96
non-interference 61–2, 65
non-intervention 74, 75–7, 80–1, 86
non-use of force 58–70, 96, 147
non-violence 61, 68
non-violent Pillar Two measures 58, 63–5
Nordic Coordinated Arrangement for Military Peace Support 2
normative ideas of UNEPS proposal 38, 40, 41–6, 48, 50; armed conflict prevention 45–6, 50; atrocities prevention 42, 43, 50; civilian protection 44–5, 50; humanitarian assistance 45; responsibility to protect 41–2; strengthening of UN as principal institution for conflict prevention 46, 50
norms 38, 39–40, 47–9; constitutive function 39; diffusion of 48; framing 49; global 39; grafting and pruning 49, 50; localisation of 48–9, 50; prescriptive 39; universal 48
North Atlantic Treaty Organisation *see* NATO
Nuclear Age Peace Foundation 25, 27, 42
Nye, Joseph S. 97

Obama, Barack 41
Office of the High Commissioner for Human Rights (OHCHR) 6
Ogata, Sadako 120
Organization for Security and Co-operation in Europe 138
Ouattara, Alassane 122
Oxfam 67

Pace, William 25, 26, 102
Packenham, Lord 17
patriotic norms 74, 77–9
Pattison, James 8, 83–4, 106
peace enforcement units 19
Peace of Westphalia (1648) 75
peacebuilding 24, 58, 60–3, 64, 68, 125, 140, 141, 142
Peacekeeping POC 44–5

Penklis, David 123–4, 140, 142
Penn, William 15
Philippines 62, 66
POC *see* Protection of Civilians
Polanyi, John 22
police 2, 3, 25, 38, 47, 50, 58, 59, 121, 123, 124, 126, 142; *see also* international (police) force
Potts, Michael 19
poverty 62, 63, 65, 78
preventative strategies 116–17, 128, 140, 141; *see also* atrocities, prevention of; conflict prevention
problem-solving ideas of UNEPS proposal 38, 40, 46–7, 50, 85, 107; inadequate personnel numbers 47, 50; rapid deployment 46–7, 50; size and cost of service 47, 50
proportionality of the response criterion 23, 44
Protection of Civilians (POC) 44–5, 58, 75, 81–3, 85, 86, 130, 142, 143–5, 150
Pugh, Michael 117
Putin, Vladimir 78

Qatar 147
Quaker UN Office (QUNO) 141
Quinn, Mariah 27–8

R2P 1–2, 7, 14, 23–4, 28, 29, 30, 38, 44, 50, 62, 85, 86, 140, 141, 144–5; and moral hazard 79; normative status of 39; Pillars 41, 42, 43, 58, 60, 63–5, 68, 75, 81–2, 84, 145; as a principle 39; state and 41–2, 60; vs POC missions 81–3
R2P-plus 58, 67, 68
radical ideology, prevention of 64
rapid response capability 14, 22, 25, 46–7, 50, 116, 117, 118, 120, 125, 139, 142
Reagan, Ronald 4
recruitment, civilian peacekeepers 139
Rees, Stuart 6, 61
regional organisations: as authorising body 43; response to crises 8
regional/sub-regional peace service 68, 100–5, 107–8, 138, 147–9, 150; advantages of 100–3; dominance by regional hegemon 103, 108; shortcomings of 103; and UN hybrid arrangement 104–5, 108–9, 148–9
Report of the Panel on UN Peace Operations (*Brahimi Report*) 3, 21
responsibility to protect *see* R2P

Richmond, Oliver 123
Rieff, David 98
right authority criterion 23, 44
right intention criterion 23, 44
Riker, James V. 39
Risse, Thomas 39
Roberts, Adam 7, 126–7, 128
Rome Statute 42
Ropp, Stephen C. 39
Rousseau, Jean-Jacques 15
Rubinstein, Robert A. 96–7
Rudd, Kevin 95
Ruggie, John 47
rule of law 60, 63, 64, 121
Russia: Crimean intervention 78; and Syrian intervention 80
Rwanda 20–1, 22, 23, 30, 85, 118, 124; genocide 1, 20, 21, 118, 127, 130; International Criminal Tribunal for 42

safe havens 45, 147
Sambanis, Nicholas 122–3
Sandholtz, Wayne 98
Saudi Arabia 147
Schwarzenberger, Georg 79
security force 123–4, 125, 137–8, 141–2, 146, 150
security sector reforms 42, 64
Shangri-La Dialogue (2008) 67
Sikkink, Kathryn 39, 48
Simons Foundation 27
size of UNEPS 47, 50, 115–16, 120, 126–7, 129–30, 131, 138
social justice 61
Sohn, Louis 17, 126
Solomon, Hussein 26, 28
Solomon Islands 101
Somalia 1, 3, 19, 20, 22, 66, 85, 96
South Africa 27, 119, 128–9
South Korea 24, 118
sovereignty 66, 74, 75, 80–1; mutual respect for 62; as responsibility 23, 42, 60, 75; Westphalian 75, 76
Soviet Union 4, 59, 129
Sri Lanka 1
standby arrangements 2, 14, 17, 19, 22, 118
Standby High-Readiness Brigade 21
Standing Police Capacity 60
Stassen, Harold 15
states, responsibility to protect 41–2, 60
structural prevention of conflict/atrocities 42, 60–3, 64
Sudan 124; Darfur region *see* Darfur

Index   167

Suthanthiraraj, Kavitha 6, 27–8
Sweden 2, 15
Syria 1, 80, 146

Tamil Tigers 1
Tang Siew Mun 82
Tanyi, Christian 28, 29
territorial integrity 66, 74, 75, 77, 81
Teson, Fernando 74
Thakur, Ramesh 98, 105
Than Shwe 79
Tobin tax 129
training, personnel 3, 25, 116
transnational advocacy networks (TAN) 26–7
Treaty of Amity and Cooperation 61
troops 38, 137, 142; numbers 3, 47, 50, 126; training 3
True, Jacqui 48
Turkey 68, 147

Ukraine 78
UN 92–100; composition of key bodies 87, 93–5; corruption 97; creation of 15; failure to follow rules 95–7, 108; ideals and moral authority, support for 98–100, 108; inefficiency/ ineffectiveness 97, 107, 108; legitimacy of 94, 95–7, 106, 120, 147; and regional peace service hybrid arrangement 104–5, 108–9, 148–9
un-armed standing service 58–69, 137
UN Assistance Mission in Rwanda (UNAMIR) 20–1, 118, 124
UN Central Emergency Response Fund 67
UN Charter 15–16, 19, 43, 93, 95, 107; Chapter (VI) 21, 59; Chapter (VII) 14, 15, 16, 17, 21, 24, 29, 43, 45, 116, 143; Chapter (VIII) 104; and creation a standing force 15–16
UN Department of Field Support (UNDFS) 118, 124, 143
UN Department of Peacekeeping Operations (UNDPKO) 3, 6, 24, 59–60, 105, 108, 118, 124, 128, 143, 144; *Framework for Drafting Comprehensive POC Strategies in UN Peacekeeping Operations* 143
UN Disaster Assessment and Coordination Team 67
UN Economic and Social Council (ECOSOC) 67, 140, 141
UN Emergency Force (UNEF), first deployment (1956) 17

UN Emergency Peace Service: activities when not deployed 115, 119–20, 130; advocacy workshops and roundtables 82–3; authorisation body 43, 44, 50, 84, 106, 144–5, 146; as complementary to other UN programmes/activities 115, 118; composition of 115, 120, 121–6, 130; contextualised approach to 27–8; cosmopolitan perspectives on 78, 80–1, 84, 86, 115, 120–6; cost of 8–9, 38, 47, 83, 115, 116, 119, 120, 127–9, 131; distinguished from other programmes/ services 145, 150; funding structure 83, 85, 86, 96, 116, 129, 131, 146; historical and legal context 8, 14–34; increasing support for 83–5, 106–8; multidimensional 38, 47, 50, 116, 121–3, 125, 137–8, 141–2; multifunctional 47, 50, 116, 121, 122, 137–8, 141–2; network of advocates 14, 25–9, 30; normative ideas 38, 40, 41–6, 48, 50; problem-solving ideas 38, 40, 46–7, 85, 107; proposal 4–5, 14, 25–9, 30; comprising of security forces 123–4, 125, 137–8, 141–2, 145; as a service 121–3, 137; size of 47, 50, 115–16, 120, 126–7, 129–30, 131, 138; and strengthening of UN peace operations 46, 108, 130; as an un-armed service 58–69, 137; and use of force 8, 43, 44, 74–87; as waste of resources 117, 119–20; UN Emergency Service (UN ES) 14, 24–5, 28, 30
UN Force Intervention Brigade in Democratic Republic of Congo 144, 145
UN General Assembly (UNGA) 17, 24, 82, 108, 140, 141; as authorising body 5, 43, 50, 146; composition of 94; Small-5 nations 27; Uniting for Peace Resolution 85, 146
UN Guard Force 4, 16–17, 59, 79, 95, 119, 128–9, 129
UN High Commission for Refugees 45
UN Legion 4, 7, 14, 15, 22–3, 150
UN Mission in DRC (MONUSCO) 144, 145
UN Mission in Liberia (UNMIL) 45, 63
UN Office of the Coordination of Humanitarian Affairs 67, 68
UN Office of the High Commissioner for Human Rights (OHCHR) 6
UN Office of the Special Advisor on Genocide Prevention 6
UN Peace Force 17, 129

168 *Index*

UN peace operations 1, 16, 17, 18–19, 107, 150; *Brahimi Report* on 3, 21; challenges facing 2–3; coordination deficits and overlaps 140; deployment delays 2–3, 21, 25, 46, 116, 118, 120; failure to follow rules in 96–7; standby arrangements 2, 14, 17, 21, 22; strengthening of (existing) 46, 108, 117–19, 130, 140, 142
UN Peacebuilding Commission (UNPBC) 62, 137, 140, 141, 150
UN Rapid Deployment Brigade 96
UN Rapid Deployment Police and Security Force 123, 142
UN Secretary-General (UNSG) 22, 43, 50; High-Level Panel on Threats, Challenges and Change 130, 141
UN Security Council (UNSC) 1, 5, 15, 19, 27, 93, 104, 108, 140, 141; as authorising body 43, 44, 50, 84, 85, 86, 105, 144–5, 146; and Central African Republic (CAR) 46; composition of 87, 94–5, 106, 146; and Iraq war (2003) 98; legitimacy 147; Military Staff Committee 15, 16, 17; and national armed forces 15–16, 19; Permanent Five (P-5) members 16, 106, 146; reform of 95, 106, 146, 147; veto power in 94, 106; voting procedures 87; Western dominance of 93–5
UN Special Committee on Peacekeeping Operations (C34) 129
UN Standby Arrangements System (UNSAS) 2, 21, 118
UN Standing Emergency Group 24
UN Standing Police Capacity 129–30
UN Team of Experts on the Rule of Law and Sexual Violence in Conflict 60
UN Truce Supervision Organisation 16
UN Volunteer Military Force 19–20, 95, 119, 120
United Kingdom (UK) 15, 27, 119
A United Nations Emergency Peace Service (2006) 26

United States (US) 22, 29, 59, 82, 98, 118; dominance in UNSC 94; Presidential Policy Directive on peacekeeping (PPD-25) 22; United Nations Rapid Deployment Act 142
Uniting for Peace procedures 43, 146
UN's Evolving Responsibility to Protect Civilians from Atrocity Crimes symposium (2010) 29
Urquhart, Brian 19–20, 22, 26, 46, 79, 95, 119, 120, 128

Van Langenhove, Luke 105
Vieira de Mello, Sergio 22, 96
Vietnam 62

Walsh, James 4
Waltz, Kenneth 77
war crimes 2, 4, 5, 26, 42, 45, 47, 148
Watt, Fergus 28
Weiss, Thomas G. 39
Wells, Pera 29
Weschler, Joanna 25
Westfall, Ted 29
Westphalian sovereignty 75, 76
Williams, Paul D. 149
Wiranto, General 85
World Federalist Movement (WFM) 25, 27, 42
World Federalist Movement (WFM)–Canada 28, 29, 44
World Federalist Movement (WFM)–Institute for Global Policy 26, 27
World Order Models Project 25
World Peace Forum (Vancouver, 2006) 28
World Summit (2005) 44, 81
World Summit Outcome Document (WSOD) 44, 64, 85
World War II 15
Wynn, Al 4

Yugoslavia, former 41

Zuber, Robert 27, 118, 145